Seeking Many Inventions

Seeking Many Inventions

The Idea of Community in America

Philip Abbott

The University of Tennessee Press

The paper in this book meets the minimum
requirements of the American National Standard for
Permanence of Paper for Printed Library
Materials. ∞ Binding materials have been chosen for
strength and durability.

Library of Congress Cataloging-in-Publication Data

Abbott, Philip.
  Seeking many inventions.

  Bibliography: p.
  Includes index.
  1. United States—Social conditions. 2. Community
organization—United States. 3. Associations,
institutions, etc.—United States. 4. Social structure—
United States. I. Title.
HN 57.A 545   1986   306.'.0973   86-11338
ISBN 0-87049-514-3 (alk. paper)

Your memories, rising, glide silently by me
—Whitman

Beryl E. Abbott
Joseph Reading, Sr.
William H. Abbott
William E. Abbott
Rufus Rudisill

Contents

Preface

Athens, Sparta, republican and Christian Rome, Jerusalem, Geneva—these are names that are the anchors of Western political thought. Other innumerable communities, villages and towns, feudal manors, monasteries, and *shetls* also form a historical testament to our ability to create forms of human association that capture a sense of moral cohesion, mutual aid, and intimacy within a place and across time.

America, as the second world of Western civilization, seems to have rejected these anchors, in practice and often in theory, in favor of other goals. There is, of course, the Puritan notion of the "City on the Hill," which still holds an enormous psychic attraction, as well as the small town, our own interpretation of the European village. But as Bradford complained, Plymouth was like an "ancient mother . . . grown old and forsaken of her children." America seems driven to pursue the consequences of a society in which the individual is his/her own community. Writers from Tocqueville to Sorel have been impressed with the sheer volume and intensity of energy released in this country by the rejection of the restraints imposed by community; many others describe America as a huge mistake.

Often overlooked in the image of America as dynamo relentlessly surging toward new futures is the fact that Americans have used this energy to create their own anchors. Ad hoc and often bizarre, these communities are the inventions of a restless and energetic people. To compare a shopping mall to the *paidea* may appear ludicrous, but the examples of American community I draw are designed not only to illustrate their peculiar character but also to show the still unfulfilled potential of our own inventions. For the idea of the saving power of these anchors has not been lost to a liberal society;

America is not yet doomed to be counted as some grotesque experiment in individualism.

Grateful acknowledgment is made to the Earhart Foundation for their continued support. The following have read portions or all of the manuscript: Michael Levy, Glenn Graeber, Robert Zieger. Their comments were uniformly helpful. Cynthia Maude-Gembler has been an ideal editor; she is a much valued advisor. I thank Patricia Abbott for her indispensable aid on the craft of quilting and for the bibliography and index. A political theorist must of necessity rely upon the words of economists, historians, and sociologists. Without the range and depth of these disciplines a study such as this would not be possible. Naturally, any errors and omissions are the responsibility of the author.

Grateful acknowledgment is made to *Polity* and to the *Public Administration Review* for permission to reprint material in chapters 7 and 8.

PHILIP ABBOTT
December, 1985

Chapter 1

Introduction

What is the common feature in this list?

the telephone
the computer
the light bulb
the shoelace
the paper bag
the elevator
the camera
the motion picture

the ouija board
the department store
the motel
the atomic bomb
the transistor
the airplane
the television

A moment's thought and one would probably be able to answer, "Why, these are inventions!" Some might also note that these are fairly recent inventions. Others might mention that many of these inventions are of American origin or at least inventions in which Americans played a major role.

But what about this list?

the penitentiary
the money-market fund
the factory
the settlement house
the revival camp
the pieced quilt

the welfare state
modern dance
rock-and-roll
the land-grant university
the town meeting

These items, too, are inventions. They are also of relatively recent origin. The American contribution is also evident. The second list, however, consists of economic, political, social, and cultural inventions. But generally we do not think of the latter in terms of invention. Technological invention is described in a language that emphasizes individual acts of creativity. An object is brought into existence where nothing directly comparable had existed before. An invention is something new, brand-new, which either helps us better complete certain tasks (the power mower) or which also opens whole new sets of activities (the telephone). We chuckle at trivial or misguided inventions because they do not alter practice. Other inventions (such as the atomic bomb) can produce an almost religious sense of awe.

It is not uncommon to extend the concept of invention to new market forms (like the department store) or even to certain techniques (like laser surgery). But political, social, economic and cultural change is not generally seen in these terms. Yet I think we fail to grasp important aspects of change in ignoring the inventive features of new political and social institutions and practices. Each entry on the second list was brought into existence as an invention. Each was the result of conscious efforts of identifiable sets of individuals. Each was designed as a solution to certain perceived needs. Each was the result of a series of creative acts. Each was in common use in a short period of time. This essay is, in part, an attempt to refocus our approach to change by examining selected American inventions.

Inventing Institutions

While few writers today are willing to expand the concept of invention from its technological base, the Western tradition of political thought does offer some precedent for this kind of thinking. Utopian proposals, from Plato's *Republic* to B. F. Skinner's *Walden II*, present new institutions and practices in the spirit of invention.[1] The Enlightenment tradition embraced political and social inventions as well as technological ones. Other theorists, "realists" to a fault, have written in the language of invention. Machiavelli's works are preoccupied with analyses of inventors in the political sphere. His portraits of Romulus, Lycurgus, and Borgia are sketches of the creators of new political institutions. Friedrich Nietzsche, too, called for new forms of culture and politics, emphasizing the role played by individual creators in these enterprises. Others—Carlyle, Sorel, Bergson—have written in the same spirit.

While I do not intend to offer a history of the idea of political and social invention, these examples suggest that a broader concept of invention is very much part of our approach to political and social

thought. Certainly all of these efforts at social and political invention have grievous flaws. The fact that they occur in analyses of
widely differing perspectives makes these faults all the more damn-
ing. For an aggressive amorality infects all these presentations. Critics are correct to condemn orientations in which the existing structure of society is treated with disdain and in which inventors of new
forms are given complete moral license. We shall return to this
important objection shortly.

There are, however, other reasons why so few writers today are
willing to employ the concept of invention. The major ideological
systems that evaluate and recommend social and political change
portray their programs in structural terms. Modern conservatism
defines itself as a philosophy that looks critically upon rapid
change. The functional approach offered by many conservatives
tells us that political and social systems somehow "adapt" to systemic strains. Liberals grant the inventive character of the market,
but they remain fixated upon theories which emphasize human
action determined by systemic variables. Robert Nozick's comment
is illustrative of this approach.

> Invisible-hand explanations minimize the use of notions constituting
> the phenomena to be explained; in contrast to straightforward explana-
> tions, they don't explain complicated patterns by including the full-
> blown pattern-notions as objects of people's desires or beliefs. Invisible-
> hand explanations of phenomena thus yield greater understanding than
> do explanations of them as brought about by design as the objects of
> people's intentions.[2]

Those liberals who pursue the extension of the welfare state like-
wise speak in terms of the fulfillment of institutional requirements.[3]

One would think that Marxism, as a revolutionary theory, would
place the invention of new institutions at the center of its political
agenda. Indeed, Marx did discuss the inventive capacity of politico-
economic systems, especially that of capitalism. He also contended
that future societies would develop new and radically different sets
of institutions. Yet Marxism is so committed to a determinist philosophy that, like liberalism, it insists that change is structurally
determined.

There are, to be sure, efforts on the part of liberals, conservatives,
and Marxists to conceive of and to recommend the invention of new
institutions. Ivan Illich has repeatedly attacked the assumptions of a

world which relies upon technological invention. He has called for what amounts to the "de-invention" of institutional structures and their replacement with new, "convivial institutions."[4] Like Illich, others have devised proposals for new inventions or attempted to refurbish old ones.[5] Some Marxists have reexamined the consequences of determinism and recommended a more sympathetic look at alternative roads to socialism.[6] Hannah Arendt, a writer who has always been preoccupied with the foundings of new societies, argued for a renewed perspective on brief-lived workers' councils which appear at the onset of modern revolutions.[7]

But each effort to recommend invention still runs counter to the general predispositions of each ideology. In fact, new determinist orientations have appeared increasingly in recent years. Neo-Freudian and behaviorist psychology, sociobiology and various versions of technological determinism provide additional justifications for a view of social and political change as being beyond human control.

One writer who has directly applied the concept of invention to political and social theory as a challenge to these determinist perspectives is Robert Nisbet. In his conclusion to the *Twilight of Authority,* Nisbet offers the concept of "social inventions" as both an approach to historical analysis and as a solution to the restoration of authority in modern society. He argues that the concept of invention is improperly limited to technological change. There are cultural inventions (the epic poem, the tragedy and comedy, the novel, the essay, the painting, fugue, ballet, and symphony) as well as social inventions. He contends that while we tend to call new forms "outcomes of 'cultural growth,' " this usage is an evasion. "Each is an invention. We invent forms of art just as we do mechanical things."[8]

Nisbet lists the following as social inventions: the walled town, the guild, the trade fair, the marketplace, the monastery, the university, the studio, the trading company, the mutual aid association, the labor union, the economic corporation. He contends that the history of social organization is the history of the rise and spread of social inventions. According to Nisbet, there have been periods of relative dearth of such inventions and other periods of relative fertility. The Middle Ages were as rich in social organization as our own is in technological ones. The monastery, village community, manor, fief, guild, university, parish are Nisbet's examples of medieval inventions. The Renaissance and Reformation were sterile, Nisbet

tells us, as producers of new social forms. By contrast, the seventeenth century was another period of social invention with its creation of institutes and academies in the arts, letters, and sciences.
The development of the "idea of the state from its absolutist to its
popular form" captured the minds of inventive women and men,
but the nineteenth century, confronted with the challenge of indus-
trialism, produced the mutual aid society in new forms, the consumers' and producers' cooperatives, the assurance societies, the
labor unions, and the business corporations. In the United States
there were waves of anarchist utopias and, on the frontier, clusters
of helping inventions. Nisbet sees the twentieth century as "sin-
gularly weak" in producing social inventions, but he notes signs of
inventiveness in the recrudescence of kinship, neighborhood, and
local community, as well as in the popularity of the contemporary
commune.

I would like to examine Nisbet's concept of social invention by
asking the following questions: Can we identify American social
inventions? Can social inventions rejuvenate American liberalism?
What would these social inventions look like? But before I attempt
to deal with these questions, I would like to propose some caveats
and extensions to Nisbet's analysis.

My first concern is with possible objections to the analogy itself.
One likely objection is that the concept of invention presents an
individualized view of social change. No one really "invented" a
trade union. The union "arose" as a result of changes in the nature
of work and the market. We tend to think of the institutions mentioned by Nisbet, as well as by Illich and Arendt, as coming into
existence in a different manner. A study of the labor union or the
university will speak in terms of its "rise," its "growth," its "development," its "formation." More likely than not, such a study would
tend to see the labor union as the culmination of or the vehicle for a
social movement. But these approaches are analogical ones as well.
They describe new institutions in terms of biological or mechanistic
metaphors. The concept of invention as a description of new institutions highlights important aspects of social change that can otherwise be overlooked. The trade union as we now know it was not the
only response available to industrialization. Even the character of
the trade union itself (its internal organization and its goals) was the
result of several possible options. In America, Bill Haywood, Wyn-
dam Mortimer, Samuel Gompers, and Walter Reuther all had differ-

ent "inventions" in mind for the trade union, and the history of the union is in part a history of these competing personal visions. Some may not have been feasible; often it is difficult to say if they would have "worked" or not. Social and political inventions are indeed collective enterprises (although it may be a mistake to underestimate the role of individual contributions). Indeed, I would argue that the major institutions of the twentieth century were not simply logical outgrowths of historical forces, but the results of the efforts of groups of determined men and women.

There are, as I indicated, important objections to the expansion of the concept of invention to include the making of new political and social forms. One might emphasize the desirability of slow, experimental and complex growth in institutions. The concept of invention suggests novelty and discovery and discontinuity, even gadgetry. In fact, Nisbet's willingness to use the concept shows his genius as a conservative. We are reminded of Edmund Burke's attack on the French revolutionaries: "By this unprincipled facility of changing the state as often, and as much, and in as many ways as their floating fancies or fashions, the whole chain and continuity of the commonwealth would be broken. No one generation could link with another."[9]

But the concept of invention is not totally inconsistent with an incremental view of historical change. The intricate machinery of the dial phone exchange is based upon thousands of "smaller" inventions. The relationship among the abacus, calculator, and computer reveals a sense of continuity. The first rocket used as a weapon in battle was launched by defenders of a Chinese city in 1232. The history of representative government shows the same kind of gradual process. Yet there still are huge "breakthroughs." Inventions like the complex set of institutions that we call the market came into existence with amazing rapidity.

Still another objection to expanding the notion of invention emphasizes the extent to which human behavior is culturally determined. Proposals for new institutions and attempts to actually build them reflect a basic naiveté, what Eugene Bestor once called a patent office model of society.[10] But again there is no fundamental contradiction between an appreciation for (or even a defense of) a society's culture and the invention of new institutions. Hannah Arendt's advocacy of the counciliar system, for example, was based upon her understanding of unique aspects of America's revolutionary tradition. In fact, one motive of the present undertaking is to attempt to show how American social and political inventions were responses and adaptations to cultural norms.

On the positive side, the concept of invention permits us to see the range of opportunities that are available in social life. As Nisbet remarks, we tend to see kinship systems as "some kind of evolutionary exfoliation of biological instincts." "We would do better," he says, "to conjure up a vision of some primitive Solon than of mere instinct in the fashioning of structures as ingeniously designed as clan, moiety, and tribe."[11] This is not to say that it is possible or desirable to invent whole new social orders, testing new inventions on unwilling and confused populations, as Burke warned against, or to believe that existing institutions ought to be casually replaced by new inventions, or to propose that such inventions do not need to be measured against basic human needs. The Burkean objection is a powerful warning, but it is one, I shall argue, that may be most applicable to political inventions. The language of invention does suggest, however, that there may be circumstances in which invention is desirable, even necessary, and that the concept allows us to break away from certain historical impasses. The latter is, I think, the current case with American society. But I do want to make a few additions to Nisbet's model before approaching this question.

Nisbet's approach suffers from two major defects as stated. First, he does not distinguish between kinds of inventions. The marketplace and the local community are complexes of institutions; the terms themselves are conceptual apparatuses for identifying whole networks of institutions. Other inventions function as supports for other sets of institutions. Moreover, the business corporation (if indeed it is a *social* institution as Nisbet suggests), along with other inventions, transformed the marketplace into an institution of quite a different kind. We shall try to present a framework for distinguishing kinds of inventions in the following chapters.

Second, Nisbet includes as social inventions, all institutions that are not expressly technological or cultural. Thus, in his conception, the corporation, the credit union, the trade union are listed as social inventions along with the commune and the university. Of course, all institutions are social in a broad sense in that they provide arenas of human interaction. The corporation provides for shares experiences that are unrelated to or may only incidentally promote the goals of the institution. But the primary character of the corporation is economic. The same sort of assessment can be made about the Communist Party. Undoubtedly, the Party performs a social function. In fact, former members often remark that they suffer most from the loss of those social relationships made possible by the Party.[12] But the Party is primarily a political institution in both its goals and activity. There are, of course, also institutions whose functions are genuinely pluralistic in the sense that the mix of economic, political, and social goals is relatively balanced. Ideally the university functions in this manner, as do some religious groups and professional organizations.

But is it as possible to identify institutions that are fundamentally committed to social goals as it is those that are committed to economic and political ones? Are there institutions whose *basic* function is the promotion of sociability leading to bonds of intimacy of friendship? These are questions we shall explore in following chapters.

Ideology and Invention

We have suggested that all inventions can be identified by function and type. Can we match up inventions to ideologies, more specifically to the great ideologies of the nineteenth and twentieth centuries, and especially to American liberalism? When we speak of technological inventions, we tend to identify inventors. Suitably qualified, it is possible to say that Eli Whitney invented the cotton gin; Samuel Colt, the revolver; Thomas Edison, the light bulb. Cultural inventions are a bit difficult in this regard, but one could match up Samuel Richardson with the invention of the novel, Horace Walpole with the Gothic novel, Arnold Schoenberg with atonal music, Lois Fuller, Ruth St. Dennis, and Isadora Duncan with modern dance. Social and political inventors, as we have noted, are often hidden in history, but one can sometimes still match up these inventions with individuals. One such pairing certainly would be Lenin and the invention of Communism. Other examples might include the "Founding Fathers" and the invention of the American system of representation, Luther and new church forms, Bentham and the Panoptican.

One of the differences, however, between technological and social, political, and economic inventions is that in a sense the latter

must be invented again and again. New institutions are rediscovered and applied to new historical situations, where they are
readjusted and revised. Inventions which were left unimplemented
are sometimes seized upon by succeeding generations. In modern
life, the task of bringing inventions into society is undertaken by
ideological systems and movements. Modern ideologies, despite
their professed commitment to determinism, are the wellspring for
new inventions; they mobilize support for these new institutions,
and refine and alter them. If we borrow from Karl Mannheim's
analysis, ideological disputes also involve the "reciprocal unmask-
ing" of the utility of inventions. Liberals attack the Communist
Party as an institution of elite rule; Marxists defend it as an agency
of economic change.

But let us begin to approach this matching up unsystematically,
in the same spirit as one would try to list the best modern baseball
pitchers. One may have one's own preferences, but boosterism is
tempered by the principle of fairness. We have already mentioned
the Party as Marxism's contribution to political invention. I can
think of no more significant modern political invention. The Marxist conception of the Party is as a generative institution. It bears little
resemblance to "bourgeois" political parties. The Party created a
new form of governmental organization. Not only has it redefined
the relationship between voluntary association and the political
system, but it has produced a historically new elite. In fact, while it
is certainly possible to imagine a Marxist society without the Party,
such a development would represent such a fundamental change
that Marxist regimes as we recognize them would cease to exist.
Either some new generative institution(s) would need to take its
place or the Party would need to be transformed into an organization resembling a liberal democratic model.

Although the concept of totalitarianism is not as compelling to
scholars as it once was, the efforts of German and American writers
to identify a new form of government (an invention, if you will) was
in part the result of attempts to assess the significance of fascism and
Stalinist Marxism. Theorists of totalitarianism attributed the invention of the new form of party to the experiences of both the
Soviet Union and Germany. Certainly the Nazi party operated in
ways similar to the Communists. There are practices common to
both regimes: the system of terror and the camps, the systematic
destruction and takeover of voluntary associations, the militariza-

tion of society. But I think the unique contribution of fascism, and of Nazism in particular, was the series of inventions that were themselves an outgrowth of the application of modern political and administrative techniques to racial ideology. Racism is, of course, not a new idea in Western thought, nor is its systematic policy application. The fascist invention was to use the concept in the context of the modern state. At the 1937 Reich party congress, Hitler announced that "Germany has experienced the great revolution. . . . in the [policies of] national and racial hygiene which was undertaken for the first time on an organized basis in this country."[13] All this was before the decree announcing the "final solution." The racial idea was incorporated into Nazi bureaucracy from the first. Recruitment to the SS was governed by models of "Aryan" type, and bureaus within the SS were assigned functions relating to racial policy. The extermination camps were planned and administered by a section of the SS. New inventions designed to deal with the race question blossomed. Each was in a sense a macabre transformation of modern institutions: eugenic institutes were created from the model of scientific research laboratories, sterilization wards from the model of the hospital, the *Lebensborn* from the model of foster homes, German farms in Poland (*Vokstum*) from the model of homesteading.

Invention is not limited to the totalitarian ideologies. Democratic socialism is an especially syncretic ideology, one which is itself an inventive blend of Marxist and democratic elements. Its distinctive contribution to the invention of institutions is, I think, those complex of institutions we refer to as the welfare state. Democratic socialists have advocated the use of the legislature as the wellspring for a series of institutional inventions: public corporations, national health insurance, social security, day care, and more recently the ombudsman. The alliance between party, legislature, administrative agency, and voluntary association (trade unions and allied groups) provides the conditions for inventions in democratic socialistic systems. These inventions have been widely accepted and adapted by both liberal and Marxist regimes. In fact, one of the unique features of the welfare state as an invention has been its ability, through creation of a political-administrative infrastructure, to establish a kind of permanent laboratory or engine of invention. This results in two factors: the desire on the part of the welfare state *appartachiki* to extend their hegonomy over society and the stresses of industrial societies which create demands for solutions to economic problems. These special features of the welfare state anger its opponents from the left and the right. It is intriguing that the commitment to the welfare state is a tentative one for many democratic socialists. It is something which must be "transformed" or "surpassed," since it seems so capable of absorbing stress through inventive reform.[14] The right, of course, focuses upon the welfare state's expansive nature. When forces which might obstruct this political structure of invention are weak or do not exist, the welfare state, for good or bad, assumes its most complete inventive character. Thus one finds in Sweden vigorous attempts to develop new inventions. New programs in female equality are one example; the proposal for wage funds as a step toward workers' control is another. From the opposite perspective, in Marxist regimes in which the Party has been weakened, the welfare state apparatus develops inventions that take on a liberal character. Hungary's unique approach to family policy—lengthy extended paid leaves for mothers, rather than day care—is an example of this sort of development.

What is the contribution of liberal ideology to political, economic, and social invention? Certainly liberals in the United States have made a contribution to the invention of the welfare state. But I think that liberalism is primarily responsible for mobilizing support for—if not more directly inventing—two great generative inventions of the modern age. One is the invention of the constitution. The other is that of the market economy. Major institutions often represent a series of inventions. This is certainly the case with both the constitution and the market. The idea of a constitutional system has been advanced and developed by generations of liberals. All the variations of the conception of constitutional government—as rule of law, as limited power, as express and written authority—were the result of a whole pantheon of liberal inventors extending from the British Commonwealthmen to Locke and Montesquieu, to Jefferson & Madison, to Constant and Tocqueville, and to Dahl. In each of these writers, the idea of constitutional government is redefined and re-invented, often with new supporting structures.

Again, it is necessary to note that liberalism is not the only defender of constitutional government. Nevertheless, liberalism has held this invention so dearly that it is largely responsible for its continued existence and development. The constitution, as a political institution, operates in only a limited number of nation-states. But its potential as a generative institution still exists.

To say that liberalism invented the modern market economy is a more complicated statement. The changes that eventually created the market economy—the breakdown of certain structures such as the guild and the commons and the invention of new ones such as finance capital and the factory—were in a large part instituted or supported by liberal writers. Locke, Smith, Bentham, James Mill certainly anticipated or nurtured or advocated the market economy. Many of them offered inventions of their own. We do not have the space to trace the relationship between liberalism and the market, but it is worth noting that liberals have not always been the doting parents of their own invention. They have worried about the social and political consequences of a market economy. Some have not supported its more recent developments. As Irving Kristol notes, while the Founding Fathers "*intended* this nation to be capitalist and regarded it as the *only* set of economic arrangements consistent with the liberal democracy they had established," the large, publicly owned corporation would have "troubled and puzzled them."[15] The corporation puzzles and troubles Kristol himself. But he concludes (as many liberals have) that "we frequently find ourselves defending specific concentrations of power, about which we might otherwise have the most mixed feelings, on the grounds that they contribute to a general diffusion of power, a diffusion which creates the 'space' in which individual liberty can survive and prosper."[16] Robert Dahl, the modern American authority on pluralism, takes a less sanguine view. He has argued that the corporation in its present form "cannot be justified."[17]

In any case, the market economy (however, modified or even transformed by the welfare state) continues to exercise a fascination for many liberals. In fact, several recent works by American liberals argue in different ways that the market economy must be supported precisely because it is itself such a dynamic inventive system.[18]

Liberalism and Invention

If we look then at the great ideologies of the modern era we find one outstanding feature. The major inventions that we identified

(the Party, racial bureaucracy, the welfare state, the constitution,
and the market) are all primarily political or economic inventions.
That this absence of social invention is not unique to liberalism but
is characteristic of all modern ideologies is cause for concern. Even
the current revival of American liberal theory explores the inventive
potential of both the constitution and the market at the expense of
social institutions. Yet this attention to political and economic institutions ignores the importance of social institutions in liberal
societies. Let me take two examples to make this point. John Rawls
begins his analysis by asking, in effect, what kind of society would
we invent if we imagined ourselves behind a "veil of ignorance" in
regard to our own personality and interests. He concludes that two
principles can be derived, one establishing equality of constitutional rights and another establishing fair distribution of economic
resources. There has been considerable disagreement as to how
radical are Rawls' principles. Robert Dahl's reaction expresses one
interpretation: "Clearly the application of Rawls' two principles of
justice to the United States would require a profound change in
public policy."[19] If Rawls' theory does require new political and
economic institutions (as I think it does), one wonders what role is
envisioned for social invention. Rawls insists that his theory is not a
justification of a "private society," a society in which "each person
assesses social arrangements solely as a means to his private
aims."[20] On the contrary, argues Rawls, "the sociability of human
beings must not be understood in a trivial fashion . . . we need one
another as partners in ways of life that are engaged in for their own
sake. . . ."[21] How will these "social unions" arise? Rawls contends
that just political and economic arrangements will provide an "am-
ple and rich structure" for many associations. "A well-ordered society . . . will presumably contain countless social unions of many
different kinds."[22] Rawls believes that the principles of justice imply
(both analytically and empirically) institutions of human sociability. But do they? Might not the invention of political institutions required by his theory of justice crowd out "social unions"? Is
it not at least possible that the two principles of justice, and the
institutions that support them, might be the governing principles of
a "private society"?

There is some evidence for an affirmative response to these
doubts. Rawls himself conceives of "social unions" as conveyor
belts for the goals of the just political order. "There must be," he

reminds us, "an agreed scheme of conduct in which the excellences and enjoyments of each are complementary to the good of all."[23] While Rawls insists that there is no dominant end, such as religious unity, to which the aims of all associations are subordinate, one wonders how much autonomy exists in a society in which "everyone's more private plan" is "a plan within a plan, this subordinate plan being realized in the public institutions of society."[24]

A similar treatment of social institutions occurs in Robert Nozick's *Anarchy, State and Utopia.* Of course the antagonism to the social in his theory arises from a different source than in Rawls'. Nozick's theory is derived from a conception of human beings as merely holders of rights. These "moral borders" are so firm that only a "minimal state" is justifiable. Nozick does argue that the minimal state would spawn entirely new forms of social experimentation; "there will be utopias of many different and divergent kinds of communities in which people lead different kinds of lives under different institutions."[25] Unlike Rawls, Nozick is willing to accept complete laissez-faire in regard to social forms. There may be no capitalist communes, or "some may have them and others don't or some may have some of them, or what you will." Nozick is not even willing to permit the state to enforce rights of egress on the part of members of these communes. Thus one does find in Nozick's work an appreciation for social institutions and even an outline of a theory for invention of new social forms. But look at how he conceives his "utopias":

> We seem to have a realization of the economist's model of a competitive market. This is most welcome, for it gives us immediate access to a powerful, elaborate, sophisticated body of theory and analysis. Many associations competing for my membership are the same structurally as many firms competing to employ me.[26]

Thus in the works of Rawls and Nozick, works which represent the range of the spectrum of liberal thought in America, the concept of the social is overwhelmed by a commitment to political and economic invention.

That both Rawls and Nozick believe that they have restructured liberalism so that social institutions can flourish only compounds their error. Let me take a moment to attempt to show why this is so. Liberals have invented and supported two extremely powerful institutions. Constitutional government and a market economy are

generative institutions of such capacity for expansion that they over-
whelm the social content of every institution they face. Many liberals have, of course, argued precisely the opposite. Limited government and allocation of economic resources by a market will
produce a free and relatively equal society. Both institutions will
reinforce one another and create vast areas of social space that will
allow individuals to pursue varied life plans. This, in essence, was
J. S. Mills' argument in *On Liberty,* the most eloquent and moving
statement of modern liberalism. For some time now individuals
have denied the validity of this proposition. Where, they ask, is
freedom in repression and equality in poverty? Many liberals have
to some degree accepted these accusations and attempted to provide
corrective institutions. In a sense, Rawls' *A Theory of Justice* is a
systemization of these efforts. The principles of constitutionalism
have thus been extended to include the protection of minorities, and
the market has mechanisms built to include provision for entitle-
ments and public goods. Radicals, of course have replied that such
measures are inadequate. But the real significance of this activity on
the part of critics of liberalism is the preoccupation with political
and economic mechanisms themselves. There is no confidence that
social institutions can be a useful corrective to the problems of
liberalism. Liberals themselves generally support this critique; in
fact, the modern reform group has become informal agent of the
liberal welfare state.

Thus, on the one hand, social institutions must submit to the
scrutiny of constitutional control (Rawls), and, on the other, their
functions are constantly being absorbed by the forces of the market
economy, perhaps the most powerful source of invention in America (Nozick). Liberalism has produced a peculiar amalgam of Lockean and Hobbesian individuals. In politics we are anxious to locate
the power quotient in all institutions and to control it by contract.
In the economic sphere we are utility maximizers. Either, and often
both, of these perspectives infect our approach to social institutions. Liberalism approaches social institutions with the eye of the
constitutional or corporate lawyer; the very concept of sociability
disintegrates under this gaze.

Even the great tradition of liberal pluralism has pursued this
approach. Tocqueville saw that liberal society produced enormous
numbers of social groups. But he also saw that associational activity
in America had a different character from that of European so-

cieties. Association rose on other than "natural" sentiments. Liberal societies produced groups that lacked permanence and stability. Yet Tocqueville argued that this basis of group formation was better than none at all. He posited the principle of enlightened self-interest as the motivation for social institutions in America. Such activity might not "inspire great sacrifices" nor "make a man virtuous," but it would create "orderly, temperate, moderate, carefree and self-controlled citizens."[27]

Modern pluralists have ignored Tocqueville's famous warning that supplemented his analysis. "I see a multitude of men," he prophesied, "alike and equal, constantly circling in pursuit of petty and banal pleasures with which they glut their souls. . . . Over this kind of man stands an immense, protective power . . . absolute, thoughtful of detail, orderly, provident and gentle."[28] These pluralists from Madison to Truman and even Dahl have written a great deal about social groups, but they have invariably treated them as politico-economic entities. Madison saw them as factions bent upon the seizure of power through "domestic convulsion" and "schemes of oppression." David Truman portrayed all groups as temporary and overlapping collections of interests. Even the category of citizenship was presented as some vast "consumer group."[29] Robert Dahl, the most imaginative and reflective of modern American pluralists, continues to see group membership in terms of marginal utility. Institutional affiliation will continue until rational self-interest requires a calculation that "the loss would exceed the gain."[30]

Viewed in this manner, it is natural that social institutions will be treated to increasing political control and domination by economic incentive. If the theory of the firm is the basis for our conception of social groups, then groups will use this as the basis for recruitment and goals, as will the political system for regulation and supervision. Such a state of affairs does create a climate for invention, but it is a climate that fosters the invention of institutions of political and/or economic control.

It is no accident that so many of our institutions today look and behave alike. Hospitals, schools, prison, professional organizations, churches, newspapers and universities not only use the same methods of institutional defense and expansion but they are increasingly internally organized on the same basis. Walk into the lobby of any of these institutions and at first you will find them

indistinguishable. There is an information desk, a waiting alcove,
clearly identified entrances and exits. The lobby is remarkably
quiet. Staff walk through quickly, information officers speak in
hushed tones, entrants sit silently. If one proceeds further, he or she
will continue to see major similarities. One confronts a receptionist
for identification and "facilitation" purposes. Then one is assigned
a staff officer, and, depending upon whether one is a visitor or a
member, the procedure of further identification, examination, and
record-keeping and processing continues.

These institutional features are, of course, the result of bureaucratization and professionalization, characteristics one would be
reminded, of all modern organization. But on another level, these
characteristics reflect adaptations to a universe dominated by political and economic perspectives; these institutions have ceased to
function as social institutions. Only pseudo-sociability is encouraged in these settings. Entrants are frequently addressed by first
name, but the structure itself permits only economic and political
behavior on the part of the member or visitor. Entrants either move
through the institution as objects, quietly responding to the next
request for information (each in itself rational and efficient), or they
challenge the system with political or economic retaliation. No
other alternatives are available.

Despite this domination of the political and economic in liberal
societies, there are possibilities for a social renewal. For the very
propositions which have created the conditions we have just described still hold out the opportunity for a different set of developments. A liberal society, even with its "social space" contracted and
withered by the hegemony of political and economic organization,
continues to allow for the potentiality for social invention. In fact, I
will argue that without new social inventions the very future of
American liberalism is threatened.

A group of theorists, writing on the edge of the liberal tradition
have focused upon this problem. Writers such as John H. Schaar,
Christopher Lasch and Wilson Carey McWilliams have attacked
liberal America as a society without a sense of social purpose.[31]
American society in Schaar's words has "lost all coherence."[32]
Lasch describes American culture in terms of a psychiatric disorder.
The narcissistic personality with "his charm, his pseudo-aware-
ness . . . his avoidance of dependence" is a defensive reaction
which has resulted from "the weakening of social ties."[33] Mc-

Williams bemoans the absence of fraternity in American life and chronicles our longings for it.

Schaar pleas for renewal in the language of invention: "The establishment of a decent common history and just relationships of power among human beings is a work of art. . . ."[34] Each writer yearns for a new "City on the Hill," the reconstruction of American society based upon "discipline" and the "work ethic" (Lasch), patriotism (Schaar) and "deep loyalty and commitment" (McWilliams). But although McWilliams argues that Calvin was correct, Americans have never really agreed. These writers are fundamentally correct in their assessment of the corrosive consequences of the dominance of the political and economic in American liberalism. They are fundamentally correct in their call for new inventions. They may also be fundamentally correct in their exposure of the often pathological character of what Americans take to be social relations and community. But the unavoidable fact is that Americans abandoned the City on the Hill as well as the virtuous republic in all its variations and recreations.

Americans have tried repeatedly to invent and re-invent social institutions, this despite the liberal agenda we outlined above. But the communities Americans have invented and supported have rarely been those which required Calvinist discipline or republican virtue. Therefore I have selected five inventions that more closely fit our historical experience: the telephone, the penitentiary, the revival camp, the motel, and the pieced quilt. Many other inventions could have been candidates for discussion, and I have been able to deal in passing with some of them. These five may not all be the sort of inventions of which we can be proud. Although they represent the fulfillment of dreams, they do not have the grandeur of the City on the Hill. But as inventions that are deeply imbedded in popular culture, these institutions illustrate the nature of America as an inventive society. They form part of our everyday lives and carry for us significant psychic force (even, as is the case with the quilt, as an artifact). The telephone is a late nineteenth-century invention, as is the revival camp. The first American experiment with the penitentiary was in 1780. The pieced quilt existed in America as early as the seventeenth century. As a popular art form it reached its zenith in the middle of the nineteenth century. The motel was an inventive spin-off of the automobile and thus is a twentieth-century phenomenon. Each invention corresponds to a basic feature of society;

the telephone as technological invention, the penitentiary as political, the motel as market, the revival camps as religious, and the quilt
as cultural invention. Most importantly, these are examples of the
kinds of inventions America creates.

But, as I suggested earlier in general terms, these initial formulations contain complex and intricate patterns. First, each of these
institutions is an example of one of three broad but identifiable
types of invention. I have called one type the *generative invention*
(the telephone and the pentitentiary are examples). Another is the
supporting invention (the motel and the quilt). A third is the *transitional invention* (the revival camp).

Second, each of these inventions does contain some social element. For each, in its own way, offers a new conception of community. The telephone provided a revolutionary new form of communication, one which is now being extended by the computer. Not
only has the phone directly created new communities, but it has
altered our conception of what a community is. The penitentiary
was a bold attempt to create a new kind of political system, self-
contained and with radical ambition. The revival camp provided a
new sense of religious community. Both the motel and the quilt were
inventions designed to meet the physical and the psychic needs of
travelers. Each, in its own way, created new "leisure" communities.

Third, there are relationships among these inventions, sometimes direct, sometimes subtle. For instance, while the telephone as
a technological invention certainly radically changed our conception of social space, making social intercourse perpetually imminent, the revival camp as preindustrial invention established similar
features through its promise of immediation conversion. The reincarnation of the camp as the "electronic church" now uses telephonic communication to expand the audience of its nineteenth-
century predecessor.

Fourth, these inventions were created through common sets of
features, what I have called an "invention matrix." I have tried to
show how this matrix works in American society, how it can explain the astonishing rapidity with which inventions—social, economic, and political as well as technological—become part of our
lives. This matrix can be found in four systemic sources of invention
in America: in the market, in the town and neighborhood, in the
reform group, and in the evangelistic churches. I shall argue that
these structures, in themselves inventions, are extremely powerful

centers for change in American society and are, in fact, the key to the renewal of the social in liberal societies.

My final point is that the community each of these inventions offers is fundamentally similar. Each presents an "instant community," a concept I try to define in the last chapter. The invention of these instant communities suggests a paradox for those who hope for basic changes in American society. On the one hand, their creation does show our historical longing for more viable and stable social relationships as well as our capacity to continually invent them. On the other, these institutions suggest that our inventions may be fundamentally flawed: For the instant communities we seek can never fully meet our needs.

Chapter 2

Five American Inventions

Let us begin our analysis by briefly reviewing the history of five different American inventions: the telephone, the penitentiary, the motel, the revival camp, the pieced quilt. Together they will provide the basic examples for American invention. We will explore the similarities among them as well as the types of inventions they represent in subsequent chapters. For the moment, we will attempt to recapture the sense of novelty each of these inventions conveyed to contemporaries. For each of these inventions, now commonplace and even in some cases obsolete, represented extraordinary claims for altering Americans' lives. Imagine a machine that "speaks" across space, a plan to change the mind of the criminal, a method to save souls, a way to live out the fantasy of "gypsy" life, a craft and social forum based upon the utilization of old rags. These inventions promised all of these things and more. Most of all, they were attempts to create new ways for us to live together. Americans immediately grasped at all of these potentialities and in the process continually transformed these initial inventions.

"Mr. Watson, come here, I want you"

The telephone is the quintessential modern technological invention. It is now a commonplace instrument, but its impact has been truly stunning. Henry M. Boettinger has described the revolutionary nature of the telephone. It was "the first device to allow the spirit of person expressed in his own voice to carry its message directly without transporting his body."[1] Today the telephone provides one with almost instantaneous contact with any part of the world. Unlike many other technological inventions, the telephone has few detractors. There is concern with phone rates and privacy, but on the whole the telephone has not produced the kind of opposition that one finds to the nuclear reactor or even the ambivalence that characterizes our reaction to the computer.

But the revolutionary potential of this device was not always evident to the inventors of the telephone. The impetus for the invention of the telephone, and even the manner of its early usage, were ultimately connected with the telegraph. Bell had, at first, conceived of his invention as a refinement of the telegraph. Western Union was searching for a way to use one telegraph wire to transmit several messages at once. Bell however, soon came to realize that he was near to inventing a different instrument. Bell's major competitor, Elisha Grey, puzzled over the new direction of Bell's research: He "seems to be spending all his energies in [the] talking telegraph. While this is very interesting scientifically, it has no commercial value at present, for they do more business over a line by methods already in use by that system." Even after Bell's demonstrations at the Philadelphia Centennial, Grey remained unconvinced: "Of course it may, if perfected, have a certain value as a speaking tube. . . . This is the verdict of a practical telegraph man."[2] Precisely so, argues one historian who believes that Grey himself could have invented the telephone had he not been so much a telegraph man.

There were also compelling reasons for the preoccupation with the telegraph. The expense of telegraph lines had already been met. By 1876 the U.S. held over 200,000 miles of wire which delivered over 30 million telegrams through 8500 telegraph offices. Specialization was newly evident. The telegraph was being used for automatic fire-alarm systems and the transmission of stock prices. The invention of automatic telegraphy promised to overcome the barrier of the expertise required to read code. In 1877 the Social Telegraph Association of Bridgeport Connecticut began installation of a home subscriber telegraph. Homes would be connected to a central switchboard. Subscribers would be able to "speak" to one another. The company would even teach Morse Code.

By contrast Bell's invention, in its initial form, did not provide complete two-way communication and functioned only over very short distances. Still, observers of the Centennial were enthralled by Bell's demonstration. They saw the telephone as a means to transmit concerts, plays, and news. Even after the two-way transmission was improved, Bell continued to use the phone as a "radio" at performances across the country, partly as a source of income, but also as a forum to explain the potential use of the instrument.

The clarity with which Bell saw the use of the telephone is revealed in a prophetic presentation addressed to "the capitalists of the Electrical Telephone Company" in 1878. He began by noting that the new instrument had an advantage over every other form of electrical apparatus in that it required "no skill to operate." He added: "all other telegraphic machines produce signals which require to be translated by experts, and such instruments are, therefore, extremely limited in their application, *but the telephone speaks, and for this reason it can be utilized for nearly every purpose for which speech is employed* [italics added]."[3] Bell went on to suggest the uses of the telephone as a means of communication between master and servant (a favorite early prediction), between bankers, merchants, and manufacturers, between retail and wholesale dealers and dock companies, and between police offices (an implied replacement for the telegraph).

But perhaps the most far-reaching of Bell's predictions was his vision of universal use. He reminded his audience that at the present, we have a "perfect network of gas pipes and water pipes throughout large cities." "In a similar manner," he suggested, "it is conceivable that cables of telephone wire could be laid under the ground or suspended overhead, communicating by branch wires with a central office where the wire could be connected as desired, establishing direct communication between any two places in the city." In the future, Bell predicted, "wires will unite the head offices of telephone companies in different cities, and a man in one part of the country may communicate by word of mouth with another in a different place."[4]

Telephone usage developed in a manner remarkably similar to Bell's outline. What is so astounding is the rapidity of the spread of telephone service. In July 1876 the *Boston Transcript* spoke of the "wonderful results" of the telephone in terms of improvements in telegraphy: " . . . if the human voice can now be sent over wire . . . we may soon have distinguished men delivering speeches in Washington, New York or London, and audiences assembled in Music Hall or Faneuil Hall to listen."[5] The public seemed better able to anticipate the radio than the telephone. By June 30, 1877, 230 telephones were in use. By July the figure had risen to 750 and, one month later, to 1300. Most of these phones were used as replacements for telegraphs. Business quickly adopted the telephone, and the public telephone emerged very shortly after. In May 1879, D.M. Finley placed an advertisement that announced that he was the "first plumber and coal dealer whose establishment had been connected with new telephone wires and that householders wanting coal the same day as ordered might telephone to the dealer from Mr. Leith's drugstore."[6] Factories installed phones to communicate between the main office and foremen on the floor. Phones were used in construction of office buildings. In 1879, the Pennsylvania Railroad became the first railroad to install a telephone. Hotels adopted the phone very quickly. By 1909 the one hundred largest hotels in New York City had 21,000 telephones from which 6 million calls were made annually.

Attempts to create general public service (to "democratize" the telephone to use *McCulure's* expression) began immediately. In 1880, four years after Bell's Centennial demonstration, 50,000 Americans were telephone subscribers. By 1900 there were 3 million, with a million miles of wire stretching across the country. By 1918 the U.S. possessed 75 percent of the phones in the world. New York City had as many as all of Great Britain.[7] Bell's lecture circuit acquainted the public with potential use. He also issued a circular reminding potential subscribers that the telephone was an easy instrument to use: "Conversation can be easily carried on after slight practice and with occasional repetition of a word or sentence." Lessons in telephone usage appeared in newspapers and magazines.

A series of subsequent telephone inventions followed to create "the grand system" envisioned by Bell and his associates. The switchboard and, later, automatic switching permitted multiple hookups and cheaper rates. Inventions in the use of repeaters and loading coils permitted long-distance telephoning. Scores of other inventions followed that have permitted an even more extensive user system.

"A little commonwealth"

Considering the great promise offered by its inventors, the prison would not today be regarded as a "successful" invention. But the

determination of success depends upon what standard one chooses
to use. And if universal use is a measure of success, then the prison is
a major invention.

The modern prison or penitentiary had a more complex beginning than the phone. The penitentiary is not exclusively an American invention. Inventors of the prison include John Howard, Sir
Thomas Beevor, and Jeremy Bentham in England, as well as those
who had worked in theoretical penology such as Montesquieu,
Beccaria, and Voltaire.[8] But the American contribution was central.
Visitors from England arrived yearly to study firsthand the American version of this new invention. Even casual foreign sightseers
included tours of Auburn or Sing Sing or Walnut Street penitentiaries as part of their itineraries.

In 1682 the first Pennsylvania Assembly banned the death penalty for all but first degree murder and prescribed instead hard labor
in a "house of correction." The political situation with England
required the adoption of a harsher code in 1718, but after the
American Revolution the invention of the modern prison began in
earnest.

America had never operated under a system of supplices (tortures) such as those have been described vividly by Michael
Foucault:

> Torture is a technique; it is not an extreme expression of lawless rage.
> To be torture, punishment must obey three principle criteria: first, it
> must produce a certain degree of pain, which may be measured exactly,
> or at least calculated, compared and hierarchized; death is a torture
> insofar as it not simply a withdrawal of the right to live, but is the
> occasion and the culmination of a calculated gradation of pain: from
> decapitation (which reduces all pain to a single gesture, performed in a
> single moment-the zero degree of torture), through handing, the stake
> and the wheel (all of which prolong the agony), to quartering, which
> carries pain almost to infinity; death-torture is the art of maintaining life
> in pain, by subdividing it into a "thousand deaths."[9]

While this "poetry of Dante put into laws" was largely absent in
colonial America, there was a system of corporal punishment. In
New York eleven offenses were deemed capital, and, for these, flogging, pillorying, branding, stocking, and carting (tying the guilty
persons to the back of a wagon and dragging them through the
streets) were prescribed. But colonial juries apparently were in-

creasingly reluctant to convict offenders on the basis of the penal codes.

On the eve of the American Revolution the only prisons in the colonies were detention "apartments" about the size of a house, which were used for debtors and an increasing number of political prisoners. In Philadelphia the large prison on Walnut Street was partially contructed by 1777 and used first for debtors (many of whom starved), then for patriots, and then for prisoners of war and Tories.

It was during this early period that organized opposition to the jail emerged. The traditional procedure required inmates to pay the jailer for food, clothing, and heat. In 1776 the Philadelphia Society for Assisting Distressed Prisoners was formed. Volunteers pushed a wheelbarrow through the streets with a sign reading "VICTUALS FOR THE PRISONERS" and solicited contributions for food and clothing. Shortly after, an amnesty for all prisoners except those convicted for capital offenses was declared by the Pennsylvania legislature, and immediate problems were averted. Reports of conditions during the Revolution reconfirmed reformers' doubts about the jail as an institution. (A particularly cruel captain had been placed in charge of the prison by Lord Howe.)

Here then was the dilemma of the Philadelphia "inventors." They were repulsed by what Benjamin Rush called the "usual engines of public punishment" (the gallows, the pillory, the stocks, the whipping post, and the wheelbarrow), but they had also seen the conditions of the Walnut Street jail. One brief alternative experiment was attempted. In 1786 a law was passed which called for punishment of most crimes to be hard labor "publicly and disgracefully imposed . . . in streets and cities and towns, and upon highways of the open country and other public works."[10] The prisoners wore a distinctive dress of red and green or black and white and were manacled at the foot with a ball and chain and around the neck with an iron collar. They were called "wheelbarrow men." "Public punishment" appeared to offer an ideal solution to the jail and corporal punishment. But not so. Quakers judged the wheelbarrow law a failure. According to Benjamin Rush, "all public punishments tend to make bad men worse, and to increase crimes" because they destroy the "sense of shame which is one of the strongest outposts of virtue." The wheelbarrow alternative produced "none of those changes in body and mind, which are absolutely necessary to reform obstinate habits of vice."[11] Philadelphians heartily agreed. Convicts would throw down their chain and ball at passersby. Pickpockets, even in irons, victimized crowds. Escapes were common. In 1790 the wheelbarrow law was repealed.

Although the American invention of the prison was based upon Enlightenment principles, two historical models appear to have been employed in its creation. One was the sixteenth-century workhouse. As an institution designed to deal with paupers on a systematic basis, the European workhouse was sometimes given a manufacturing monopoly and administered either by the government or by contract to private businessmen. Today we wince (and properly so) at the concept of the workhouse with its penal discipline and administrative corruption. But during this period the workhouse was admired by many reformers. It provided work in return for alms, and it turned a profit. John Howard recommended the workhouse as proof that prisons could be more than places of idleness and corruption.

Another model, less obvious but still influential, was the monastery. In the Middle Ages, the Church's criminal jurisdiction permitted ecclesiastical courts. For those who enjoyed the "benefit of clergy," sentence included monastic seclusion as a means of expiation and atonement. Penitence required sexual abstinence, simple food, special clothing, manual labor, and sometimes a vow of silence.

From these two institutions, the workhouse and the monastery, the basic principles of the penitentiary—work and solitude—were derived. The Philadelphia Society for Alleviating Miseries of Public Prisons, formed in 1787 and influential in repealing the wheelbarrow law, drafted a *Memorial* in 1788 to the state legislature recommending "punishment by more *private* or even solitary labor." The legislature asked for more information. On December 15 the Society responded with a bill of particulars. It is at this point that we can say that the American version of the invention of the penitentiary occurred. The Philadelphia Society paraded before the legislature the defects of the Walnut Street jail: corrupt administration, barred windows, prostitution, (women "procure themselves to be arrested for fictitious debts in order to gain admission among the men"), intermingling of felons and debtors. It recommended separation of debtors from criminals, sex segregation, abolition of liquor and proposed "solitary confinement to hard labor."

Three months later these recommendations were enacted into law. A complete revision of the penal code and the reconstruction of the prison system was made in April, 1780. The Pennsylvania penitentiary system had been invented. Not only the concept of a new prison now existed, but what was to become a system of political architecture. The Act of 1790 called for the construction of "a suitable number of cells . . . each of which cells shall be six feet in width, eight in length, and nine feet in height and shall be constructed with brick or stone . . . and said cells shall be separated from the common yard by walls of such height, as without necessary exclusion of air and light, will prevent all external communication for purpose of confining therein the more hardened and atrocious offenders."[12]

Finally, said Caleb Lownes, a Quaker reformer and a member of the new Walnut Street penitentiary's board of inspectors, there was a system which recognized the prisoner as a "rational being." For ten years the new structure on Walnut Street would have visitors. Robert Turnbull described the prison as the "wonder of the world." An anonymous Philadelphia woman called it a "sort of little commonwealth," a place where "virtue will display her charms, to beings who have never before beheld her."[13] LaRochefourd, a French visitor whose travels preceded Tocqueville's famous tours, compared the prison to a microcosm of bees. Walnut Street did indeed become a commonwealth. Flogging had been eliminated in favor of solitary confinement. Prisoners were placed in four classifications, and a system of incentives was introduced that allowed for early release. A uniform diet was provided at the expense of the state. And, of course, there was the system of labor and silence. A "piece-price" system was instituted, and the prison inspectors entered into contracts with businesses to provide finished products. In addition, prisoners made all their bedding and clothing. Here is Benjamin Rush's diary entry describing the "New Jail":

> January 30, 1794: Visited the new jail with Caleb Lownes. The prisoners, fifty of them from the whole state, convicted of slight offenses, the same pains taken now to convict as formerly to acquit. All busy and working hard at first, carving marble; second, grinding plaster of paris; third, weaving; fourth, shoemaking; fifth, tailoring; sixth, spinning; seventh, wood turning, eight, cutting and chipping logwood.
> Care of Morals: Preaching, reading good books, cleanliness in dress, rooms, &c., bathing, no loud speaking, no wine, and as little tobacco as

possible. No obscene or profane conversation. Constant work, familiarity with garden, a beautiful one, 1200 heads of cabbage, supplies the jail with vegetables, kept by the prisoners.

Product of labor: One man carried 60 dollars out with him. All carry some. One made restitution for a stolen horse. They work from daylight till six o'clock, go to bed early, have no candle.

Conviction for small offenses. All express a wish to be released, and all confess that they are happy. A silence pervades them. Easy to tell by countenance who have recently come in. Never quarrel or steal from each other.[14]

A new board of inspectors, unpaid and meeting monthly, supervised the penitentiary. Ten of the original twelve inspectors were members of the Philadelphia Society. These men performed their new duties in great earnest. They fined themselves twenty-five cents for failing to appear at a meeting, and one or more members visited the prison daily. New institutions were added to complete the creation of this new "commonwealth." Public worship was provided, and in 1798 a prison school was instituted. Books were furnished, a lecture system was begun; a part-time physician was hired. Walnut Street penitentiary became known as the "Pennsylvania system" of incarceration.

As early as 1800 reformers were well aware that the Walnut Street facility was a failure. Escape attempts, assaults, and even riots occurred with greater and greater frequency. But the disillusionment with Walnut Street was traced to overcrowding and political disputes. The Pennsylvania system was tried again, with major additions, at the new Eastern State Penitentiary at Cherry Hill, and was replicated in several other states, including New Jersey, Maryland, and Virginia.

Eastern State featured a system of cells, each with its own furniture, plumbing, and courtyard. Here prisoners worked in complete solitude except for visits from prison officials and representatives of philanthropic societies.[15] The Pennsylvania system was characterized by solitude and handicraft labor. But this system soon would be challenged by a variation of the invention of the penitentiary, a competing invention called the Auburn system.

The foundation of Auburn State Penitentiary was laid in 1816. The new prison was originally designed to deal with overcrowding at the Newgate (N.Y.) facility. Newgate had been built in 1797 along the lines of the Pennsylvania system. Orlando Lewis reports that Auburn "did not start as an inconoclastic, insurgent institution."[16] But William Britten constructed a new north wing in 1819 that was to become the "most frequently copied prison structure in the world." This new cell-block model consisted of tiers of cells seven feet long and three-and-one-half feet wide. There were five tiers, each consisting of two rows of cubicles placed back to back. Surrounding these tiers was a wall. Such was the structure of the Auburn system, a prison within a prison and a true refinement of LaRochefourd's beehive.

On Christmas Day, 1821, officials at Auburn began an experiment authorized by the state legislature. Eighty criminals were placed in these north-wing cells. They were not permitted to work or to lie down in these cells in the daytime. The idea was to produce a kind of shock treatment that would "force convicts to reflection, and let self-tormenting guilt harrow up the tortures of accusing conscience, keener than scorpion stings; until the intensity of their sufferings subdues their stubborn spirits, and humbles them to a realizing sense of the enormity of their crimes and their obligation to reform."[17] Reflect the prisoners did; a large number went mad. In 1823, the governor conducted an investigation and chose to pardon most of them.

But the reformers would not be defeated. In the next few years a new system of discipline was developed to supplement the Auburn architectural design that would become world famous. A team of three legislators, George Tibbets, Samuel Hopkins, and Stephen Allan, along with the voluble Elam Lynds, the warden who so fascinated Tocqueville, complained about the work of "recluse and studious men" who wrote of the potential "virtues of felons." Reform had taken a significant turn, no less earnest but much more severe in its attempt to create a new kind of commonwealth. Auburn instituted a system of congregate labor at day and solitary confinement at night. In a general way, this system was not different from that practiced at Walnut Street. But Auburn substituted factory industrial methods for the handicraft approach, and prisoners only used their cells for sleeping.

Most important, however, was the Auburn system's attention to uniformity of detail. Every prisoner wore the same uniform. "A convict should have the same cell at night, the same place in the shops, and these same relative position in the column."[18] No visitors were permitted, nor were books allowed except for a Bible.

The Walnut Street program of individual incentives for work and good behavior was abandoned. Nothing epitomized the Auburn system more than the lockstep, invented by prison reformer, John Cray. Prisoners marched single file, each with his right hand on the other's shoulders and his face turned toward the jailer who watched for any movement of the lips. The technical invention of the "compound lever lock," which could close fifty cell doors at a time and was used first at Sing Sing, paralleled the marching procedure, as did the installation in the 1890s of peep-holes for secret surveillance at Auburn workshops.

The Auburn system was immediately and immensely popular. By the 1830s it was employed in Maine, New Hampshire, Vermont, Massachusetts, Connecticut, District of Columbia, Tennessee, Louisiana, Missouri, Illinois, Ohio, and Canada. One reason for its widespread adoption was economic. A cell built on the Pennsylvania model cost $1650, while the Auburn system cost $91 per unit. Nevertheless, the competition between the promoters of these two inventions was intense. Tocqueville's assessment is a balanced summary of the debate.

> The Philadelphia system being also that which produces the deepest impressions on the soul of the convict, must effect more reformation than that of Auburn. The latter, however, is perhaps more conformable to the habits of men in society. . . .
> If it be so, the Philadelphia system produces more honest men, and that of New York more obedient citizens.[19]

In any case, America, collaborator in the invention of the penitentiary and inventor of the Auburn system, had also created the first modern total institution. Again it was Tocqueville who appreciated its significance: "Whilst society in the United States gives the example of the most extended liberty, the prisoners of the same country offer the spectacle of the most complete despotism."[20]

"Thoreau at 29 cents a gallon"

Today the motel is as much a part of American everyday life as the telephone. And, like the telephone, its invention was swift and dramatic. But the history of the motel places it in an entirely different order of invention. For the motel is part of a whole string of inventions that were adapted to meet the demands created in the culture by the automobile.

When the invention of the automobile revolutionized travel, the motel, as a new kind of inn, did not exist. The new "auto tourist" of the early 1920s had no travel infrastructure to aid his journey. This vacationer moved slowly (about twenty miles a day) across many primitive roads and with frequent stops for repairs. There were three basic forms of temporary residences available to the motorist: the large urban hotel, the small town "drummer" hotel, and the vacation resort. Each in its own way was unsuitable to the new form of travel. The established hotel, conservative to a fault, with its dress regulations, officious clerks, and venal bellhops, clearly embarrassed the casually attired new auto travelers. As one diarist recalls:

> I feel yet the sense of shame that suffused my cheeks under that thick layer of dust as the bellhop held open the door and eight grimy intruders walked in, single file. Had we been clean, we should still have been objects of hostile suspicion, owing to our bizarre camping togs. But the bellhop, whatever his mental reaction, let us in, and we slunk off to our respective washrooms.[21]

The grand vacation hotel with its gingerbread-peaked verandas and formal dining halls effused an atmosphere, delicate, sedentary, and restrained, that made the new autocampers just as uncomfortable. But perhaps most dreaded was the small town hotel. These establishments catered to the traveling salesman who leered at women who passed through the lobby."[22] Food was unpredictable, and bedding was often left unchanged through the week.

Yet these new travelers tended to avoid the traditional wayside businesses for other reasons. Until the 1920s auto travel was still a sport, and a sport limited to the affluent American. The distinctive character of automobile travel produced a special attitude on the part of this new kind of tourist. Warren Belasco has discovered that early autocampers saw themselves as "gypsies" and "hobos." The car permitted people to be free of the "shackles of railway timetables." Enthusiasts compared their new cars to stagecoaches, ships, and gypsy caravans. One traveler described the automobile vacation as "Thoreau at 29 cents a gallon."[23]

Discouraged by the ambiance of the hotel and buoyed by images of primitivism and freedom, the autocamper spent his nights off the roadside on a farmer's pasture. The family would pick flowers

(some would even chop down a tree as an awning for shade), cook a
light dinner, and enjoy this new bourgeois fantasy of gypsydom. At
first, farmers encouraged this arrangement. Tourists would often
buy eggs and milk in the morning and sometimes offer a small tip.
As auto travel increased, however, attitudes changed. One magazine
inverted the new automobile pastoral: "They are pioneers, ex-
plorers all. Yea, some of them may be termed vandals, slaying and
burning as they go, bringing upon innocent nomads of the road the
justified wrath of injured farmers."[24] There were reports of tourists
using streams as toilets or emptying their latrines too close to drinking water. Typhoid scares forced campers to begin carrying their
own water.

But as one adaption proved troublesome, another was called
forth to take its place. Small towns, anxious to profit from a new
market source, allied themselves with those anxious to segregate
these new tourists. The municipal autocamp was the invention that
met both needs. The autocamps were free, supported by local reve-
nues, and included cold water spigots, outdoor privies, and cooking
facilities. One of the largest, Denver's Overland Park, was described
as "the Manhattan of auto-camps, the middle-western metropolis
of the thermos bottle and khaki lean-to." It held 800 lots on 160
acres along the Platte River and could accommodate 2,000 autocampers. Most parks were smaller, 10 to 15 acres, and, by the early
1920s, there were nearly 6,000 such parks in the United States.
Autocampers appeared to revel in this new invention. Camps were
"one of our greatest modern let's get acquainted institutions," the
Saturday Evening Post concluded.[25]

Again, there was trouble. As the camps grew larger, sanitary
problems occurred. Towns people began to resent the money spent
for plumbing and garbage removal. Hotel owners were outraged at
the loss of customers. But perhaps most of all, the camps were
threatened by the democratization of auto travel, which encouraged
a class of "undesirable" autocampers. These "tin-can tourists" challenged the principle of "pal-ship" at the new parks. Migrant workers began using fourth- and fifth-hand autos as a means of travel.
The traveling salesman, now more peripatetic than ever in the auto
age, frequented the autocamp. *The Motor Camper and Tourist*
abandoned its gypsy analogy and reminded its readers that "Fun
and Funds are intimately related."[26]

As a result, important innovations were added. The municipal camp initiated a series of new practices instituting mechanisms of bureaucracy and social control. Fees were charged (twenty-five to fifty cents). Time limits were established. Permits were required, revocable upon unacceptable behavior. And registration, the hotel practice so disdained by the "gypsy" autocamper, was added. These new regulations now opened up the wayside market to entrepreneurs who could not previously compete with the publicly subsidized autocamp. For instance, in 1925, 9 of Colorado's 64 camps were private. Three years later, 65 were privately owned and 20 public. The conditions were now in place for the invention of the motel.

As an institution, the motel had a whole army of individual inventors. One of them, Clara Keyton, wrote an account of her experiences in the 1920s in the development and perfection of the form.[27] Others have done the same. Paul Lancaster tells the story of one such inventor.[28] In 1919, at a grocery store along a highway near Dodge City, travelers would stop in for food and gas and ask for directions to the municipal autocamp. The owner-entrepreneur decided to offer a similar but more enticing product. He built fifteen "tent houses" with dirt floors and a cold water tap. Matresses could be rented. His fee was one dollar a night. Almost immediately, the owner found that the fifteen cabins were always filled by dusk.

While early motels were quite primitive, they were more comfortable than the camps. Yet they still met the demands of the motor traveler that the hotel could not provide: no registration, clerks, tipping, or formal dress. The immediate popularity of the motel is revealed by the rapid decline in tent sales which fell from a 1923–24 peak to a pre-1916 level by 1929. The Great Depression kept the motel as a cottage industry, but after World War II, the motel experienced large-scale national development and franchising. In the postwar period motel owners added innovation after innovation: radios, televisions, bars, swimming pools, restaurants, telephones, room service. The great chains systematically dotted the country— Howard Johnson's, Mariott, Sheraton, Ramada, Holiday Inn. Motels began to specialize. There was the airport motel with limo service, the convention motel with banquet and meeting rooms, the "adult" motel with closed circuit cable and its own specialized clientele. In fact, the motel has begun to look a lot like a hotel. As rates have risen, new innovations have been made such as the "no frills" motel. Moreover, many Americans have begun to develop the same attitudes toward the motel as an earlier generation had toward the hotel. Trailer campers now hold the claim to gypsydom.[29] Their patrons are the new democrats of the road who eschew air-conditioning for open air, isolated comfort for comradeship.

"Scattering the fire"

Ralph Gabriel had described the camp meeting as the "unique American contribution to Christianity." It is difficult to convey the impact of the camp meeting on American religious and cultural beliefs: It permanently transformed American Protestanism. The camp meeting was the key organizational structure of revivalism. Even Benjamin Franklin, confirmed deist, was impressed with its capacity for social change:

> The multitudes of all sects and demonstrations that attended were enormous . . . it seemed as if all the world were growing religious, so that one could not walk through the town in an evening without hearing psalms sung in different families of every street.[30]

But it was not until the beginning of the nineteenth century that the camp meeting broke across the United States. Several sets of conditions provided the background for its phenomenal success. Calvinist beliefs in election and original sin were being eroded by more optimistic religious doctrine. Unitarians proclaimed a simple doctrine of human goodness, Godly love, and reason. In William Ellery Channing's words, "The adoration of goodness—this is a religion."[31] Whole congregations, including clergy, converted to Unitarianism. Church property, formerly Congregationalist, Episcopal, or Presbyterian, was determined by the courts to belong to the newly constituted congregation. Universalism was the poor man's counterpart to this abandonment of Calvinist doctrine by the New England middle class and was to become a focus of attack by evangelists. The Universalists also emphasized universal salvation and were preoccupied with denying the existence of hell. The frontier provided an open battleground for Universalists and established Calvinists. Methodists, only formed in 1784, fought both groups with zeal. The Rev. James B. Finley complained in his autobiography that in almost all frontier towns, "Calvinism and Universalism had intrenched themselves." Their influence was so great that "Methodism could scarcely live."[32] The competitive atmosphere in the West was paralleled in New England by the gradual disestablishment of local churches. "Voluntarism" implied that all churches were potentially equal; each had to support themselves without taxation.

It is not surprising then that the Methodists would invent means to attract adherents from more established denominations. The invention of the circuit rider was one such effort. Young men would travel from settlement to settlement to hold prayer meetings in homes and, if permitted, offer sermons in churches. The camp meeting was another of its inventions. Methodists would claim that a revival was in every church's interests and invite other denominations to participate in the camp meeting. There was a Machiavellian element to this approach. As Peter Cartwright admits in his autobiography, the Presbyterian ministers, "not accustomed to much noise or shouting were not likely to present themselves well."[33]

The Great Revival began in Kentucky and Tennessee and moved South and East. The number of participants at camp meetings was very impressive, even in our age of rock concerts and demonstrations, especially considering the available population: Cabin Creek (20,000), Pt. Pleasant (4,000), Indian Creek (10,000), Paint Creek (8,000), Cane Ridge (20,000).[34] By 1805 the frontier camp meetings slackened and became annual affairs. But as they spread to New England and New York they initiated new revivals.

The camp meeting itself was ingeniously simple. As an organizational form it was immediately replicable and easily adaptable to new circumstances. Charles A. Johnson has remarked that the "very lack of artificiality gave the open air revival its great religious power."[35] They were set at forest clearings usually along a river for drinking water. A tent was erected from timber hewn on the grounds and sheets and quilts sewn together by frontier women. Sometimes "log tents" were even constructed. An amphitheatre was arranged with logs as pews.

People slept in wagons or on the ground. Lighting was provided by candles and "fire altars" (fires from bark and twigs atop a platform covered with sod). The illumination itself created a sense among the participants that God was present. At the larger meetings a dozen preachers would deliver sermons at once. Usually the

revival would last four or five days. But sometimes meetings ran on
for weeks. James Finley's eyewitness account gives some notion of
the power of the camp meeting:

> We arrived upon the ground and here a scene presented itself to my
> mind not only novel and unaccountable, but awful beyond description.
> A vast crowd, supposed by some to have amounted to twenty-five thou-
> sand, was collected together. The noise was like the roar of Niagara. The
> vast sea of human beings seemed to be agitated as if by storm. I counted
> seven ministers, all preaching at one time, some on stumps, others in
> wagons. . . . Some of the people were singing, others praying, some
> crying for mercy in the most piteous accents, while others were shouting
> vociferously.[36]

The camp meeting was designed to place people on an emotional
rollercoaster. Finley, who later became a Methodist circuit rider,
reported his reaction at Cane Ridge thusly:

> While witnessing these scenes, a peculiarly strange sensation, such as
> I had never felt before, came over me. My heart beat tumultuously, my
> knees trembled, my lip quivered, and I felt as though I must fall to the
> ground.[37]

He went to the woods and "tried to philosophize" his reactions,
"resolving them into mere sympathetic excitement—a kind of religious enthusiasm, inspired by songs and eloquence." Returning to
the meeting, Finley saw "at least five hundred swept down in a
moment, as if a battery of a thousand guns had been opened upon
them." He fled to the woods again, staggered to a tower for a drink
to steady himself, and still finding himself panicked began his conversion: "Then it was that I saw clearly through the veil of Universalism, and this refuge of lies was swept away by God . . . I realized
in all its force and power, the awful truth, that if I died in my sins I
was a lost man forever."[38]

It was this physical aspect of its conversions that so angered the
critics of the camp meeting. Actually, Finley's experience was a
rather mild one. "Falling" to the ground was a common reaction to
the sermon, and those thus "slain" would convert. The "jerks" was
another affliction. Peter Cartwright, an extremely popular and ef-
fective preacher reports the following. Notice the dollop of class
resentment in his account:

To see those proud young gentlemen and young ladies, dressed in their silks, jewelry, and primella, from top to toe, take the jerks, would often excite my risibilities. The first jerk or so, you would see their fine bonnets, caps, and combs fly; and so sudden would be the jerking of the head that their long loose hair would crack almost as loud as a wagoner's whip.[39]

People would be awed when "scoffers fell at the services 'as suddenly as if struck by lightening' sometimes at the very moment they were cursing the revival." Some participants would "bark" until they were hoarse. Others would run about madly; some engaged in a swooning dance.

The detractors of the camp meeting reported these acts with alarm and disgust. Accounts of sexual behavior at the meetings confirmed their worst fears. The established clergy were the most unsympathetic. Lyman Beecher, who later was to make his peace with the Great Revival, once warned Charles Finney: "I know your plan and you know I do—you mean to come to Connecticut and carry a streak of fire to Boston. But if you attempt it, as the Lord liveth, I'll meet you at the state line, and call out all the artillerymen, and fight every inch of the way to Boston, and then I'll fight you there."[40] But overall, there seemed to be a certain ambivalence to the camp meeting. Margaret Bayard Smith's description of the preachers at a 1822 meeting in Washington is not atypical:

Whether all these excessive efforts will produce a permanent reformation I know not; but there is something very repugnant to my feelings in the public way in which they discuss the conversions and convictions of people and in which young ladies and children display their feelings and talk of their convictions and experiences. Dr. May calls the peculiar fever, the night fever, and he says almost all cases were produced by night meetings, crowded rooms, excited feelings, and exposure to night air.[41]

Thomas Hamilton reminded readers that "in a free community the follies of the finatic are harmless," and that, after all, the introduction of religion "in a newly settled country . . . is on the whole beneficial."[42]

Those so distressed with "night fever" did in fact find themselves in a curiously defensive position. American Protestianism placed great emphasis upon the conversion experience. In fact, conservative Calvinists had insisted upon a sign of election as the basis of

church membership. The revivalists accepted this position, in opposition to the Unitarians and Universalists, and as Margaret Smith
noted, pursued it ruthlessly. Aside from the extravagant behavior of
the camp meetings, what so upset the opposition was the democratic reinterpretation of election. In order to repeat and "come
through," the participant need only confess his/her sins and rededi-
cate his/her life. The camp meeting itself was the perfect democratic
agency for this belief since it was based upon the principles of mass
conversion and mass admission. Conversion became an act of free
will, and it was the preacher's task to create the conditions for it to
assert itself. Again the camp meetings proved to be the ideal vehicle
for the new doctrine. Ministers must be able to converse with the
people on their own terms. A seminary education which emphasized fine theological points and erudite sermons proved to be a
positive disadvantage in the context of the camp meeting. Charles
Finney insisted on addressing people in "such language as they
would understand: Among farmers and mechanics, and other classes of men, I borrowed my illustrations from their various occupations." When critics would ask, "Why don't you illustrate from
events of ancient history, and take a more dignified way of illustra-
ting your ideas?" he would defend himself by saying that his object
"was not to cultivate a style of oratory that should soar above the
heads of the people, but to make myself understood. . . ."[43]

It was Finney who was responsible for making the most important innovations in the invention of the camp meeting. Whitney
Cross has said that he "has seemed to some historians, as to many of
his contemporaries, to be one of those rare individuals who of their
own unaided force may on occasion significantly transform the
destinies of masses of people."[44] As we noted, Finney consciously
adopted the new style of sermonic oratory. He, along with other
innovators, developed the Eastern version of the camp meeting.
Different cultural dispositions, village life, as well as climate made
the frontier camp meeting more limited as a means of revival. Finney became the leader of what came to be known as the protracted
meeting. He made scores of trips up and down the East coast, but
especially in Western New York. Finney would respond to requests
from congregations or clergy in the winter, when, as Cross notes,
"commerce ebbed and ceased while an apathetic but pentitent
Yankee community contemplated its past and present sins."[45] More

than ninety letters to Finney have survived, detailing such communities' felt need for revival. Evangelists like Finney employed the metaphor of fire for their mission: the "explosion" of Rome, New York, "scattered the fire over all this region." Revivals did indeed seem to move in widening concentric circles.

The protracted meeting was made up of what were called "New Measures." It began with a daily sunrise meeting. A "little band of sisters" or "holy band" would provide a kind of organizational cadre for the revival. "Where there was a sinner unconverted, especially if he manifested any opposition, you would find some two or three brethren or sisters agreeing to make him a particular subject of prayer."[46] The band would press villagers to attend every prayer meeting. These groups would also act as monitors and facilitators at the large meetings later in the day. The recruitment of women was regarded as essential to a revival. Their pivotal role was soon acknowledged, as women often came to lead the assemblies in prayer (much to the consternation of conservatives).[47]

Great emphasis was placed upon the "prayer of faith" at the nightly meetings. A "new system of particularity" was created. Requests from God must not be vague or general, but for a special object. Finney would "dissect" the prayers offered and mock them for their formality. During the days, as the number of converts grew, visits would be made to homes either to help those in the agonies of conversion or to urge participation by the unrepentant. Ideally, itinerant preachers wanted complete local attention focused on the revival. Finney thought that merchants should lock up their stores. In many towns, business after business would close until the whole community was transformed into a camp meeting.

Perhaps not surprisingly, the very success of the camp meeting was the basis for its demise. The protracted meeting began to assume a bureaucratic character as adaption and experimentation came to be seen as stock measures. The process worked, in Cross's words, much like modern juke boxes which kill a new tune with repetition. But the bureaucratization of revival went even deeper. The invention of the camp and protracted meeting had produced a new class of professional evangelists, formally unschooled perhaps, but as ruthlessly efficient and rational as any manager.

E.M. Forster once visited a Shaker Commune with a group of
American friends. After the tour, the Shakers gave him a ruler as a
gift. The other members of the party marvelled at the small object.
They remarked upon its simplicity, its originality of design, its balance. Forster, who was anything but an insensitive man, puzzled
over the object and wanly concluded that to him it was just a
ruler.[48]

This same reverence forms the reaction of the American who
views a pieced quilt. One is overwhelmed by its combination of
simplicity and intricateness, its boldness of design, its colors, its
balance, and perhaps most of all, the amount of time it must have
consumed to complete. This is not to say that other cultures could
not appreciate the art of the American pieced quilt (although for
some time it was regarded as inferior to its European counterpart).
But this reaction on the part of an American is in large part derived
from an appreciation of the pieced quilt as a uniquely American
cultural artifact. For the quilt is an invention of the American preindustrial past. It awakens pastoral longings in a nation in which a
craft less than three hundred years old can be deemed archaic. One
recent book on quilt-making unreservedly evokes this romance:
"indigeneous as Vermont maple sugar, picturesque as a split-rail
fence in Appalachia, dignified as a New England sea captain's man-
sion, romantic as the white pillored plantation houses of the deep
South . . . within the fields of the quilt are pieced the dreams of the
men and women who were wresting a place of their own from the
unsubdued wilderness. . . ."[49]

The concept of the quilt itself is actually a primordial invention,
a response to human vulnerability to the environment. An animal
skin forms a basic quilt with hair as a layer against the cold. A sack
stuffed as a means of protection was probably the first consciously
constructed quilt. These Rousseauean musings aside, remnants of
quilts have been found in ancient Egypt. The Museum of Cairo
displays a quilt of dyed Gazelle hide dated at 960 B.C. that was used
for decorative purposes, as a canopy for an Egyptian princess.

The craft of quilt-making reached spectacular decorative levels in
the Middle Ages, in part as the result of world commerce opened by
the Crusades. Quilts were used as padding for armor, as bedding, as
curtains, as hangings in churches, as gowns, as cloaks, as banners.

Medieval and even late Elizabethan quilts were of three types: the plain quilt composed of two single sheets of material and filled with straw, wool, feathers and later cotton; the appliqué, also composed of single sheets but with forms stitched on the top; and the pieced quilt, composed of separate swatches of material stitched together.

International trade produced the second major revolution in quilt-making in the seventeenth century with the importation of Indian chintz. Easier to sew than wool or silk, brighter, colorfast and washable, chintzes were immensely popular. The new cloth produced waves of innovations in quilting based upon bright colors and new designs. In 1700, English and French woolen and silk manufacturers struck back; a law was passed banning the importation of cotton. In 1721 harsher measures were added, including a provision which made it unlawful to wear chintzes.

It is at this point that the patchwork quilt as we know it was invented. Traditional piecing used large portions of material combined with appliqué or pieced borders surrounding appliqué. The scarcity of the new and technically superior material created a new craft. As cotton was now only available in small pieces, patterns of small blocks were the only alternative. Jonathon Holstein has carefully traced the origin of the patchwork (blocked piece) quilt in an attempt to determine its American origins. He notes surviving quilts using pieces of Indian chintz at Levens Hall in England which were completed early in the seventeenth century. They do not bear a great resemblance to American counterparts. The pieced designs (circles and crosses) float atop a white background. Holstein believes that these quilts were not the first patchwork quilts: "They are too 'finished' in the sense of sophisticated technique and design not to have precursors."[50] It is possible, he continues, that some lost missing link connects the Levens Hall and the American quilts. It is also possible that the new pieced quilts were a later invention, independently developed in the New World. Holstein also considers the possibility that the blocked piece quilt was a well-developed craft in England and was brought to America by its first settlers. But it is really not possible to locate this craft as to national origin with any real certainty. The earliest surviving American quilt does employ a central medallionlike design which corresponds to an English style, but its inscription shows a very late date: "Anna Tuels her bed quilt given to her by her mother in the year Aug. 23, 1785." In some ways, this historical question is a moot one. American quilts are so unique in design that as an artistic craft they are clearly an American invention.

Political and economic developments forced this originality. The American patchwork quilt was an invention of the immigrant experience. Colonists were repeatedly warned to pack as many quilts as possible. After arriving, however, settlers found replacement quilts to be quite scarce. The first cotton mill did not appear in America until 1790 when Samuel Stater established a plant on the basis of secretly memorized British plans. England jealously protected its right to a monopoly of textile production. In defense, seventeenth-century towns set quotas for each family in the production of spun yarn. But these "homespun" goods were no competition for the new dyes and block prints of British mills. We don't know what very early American quilts looked like. Very likely, colonists patched existing quilts with worn-out clothing or created new ones from fabrics too tattered for wear. We can see, however, that the pieces available were likely quite small and, from traditional European perspectives, very mismatched. What does one do with a "scrap bag" of brown fabric, mixed, say, with a few pieces of blue? The most likely alternative would have been to cut these remnants into some kind of geometric shape and arrange the colors in a pattern (a blue border, for example). If the remnants were too small and ragged, a random pattern would be possible, as in the crazy quilt.

Progressively pieced blocks were technically the easiest to work. They took less time, were sewed in laps, and permitted the least amount of waste. Several types of blocking were invented: symmetrical blocks, split blocks (composed of triangles), and asymmetrical blocks. Strips of material could also be used.

With these severe limitations, quilt-makers invented thousands of designs, many of which produce breathtaking patterns. Let me talk about just a few that in my mind are most pleasing to the modern eye. One of the most popular was the Log Cabin design. It is composed of a series of blocks, each with a central sequence to represent a chimney. What is so fascinating about this pattern is its use of light and dark shades diagonally dividing each square. Frequently, these shades were sewed to visually "hook up" with the next block, so that the quilt shows an overlay of larger log cabins at right angles to the smaller blocks. The Log Cabin is a design that evokes order, but the visual overlay produces an effect that, while hardly jarring, suggests another pattern emeshed but also partially at odds with the first. Since the design is derived from the architecture of the home, it offers a complex cosmology composed of discrete and simple parts.

Many designs employed stars of all shapes and sizes. One of them, the Star of Bethlehem, is an eight-pointed design that frequently takes up the whole quilt. The eye catches an opposite effect from that produced by the Log Cabin. Here one sees a huge design of reds and oranges that seems to almost burst both up and out of a rectangle that barely encloses it. Then one notices that the design is composed of tiny diamonds arranged in rows of complementary shades. Sometimes the center star is surrounded first by four smaller stars and then bordered by a sea of tiny celestial objects. The tiny scraps are used to create a gloriously large figure without hiding the humble pieces which form it.

One of the most astonishing designs is one called Baby Blocks, a nineteenth-century invention. Pieces are cut in differently shaded parallelograms to create cubes. The optical effect is strikingly reminiscent of modern cubism. In some variations, the shades selected for the blocks are so arranged as to produce the effect of a larger cube (also three-dimensional). One quilt made in Oklahoma about 1875 features five rows of clusters of cubes that appear to be gliding down a polka-dot background. It was named "Tumbling Blocks."

These three designs are only three of thousands. The simplicity and directness of the names themselves prick a sense of longing in the modern mind. Quilts were named after tools that are now archaic: Anvil, Saw-Tooth, Ship's Wheel, Carpenters Wheel, Water Wheel, The Reel, Chain Dash, Dusty Miller. The pieced scraps were abstractions from everyday objects. One woman gives us the emotional background for her version of the Windmill quilt, consisting of semicircles within circles over squares:

> I didn't use a compass to plan out my circles. Sometimes I draw a plate if its the right size. . . . Then I plan whatever piece I'm gonna do inside the circle. . . . Back then I slept in the attic room. There were windows at each end and I had my bed under one of them. I could hear the windmill at night. That sound was my lullaby. The windmill seemed like the biggest circle then, bigger than the moon or a wagon wheel, and always in motion.[51]

Many designs were derived from nature: Garden Maize, Sun Dial, Autumn Leaf, Spider Web, Rolling Stone, Flying Bats, Dovein-the Window, Ocean Wave, Gray Goose, Wild Goose Chase, Sunburst, Love Apples. Flowers, sometimes geometrically abstracted and sometimes appliquéd on blocks, were common. When one woman was asked how she designed roses, she replied that she went outside, plucked some petals and leaves and impressed the form on the patches and traced it.[52] Religious designs were also widely used. The cross was especially popular, no doubt because of its geometric form as well as its religious power. Crosses and Losses was a particularly poignant pattern, composed of shattered and solid triangular pieces. Political themes were given quilted abstractions: Lincoln's Platform, Whig's Defeat, White House Steps, Elephant, The Little Giant.

The need for quilts was pressing. Every bed required several quilts. For frontier families, quilt-making was a matter of survival. As late as the 1880s three-fourths of American bedcovers were quilts.[53] In 1930 Kathryne Travis reports visiting an old woman in the Ozarks who revealed a frank utilitarian approach to quilting: "I managed to give all my four sons and three married daughters enough quilts to keep'em warm and now these here (pointing to a stack) belong to Emmie and Pearl. Leastways they will as soon as they git them a man. I don't want any o'my chillern a-sayin' I ain't done right be'em by not givin'em plenty of good warm beddin'. "[54]

But in addition to this basic protective use, the patchwork quilt was used for social and ceremonial purposes. In fact, in the history of American quilt-making, these protective and social uses rest side by side, sometimes forming two separate crafts. In their oral history of quilt-making Patricia Cooper and Norma Bradley Buferd provide us with an example of this distinction:

Oh, I don't like to think about my quilts. I lost them all in the fire. . . . We lost all the kids' things too. My momma's quilts was in there with mine. Well, I didn't have the heart to quilt after that . . . at least no fancy quilts. We was always quilting for cover, making up warm block quilts from old wool and work clothes. But I just tacked them. They was serviceable all right. Everyone put their hand to piecing in the winter. All my boys pieced right along with the girls. It was work that had to be done.[55]

The social tradition of the patchwork quilt was related to the "work that had to be done," but it also transcended the simple protective function and produced quilts that corresponded to the major events of life (birth, marriage and adulthood, and death), as well as commemorating special relationships (friendship, gratitude, hospitality). The social tradition elevated the humble and utilitarian patchwork quilt to the status of gift giving.

The center of this tradition was the Bride's Quilt. While practices varied slightly, the bridal quilt actually included a whole set of between ten and thirteen quilt tops. Many were made years before and kept in a hope chest to be brought out when a design was selected. Heart motifs were reserved exclusively for bridal quilts. Other patterns included arrowpoints, linked rings, crescent moons (symbolizing virginity), and oak leaves (longevity). Sometimes the design would be selected by the engaged pair, and the groom-to-be would be presented with a "Freedom Quilt" (completing the dozen or bakers dozen) by a sister or a friend.

Mourning, Memory, and Widow's Quilts, with designs composed of willows, black darts and coffins, may appear excessively maudlin to us today, but they had a therapeutic and communal function. Memory quilts featured a central wreath with squares composed of the clothing of the deceased. They often were inscribed with the date of death. If a family did not own one, neighbors would lend the bereaved their own memory quilts for display at the viewing.

Each of these social traditions as well as others were community arrangements. One poignant recollection follows:

> When I was about four years old the neighbor's baby died, and all the women was called in to help. Mama knew what her part was because right away she took some blue silk out of her hope chest. I remember that silk so well because it was special and I got to carry it. When we got to the neighbors some of the women was cooking and the men was making a casket. Mama and three other women set up the frame and quilted all day. First they quilted the lining for the casket, and then they made a tiny little quilt out of the blue silk to cover the baby.[56]

Many of these gatherings, however, were organized around more pleasant occasions. Designs for bridal quilts were sewn by groups of women. Each participant in the "quilting bee" would bring a quilt block, often with a signature, and the host would receive the finished product as a gift. Quilting bees also made bedding for the circuit riders discussed in the section on the revival camp.

Quilt-making as both a social and an art form reached its peak in the middle of the nineteenth century. Ironically, the craft of quilting blossomed at precisely the point at which it was to rapidly decline. At first quilt-making directly benefited from industrialization. Machine-printed fabrics (including roller painting) and aniline dyes produced cheap and brightly colored prints. Holstein reports that Americans responded with a "flurry of quilt-making." "In terms of design, it was the most important period, since after a long evolution, a distinctive American style had been achieved, and its possibilities were thoroughly explored during more than a half century."[57]

Until the 1840s, quilt-making was independent of market inventions. As a salvage craft, quilting was performed outside the market for home and social use. The actual making of the quilt, of course, remained part of this vernacular craft. The sewing machine pushed quilting even further into the grasp of the market economy. In 1855 *Godey's* magazine told readers that sewing machines were "valuable aids to female industry." By 1860 it had described them as "indispensible." After the 1860s one-half of American quilts were machine stitched. Quilting came to be regarded as a genteel activity and was seen in terms of a leisure-time pursuit. "The aim," writes one authority, "was to see who could lavish the greatest amount of handprinted adornment and intricate stitchery upon her silk and velvet masterpiece." Lessons were given in handpainting quilts. Magazines supplied "how-to" articles on "Fancy Designs" and "Oriental Work" as well as new stiches. Quilts, at least those in urban areas, took on a baroque quality. The crazy quilt was transformed into a parlor decoration.[58]

Further industrial invention brought about the demise of the quilt. Many households featured the new white bedspreads from the Jacquard looms which produced computerlike weaving. The most devastating treatment of the handicraft was the practice of placing a quilt on a bed wrong side up in imitation of the new "machine-made" cover. Handmade became a derisive description even for the ornamental quilt. Those who had hand sewn utilitarian quilts now saw "store bought covers as eminently practical."[59]

The "de-invention" of the quilt was rapid but uneven. Spectacular quilts were made well into the twentieth century. But increasingly the quilt, as both a salvage art and social institution, was to be found only in backwater communities: in Appalachian hill towns, in conservative religious communes (most notably among the Amish and the Mennonites), in isolated farm communities.

In the 1930s, Eleanor Roosevelt attempted to re-invent quilt-making as a project of the WPA. Remains of these quilting co-ops still survive in some Appalachian towns. The plan was to reconstruct quilt-making to correspond to the American fantasy of a cottage industry. But WPA administrators were so concerned about unemployment that they neglected the problem of marketing the finished product. In any case, war production seemed more attractive than quilting as a source of income. Today charming stone buildings that briefly housed these craft centers stand as garages and restaurants.

Later War on Poverty officials would rediscover the same region and craft. Using VISTA volunteers and OEO grants, the Mountain Artisans Co-op was formed. With the help of *Women's Wear Daily* they sold their quilt spreads and dresses to fashionable New York retail outlets. Even more recently a group of eighteen women artists, supported by an NEH grant, collaborated with traditional quilt-makers to design a series of quilted pictures. The quilt was also brought to the attention of the avant-garde when Ralph Lauren used pieces of antique quilts in skirts.[60] The innovation caused a great deal of horrified reaction, although it must be said that Lauren's use was very much in the quilting tradition as salvage art.

Quilt-making has now recaptured the imagination of the American middle class.[61] But "hand-made" is firmly linked to the market. "Craft" books, patterns and quilting alcoves in fabric stores vie for consumer attention. A commercial cuteness infects many of the designs. Sun-bonnet Suzie, Grover, and E.T., calico roosters and sky blue cows are the new motifs. No doubt, however, the American woman who quilts in front of her television set and will hang her creation on the wall or use it to adorn her nursery thinks of log cabins, quilting bees, and Vermont maple sugar as she participates in some vague way in the "feminine art" of her American sisters.

Chapter 3

The Invention Matrix

The inventions under consideration, as disparate as they appear to be, reveal certain basic common features in their development. Each had immediate as well as remote forerunners. The telephone appears to us to be the most revolutionary, in part because we are used to accepting novelty in technology. But innovations in the telegraph were producing an instrument close to the telephone at the time of the latter's invention. The telegraph had acquired some expansive specialization (fire alarm systems, stock ticker tapes), unskilled-use techniques (autographic telegraphy), and private-use capability (the formation of the Social Telegraph Association). The penitentiary had predecessors in the workhouse and the monastery as well as in early experiments at Walnut Street and at Newgate, England. The motel was, in general way, a modern reincarnation of the inn and, as we saw, had a whole series of immediate experimental forerunners. The revival camp meeting in some ways reinstituted the techniques of the European Reformation. It was used with success during the Greak Awakening. Not only was quilting a well-developed craft with a long history, but British women had already invented new forms of the pieced quilt in response to shortages of cotton.

Yet despite these precedents, each of these inventions, when fully perfected, brought about rapid change—and in a very short period of time. In each case, the invention was in wide use within ten years. The impact of the telephone, penitentiary, motel, and camp meeting was clearly momentous. And such impact, after all, is part of the grand definition of invention. Not surprisingly (and in support of the Burkean objection), each invention produced consequences quite unforeseen by its inventors, early proponents, and users.

There are more similiarities. Together they form what we can call an invention matrix. For an invention, any invention, represents more than the acts of inventors, more than efflorescence of the cultural beliefs of a society, more than the output of economic demand. An invention is part of a complex set of elements, each feeding upon the others. Let us review what seem to be the essential parts of the invention matrix: problem construction and a solution apparatus, a use community, a replication procedure, promotion groups, and invention linkages.

Problem Construction

An invention arises from a series of attempts to solve some perceived problem. Certain structures are seen as inadequate and/or incapable of improvement. Of course, especially in the case of social and political inventions, these perceptions are subject to complex variations. The problem itself can be quite intricate. But the effort of the inventors at problem construction are often animated by very rudimentary concerns: How can we transmit the human voice across a distance? How can we treat the criminal as a rational creature? How can we travel the way we want? How can we save the unrepentant? How can we keep warm? Surrounding these questions are layers of cultural assumptions, often only vaguely understood, but the question itself as part of the process of problem construction is very basic and compelling. Thomas Kuhn in his analysis of scientific discovery calls a process similar to this the perception of anomaly.[1] A theory does not explain some occurrence. Invention requires the same kind of perception, but here the concern has a much closer relationship to practice. The questions revolve, not around explanation (although this concern is certainly part of the formulation), but around action.

Perhaps most importantly, however, the inventor, unlike Kuhn's scientist who resists the perception of anomaly, embraces novelty. Bell's invention began modestly as an effort to perfect telegraphic transmission. In fact, the telephone was in a sense an invention of the telegraph. Some historians contend that Morse and Henry should be regarded as co-inventors of the telephone. In any case, it was the telegraphic system that provided the basis for Bell's efforts. No doubt Bell's background in speech therapy acted as a prod to his work. But what appears crucial to the invention was Bell's own perception of novelty. The fact that Bell believed that he could produce an instrument with new and extraordinary capabilities appears to have been essential to his invention. His lectures attempted to convey this sense of novelty to audiences.

The modern prison was the invention outcome of several elements that constructed a problem. One was a disgust with corporal punishment, a disgust derived in part from religious principles. In Philadelphia, the prison represented an application of the religious methods of Quakers to the case of lawbreakers. Another element was the Enlightenment confidence in the ability to invent new institutions. Every modern revolution seems to have added new innovations in the prison. In America the invention of the penitentiary was an act of self-confidence, a belief in the ability to reform the criminal. But the prison also arose as a solution to the problem of social control. Particularly in western New York, reformers were concerned about the ability of transplanted New England institutions to produce a stable social order.[2] On the one hand, the prison involved a recognition of the possible failure of the village and the church as agencies of control; on the other, it applied the principles of self-control in a free society to the problem of criminality. The prison would teach self-control through a carefully managed environment. The penitentiary, as an institution incorporating the principles of segregation, work, and solitude, represented an "ideal" solution.

The motel, as an invention, was the result not only of a redefinition of time and space as a result of the automobile, but also of the special social psychology of the new auto travelers themselves. These "gypsies of the road" held a particular set of attitudes toward travel. They were immersed in an experiment in the fantastic. Early auto travelers wanted to capture the romance of an adventurous and leisurely pastoral. The hotel did not fit this vision; some solution was necessary.

The revival camp, the most explosive of our invention examples, was, in at least one of its forms, a response to the circumstances of American frontier life. There was a concern over the absence of churches and religiosity in general on the frontier. As we noted, the frontier also provided a huge, new, and highly competitive arena for denominational activity. The camp meeting was the solution to these problems. It fit the informality of frontier life, provided access to sparse populations spread out over long distances, and most importantly, provided the structure for immediate church admission.

The American craft of quilting was invented from a humble need: the need for protection. Writer after writer complains about the discomfort of the colonial house in winter. Judge Sewall noted that his morning bread was too frozen to eat. Cotton Mather could not write one winter day: " 'Tis Dreadful cold, my ink glass in my standish is frozen. . . ."[3] But the quilt, now pieced from fragments and rags, was also a solution to the need for social and cultural expression for a dislocated people without, especially in winter, a great deal of daily human contact. Accounts of frontier life contain more complaints about loneliness than the weather. The quilting bee was an invention designed to meet the needs of the woman "starved for female companionship" as well as of those entering new communities.[4]

The Use Community

While I do not wish to treat inventions as part of some simple marketing enterprise, it is important to note that an invention does require some sort of use community. The use community need only be a potential one, as in the case of the telephone. But some conception of users is as essential to the success of a social or political invention as it is for a technological one.

Bell saw the significance of this point when he emphasized that the advantage of the telephone over the telegraph lay in the fact that the former could be operated by anyone. When the phone was first used to relay presidential election returns in 1896, one journalist marveled over the simplicity of its use: "Thousands transmitted the vote of the country townships that had never operated a telephone, and thousands sat with their ear glued to the receiver the whole night long, hypnotized by the possibilities unfolded to them for the first time."[5]

The success of the revival camp can be partially explained by the relative lack of resources it required. The camp itself was a modest enterprise. As we noted, a clearing and some basic labor and cooperation were all that was necessary. More importantly, the camp meeting used the services of unlicensed ministers, much to the dismay of established denominations. Speaking ability was, of course, a premium, but it did not require a seminary education (Finney, in fact, rejected a scholarship to Princeton, regarding it as a liability) and could be developed experimentally. In this respect, both the telephone and camp meeting are democratic inventions. They require little or openly obtainable skills.

The character of the use community for the American pieced quilt is somewhat different from that of both the telephone and the revival camp. It is true that, contrary to the European appliqué tradition, the American pieced quilt required few basic skills. Sewing is a democratic craft, and the utilitarian tradition of the pieced quilt as protection illustrates this point. But as a craft, quilting allows for excellence and creativity in design and execution that is not equally distributed across the population. Communities recognized these skills by referring to one or two women of a town as master quilters. In fact, I think part of our awe of the quilt today is the result of an immediate appreciation for the creation of so magnificent an object by people whom we sense vaguely as having been ordinary, if not primitive.

Another aspect of quilting worth noting is that the activity occurred outside the market. The pieced quilt is an invention of a household economy relatively unpenetrated by the market. Today, this economy is part of a market consumption system. We buy clothes, heat, food, medical care, entertainment. Of course, except in certain periods, the quilt was never completely isolated from the market. Thread was purchased; swatches of material were bought to "dress up" the quilt. But to a greater or lesser degree, the pieced quilt represents a use community that has contracted to the point of extinction.

Universal use is, of course, the goal of the inventor, one which the prescient Bell foresaw. Although we should mention that the development of a universal and unskilled usage community need not be the only avenue for insuring the success of an invention. The opposite approach can be pursued, in which an invention with a clearly defined and limited use community can nonetheless effectively maintain itself, particularly if its administration requires skilled licensure and/or if the usage is formally or de facto somehow restricted. An example of the latter is the user reliance upon oil or natural gas heating. In fact, one way to access the democratic characteristics of inventions is to think of them in terms of the manner in which administrative and consumer use groups are implemented. In a way, the history of the invention of the prison and the motel illustrates this alternative. At one point, the auto traveler rejected the universal use of the auto camps. Efforts were made to disestablish the democracy of the camps so that vacationers could rid themselves of "tin can" fellowpatrons and cultivate a more select company. On the other hand, the volunteers who composed the Philadelphia Society represented a broad spectrum of the urban bourgeoisie. Today, the idea of a penitentiary's being managed by unpaid amateurs appears quaint. Prisons are run by professionals—psychiatrists, social workers, criminal justice administrators—and general access to the prison itself is carefully limited. The very concept of the penitentiary involved a "closing off" of the prisoner from the rest of society for the purposes of conversion. Still, at Auburn, for a small fee, visitors could tour the penitentiary any weekday. From a contemporary view, this practice does seem voyeuristic and cruel, but it nevertheless did represent an institutionalization of public access to this newly constructed society.

The Promotion Group

Central to the creation of a use community is the formation of promotion groups as sponsors of new inventions. In a market society, the firm itself undertakes the role of conveying the advantages of a new product and identifying a use community. Bell's address on forecasting that we have been quoting was presented to a group of British industrialists. In the case of social and political inventions, the task of promotion is also assumed by collections of organized groups. In chapter 7 we shall discuss the historical roles of these groups as inventive communities in their own right. For the moment, we can illustrate this aspect of invention through the examples we have just discussed.

The American contribution to the invention of the prison offers an ideal example of the function of a promotion group. The general social condition of colonial urban society provided the background for invention. Here was a fluid and aggressive society with special internal bourgeois conflicts. Eric Foner's description captures the economic background of ideological activity during this period: "Philadelphia's artisan culture was pervaded by ambiguities and tensions, beginning with the inherent dualism of the artisan's role

on the one hand, as a small entrepreneur and employer and, on the other, as a laborer and craftsman. Culturally, there was a recurrent tension between the sense of mutality and community, whether confined to a specific craft or extended to all artisans, and the strong tendency toward individualism and self-improvement."[6]

An attitude of concern and common interest as well as competitiveness characterized the relationships of the artisans themselves and the laborers who worked in their shops. These artisans, self-educated and potentially mobile, frequently turned to participation in public projects as a mode of self-actualization and solidarity. These conditions made possible an extremely successful kind of promotion group, one which we would identify today as a reform group. No single individual was more aware of the potentialities of this version of a promotion group than Benjamin Franklin. Franklin, of course, was a creator of technological, social, and political inventions and was himself a contributor to the invention of the penitentiary. In his autobiography, he recounts his own organization theory. He describes the implementation, telling how he collected a small group of men from decidedly petit bourgeois backgrounds, men with strong aspirations for individual success, who would meet regularly to discuss new books and ideas. The "Junto" was a semi-secret society, in many ways not unlike a front group. Members would organize their own groups whose members were kept ignorant of the group's relationship with the Junto. Franklin or another member would write an anonymous article "to prepare the minds of the people." Junto members and affiliated organizations would discuss the new proposal, and a campaign would be planned for the legislature to undertake the project. Very often, at this point, Franklin would propose some matching grant to initiate the project on an experimental basis. In the case of the plan for Philadelphia's first hospital, he proposed to the legislature that, if £2,000 were donated privately, another 2,000 in public funds be appropriated. The Junto provided the organizational structure for fund-raising. In the same manner Franklin claimed credit for the reform of the constable system, for the creation of an orphanage, a cooperative library, and an academy, and for more prosaic projects such as street paving and lighting.

Franklin's curious combination of cynicism regarding human motivation and optimism about reform was not shared by the religious and earnest Philadelphians. But this general model of a promotion group (itself an invention for which Franklin shares credit) is universally applicable in liberal societies. The Philadelphia Society for Alleviating the Miseries of Public Prisons promoted the idea of the penitentiary, wrote the enabling legislation, administered its new invention, and served as a promotion group in other states. When New York reformers invented another model, open warfare between promotion groups broke out. Today, the reform group recruits from a different stratum of the bourgeoisie, but the general function of the promotion group remains the same. Whatever new policy initiative or institution is advocated, the reform group offers new communities for its own members and its clients.

The revival camp, of course, created informal networks of promotion groups among the converted. Finney, Cartwright, and Finley were all converted through camp meetings and became independent evangelists themselves. Congregations in the East served as promotion groups for revivals. They sought out evangelists to "light fires." The churches themselves were the most powerful promotion groups. As we noted, Methodists aggressively encouraged camp meetings and challenged other denominations to participate. In fact, the revival camp was one aspect of a massive and complex institutional network of American Protestantism which Ronald G. Walters has called a "benevolent empire."[8] Walters describes these religious associations as "formidable instruments of propaganda." They include the American Bible Society (organized in 1816), the American Sunday School Union (1824), and the American Tract Society (1825). Formally interdenominational, these benevolent enterprises were connected to parent organizations whose executive boards were frequently interlocking. Annual conventions established an upcoming agenda. Whitney Cross has pointed out that the interdenominational character of these associations was challenged on occasion. One activist wrote in 1828 that "whatever . . . may be said . . . these national institutions . . . are sectarian. One denomination has a predominating influence . . . and just enough from other denominations are introduced to save appearances and give a tone to the sound of catholicism." The amount of written material issued by these promotion groups was staggering. For example, in two years the Geneva agent of the American Tract Society covered 200 towns monthly, reaching 500,000 people and leaving behind 4 million pages of religious material. In 1824 the

New York state chapter convinced the secretary of state to request

systematic use of its publications in the common schools. The order
was later rescinded after other groups petitioned the state legislature.

The history of the invention of the motel shows its own clusters
of promotion groups. The auto vacationers circulated privately
printed accounts of their journeys. Later more professional guide-
books appeared, including advertisements for appropriate travel
gear, and were supported by small-town chambers of commerce
and by the auto industry. Trade publications helped motel owners
to identify new markets. The formation of the National Tourist
Lodge and Motor Court Trade Association (NTL-MCTA) indicated
that the motel had arrived as an established American economic
institution. Its first major act involved the drafting of a price-
stabilization proposal for the consideration of the NRA.

The central promotional group for quilt-making was the bee or
party, whose role in the engagement reception we have already
described. The bee was only one of many ad hoc communal self-
help groups in new settlements. Cornhusking, and barn- and
school-raising were activities that required mutual cooperation.
The quilting bee was a more regular affair. One New England woman recalled attending twenty-eight bees in a single winter. The quilting bee assumed a more formal function in the nineteenth century as
an adjunct to the local church. Quilts were sent to missions, to the
poor, and to those whose homes had been destroyed by fire. These
service groups also auctioned quilts at fairs to support church activities. Communal quilt-making, then, had become attached to the
service tradition in American towns. When one finds evidence of its
survival today, it is preserved within service groups—among Men-
nonite women, in associations like the newly transported Quilters
of Miami Beach.

A history of invention in America is in large part a history of the
activity of promotion groups in the marketplace and in social and
political communities. Those who concentrate on the bourgeois
hegemony in American society tend to overlook or underestimate
this aspect of change. But the American middle class, so swollen in
numbers, at least in a psychic sense, represents a vast reserve army
for the support of inventions, awaiting a call by promotion groups.
We shall explore this point further, but it is appropriate here to note
that the bourgeois sensitivity to reform and innovation, especially

when it is not contained by the restraint of other classes, will foster wave after wave of invention.

Replication Procedures

I have noted that our contemporary focus on technological invention shapes our approach to all invention. Sometimes that preoccupation is advantageous. One of the major breakthroughs of the industrial revolution was the invention and perfection of interchangeable parts. By creating a system in which component parts could be made in massive numbers and could be reliably uniform, the manufacturing process could be made vastly quicker and cheaper. Interchangeable parts, along with the factory system itself and the assembly line, were inventions that created a new replication procedure for any technological invention. The existence of an economy based upon capital expansion was also an essential element of modern technological invention. Whatever one's attitude is toward these changes, they highlight for us an important feature of social and political invention. For *any* invention requires some replication procedure, some plan or set of plans that reproduces the invention. Without a successful replication procedure, an invention remains in the realm of novelty or gadget. This, you will recall, was the initial view of the telephone even after its use community could be identified. However, although complex to put into practice, the replication procedure for the telephone was easily identified. Here the instrument itself, once perfected, posed no problems. It was the system of telephone lines and switchboards that provided the necessary element for reaching that universal use community. Initially, only clusters of business establishments were connected telephonically.

The example of the telephone illustrates the two-layered nature of invention and replication. In a broad sense, the replication procedure of the telephone was made possible by the inventions of the Industrial Revolution and the market system in general. In a more immediate sense, a specific replication procedure was required for the telephone. The invention of the motel provides a similar example. The tourist cabin required little capital investment, no technological innovation, and little economic expertise. Thus, when the desire for selectivity, together with new resource demands arising

from overcrowding, created the fee camp, private sector entry was
provided with ideal circumstances for replication. In fact, the motel
industry was one of the few growth sectors in the Depression economy. It was an ideal family enterprise; retirees were especially attracted to the new business. The tourist cabin was so accessible as a
business that many hard-pressed families would place signs in their
homes advertising "rooms to rent by the night." These "tourist
houses," boarding houses of the early automobile age, were naturally regarded as a threat by the new motel entrepreneurs.

The conditions that provided for the easy replication of the invention of the motel (low overhead and investment in a depressed
economy) began to change in the late 1930s. It is at this point that
shrewd entrepreneurs began to see the possibilities for a transformation of the industry in the direction of a new replication procedure. In 1937, J. C. Stevens, the former president of the NTL-
MCTA, called for the replacement of the administration of motels by
"individualistic drifters" to businessmen who could assure accom-
modations of a "reasonably high class."[9] Again, the psychology of
the auto traveler, the factor that helped promote the success of the
tourist cabin over the autocamp, was now an impetus for the modern motel. The American vacationer, like all bourgeois, straddled a
psychic line between a longing for simplicity and convenience, adventure and security, thrift and comfort. And like all bourgeois, the
motor tourist found that in each case the latter was an irresistible
temptation. The postwar motel industrialists promised all manner
of convenience and comfort (from hot and cold water to free parking and reassuring decor) as well as uniformity. Belasco notes that
"Mama-Papa courts would give way to larger 'motor-hotels.'"[10]
The current advertising campaign of Holiday Inn which promises
"no surprises" was predicated upon decades of experience with
consumer anxieties. Only in resort areas has the motel maintained
itself as cottage industry in a "backward" economy. Limited access
freeways gave the old replication procedure its death blow. Hitch-
cock's *Psycho* (1960) confirmed the modern auto travelers' worst
fears about independent motels by showing what short of adventure
was in store for those who gypsied too far from the freeway and
Howard Johnsons.

As we have discussed, America produced two versions of the
penitentiary. We are in a position, then, to see in this case how one
version won out. Both the Pennsylvania and the New York systems

had experienced and dedicated "promotion groups." In fact, for a time the New York penal authorities actively sought the advice of their cohorts in Pennsylvania. The key to the success of the Auburn model was the superiority of its replication procedure. One decisive factor, as we have already noted, was an economic one. Eastern State Penitentiary cost the State of Pennsylvania a staggering $432,000.

But I do not think that economic considerations were the only, or even overriding, flaws discouraging replication of the Pennsylvania model. One could argue that the success of the Auburn model lay in its anticipation of new forms of industrial organization. W. David Lewis contends that "the techniques in the Auburn shops were somewhat similar to those used in many factories; the methods employed at Philadelphia smacked of the past, of an industrial era that was dying."[11] Auburn not only used piecework rather than handicraft labor, but it adopted the organizational structure of the factory itself: the day was divided in precise units, work supervision was extensive, uniform routine was scrupulously engineered. But I think the explanation for the success of Auburn lay in another direction. I shall discuss this point more fully in the next section, but for now let us state that the Auburn plan established a replication procedure that was based upon the fulfillment of its initial premises. Contemporaries seem to have focused upon the structural and especially the architectural differences in each of these correctional inventions. This preoccupation was not completely misleading, for in a total institution architecture is organization. As a minuscule society, the penitentiary sought to create human beings anew. The Pennsylvania model, with its cellular apartments, sought transformation by means of the principles of solitude and reflection. The visits to individuals by the Philadelphia Board of Inspectors illustrates the determination to recreate human personality. Auburn, on the other hand, was at once both more and less ambitious in its aims. It abandoned a belief in the capacity for individual conversion and instead sought mass self-discipline. The promoters of each system represented a different approach to reform. The invention of the Pennsylvania model reflected a "soft" reform and the Auburn a "hard" one. This is not to say that Eastern Penitentiary offered casual or easy-going treatment. On the contrary, inmates were subjected to a rigorous system designed to reconstitute their person-

ality structures. The supporters of Auburn were, in fact, far less
optimistic about the possibility of human reform. When Beaumont
and Tocqueville interviewed Elam Lynds, administrator of both
Auburn and Sing Sing, he insisted that he did not believe in "complete reform" (except for juveniles) in the sense that a "mature
criminal" would become a "religious and virtuous man." But it was
possible that a great number of convicts could become "useful
citizens, having learned a trade in prison and acquired the habit of
steady work." "There's the only reform that I have ever hoped to
produce," concluded Lynds, "and I think it's the only one which
society can demand." This sense of the limits of reform permitted
Auburn administrators to de-individualize the prison and to concentrate upon methods designed to enforce mass discipline. Auburn
was, in the words of Lynds, "the result of a daily succession of
efforts . . . one has to attend to business all the time, watch the
keepers as well as the inmates, be pitiless and just." Lynds' summa-
tion was chillingly informative: "Once the machine is built, it runs
with great ease."[12]

Auburn developed a replication procedure that was based upon
the creation of a total and mass society. It was successful, I think,
because it more consistently developed the principles of a total
institution that its competition did. By rejecting the goal of creating
virtuous citizens, it was able to invent a series of procedures, easily
replicable, to meet the new goal of "passive obedience." The Pennsylvania model took men and women away from society and demanded solitude and labor so that they could return to it. Auburn
left men in a society, but destroyed the entire basis of social interaction. Inmates worked and acted together under a system of perfect
unison, but they were forbidden to talk or even look at one another.
In short, Auburn had invented a new kind of society. Visitors at
Auburn were fascinated by the spectacle of large groups of men
working together, often without overt supervision. When Beaumont spied on prisoners from a gallery, he was amazed to see the
faultless conduct of inmates. Some observers of the same behavior
were distressed. One was struck by the look on the inmates' faces: "I
walked through all the shops in which the prisoners were at labor
and I must say that so miserable, jaded, desponding a row of faces I
never beheld—such sunken, lack-lustre eyes I never encoun-
tered."[13] Another visitor offered an incisive analogy comparing the

demeanor of prisoners to those of the deaf. "Struck with the similarity of expression in all the countenances of the prisoners," he asked, "does this arise from the identity of their condition, as we see a peculiar resemblance of features or expression in the faces of almost all deaf men?"[14]

The success of the revival camp can, I think, be explained by three aspects of its replication procedure. First, the ingeniously simple structure of the camp itself was easily replicable. In the West the camp provided for an arena of religiosity in the absence of a village church. During the Eastern revival, the local church itself could be transformed from a place that held conventional services to one that housed the more informal and experimental meetings. In fact, in New York the village itself, which had copied the basic compact structure of the New England town, provided the perfect setting for transforming the whole town into a revival camp. Second, of course, was the role of the "benevolent empire" of the American evangelistic communities. As we noted, a vast organizational structure of Protestant denominations was already in place by the time of the Great Revivals. The camp meeting was an ideal invention to meet the highly competitive religious environment. It was, in a sense, itself a replication agency for Protestantism. The third basis for the success of the camp's replication procedure was the psychology of the camp and of the protracted meetings. Both were based upon a principle of psychological contagion. We reported how the Reverend Finley had been so unwillingly affected at Cane Ridge. Scoffers who attended the meetings found themselves afflicted with the "jerks" suddenly "as is struck by lightning." The camps were an invention of spectacle, a mix of mass joy and mass terror that so characterizes evangelism. Some in "the transport of their feelings" embraced and kissed everyone around them. Rejoicing filled the air. But, as John McGee, Methodist minister reported, the nights could be "truly awful. . . . The campground was well illuminated; the people were differently exercised all over the ground, some exhorting, some shouting, some praying, and some crying for mercy, while others lay as dead men on the ground."[15]

The process of contagion by which the camps were filled also provided the conditions for attendance at new meetings. Thus the camp and protracted meetings, as organizational forms, were able to use to advantage the isolation of frontier settlements and villages. People would travel to the site of a camp meeting upon hearing of

some past spectacle or, in the East, invite an evangelist to ignite
a revival in their community. These acts themsevlcs created a sense
of vulnerability in the participants. Once the revival began, relative geographic isolation heightened the likelihood of emotional
responses.

In very general terms, it must also be noted that the Great Revival
and the meetings that spread its message were themselves replica-
tions of basic cultural norms for religion. The doctrine of universal
redemption and full and free salvation represented a complex process of religious democratization that had shattered the clitist ten-
dencies of Calvinism. The camp meeting promised immediate conversion and salvation and, as such, represented a cultural adaptation of Protestanism to democratic trends in American society. This
process was not, however, a simple one, since the Revival was also a
conservative force as well. We shall pursue this point in chapter 5,
but it is worth noting here that the camp meeting as an institution
owcd a portion of its success to the fact that it was a religious
replication of the democratic norms.

As a craft, quilting employed the vernacular replicative traditions
of any folk art. Its geometric base provided for a very large potential
number of designs, and, before the intrusion of the market, patterns
were freely exchanged. Patterns of prize quilts at fairs were hur-
riedly sketched or quickly copied from memory when women returned home. It was a practice for older women to bequeath single
blocks and sketches for quilts to their friends and daughters, many
of whom they had taught.[16]

One of the unique aspects of quilting as a craft was, in fact, the
truly explosive potential for variation of patterns and stitches. Generally, vernacular crafts change very slowly. The constant geographical movement of Americans introduced women to new designs.
Regional patterns streaked across America, undergoing variations
on the way. The exchange of patterns was part of the social tradition
of quilting. The quilting bee was a simple affair. Food was shared,
quilting frames were quickly set up and, most significantly, quilting
itself provided an ideal setting for women who were not always well
acquainted with one another. Thus, the urgent social needs of wom-
en could be met by the replication procedure of the craft.

Each of the five inventions we have selected, besides having a procedure for replicating itself, also possesses the ability to expand by "adding on" other new inventions or even by creating new adjunct inventions of its own. We are easily able to see the principle of invention linkages in regard to technological invention. The telephone has been especially productive in this regard, having linked itself to the invention of the computer, coaxial cable, and satellite communications. The telephone has, of course, its own engine of invention, the Bell Telephone Laboratories. Bell Labs has had a formal existence since 1925, but grew enormously as a result of World War II military contracts. Today, it employs almost twenty thousand people and by 1975 had been issued over eighteen thousand patents.[17] Self-described as a "mission-oriented" organization, Bell Labs had produced a series of basic inventions which have spilled over into communications technology. Perhaps the most spectacular was the invention of the transistor by William Shockely and Walter Brathain in 1947. The transistor not only provided Bell with its much needed-system of electronic switching but also created the basis for the modern computer.

The motel, as an invention of the market, has added every technological invention of convenience produced since World War II.[18] The essential motel room now contains a color television, often with cable, pulsating shower head, vibrators, infra-red bathroom lights, disposable sanitary glasses. It has used the franchise system and new techniques on construction to expand as well as link up with new forms of travel such as the freeway and the airplane. In fact, while the drummer hotel died because of auto travel, the motel has managed to adjust to travel innovations, becoming the accommodation which provides for the new airborne salesperson.

Social and political inventions appear to be lacking the equivalent of a Bell Laboratory system. But this is an appearance only. These new institutions have their own engines of invention. In the case of the prison, professional organizations of corrections specialists perform the role of researchers. Their goal is to create a combination of technological, architectural, and behavioral innovations that will perfect the prison.

A recent example of these efforts is the new maximum security penitentiary at Oak Park, Minnesota. Corrections officials have described this new facility as "the best prison ever built," one which

represents "state of the art technology and theory."[19] This "prison of the future" is a trapezoidal structure deftly hidden from public view. It is advertised as the "invisible prison" and is designed to house high-escape risks and prisoners with records of rape and assault ("predators" in the terminology of current penology). Oak Park employs all the latest technological inventions: bullet-proof and flame-resistant glass, computer monitoring, and an "escape proof" roof of a new taut wire made in Israel. Innovations in architectural design are wedded to those in behavioral control. A Dallas-based architectural firm that specializes in prison design has created a 406-bed structure divided into eight complexes with three levels each. Oak Park is based upon a theory of control which uses "classification by compatibility." Prisoners are grouped by age and type of offense. Each group has its own dining and recreational areas. One-person cells are divided into groups that Warden Frank Wood calls "defensible living spaces." Solid steel doors can isolate fifty-two inmates at a time. Oak Park is designed to be riot-proof. It is not yet clear that "management by small groups" will indeed be the prototype for future prisons. But the pattern of invention linkage illustrated by Oak Park suggests that the prison is still an invention capable of absorbing innovation.

The revival camp, by nature an ephemeral institution, nevertheless created significant sets of inventions—despite the best efforts of its organizers. In fact, it proved to be a particularly explosive institution that threatened to completely outstrip the goals of those groups who most benefitted from it.

The revival camp's inventive linkages lay in its claim that salvation was a question of individual commitment. Richard Niebuhr, in his study of American Protestanism, provides some focus to this point. He speaks of the important difference between a sect and a church. The latter is a natural social group akin to the family or nation. The sect, however total its internal organization, is a voluntary association. Thus, Niebuhr argues, one joins a sect but is born into a church.[20] Of course, the revival camp did not "invent" the sect as a form, but it was a major force in its proliferation in America and perhaps set a historical pattern in American Protestanism. For the camp meeting had made religion a matter of individual choice. While it freed people to reject the religion of their birth to become Methodists or Baptists, it also freed people to form their own sects or even new religions. And choose they did; sects formed around every imaginable doctrinal point. As the camp and the protracted meeting evetually became subject to routinization, new converts would seek other realms of individual choice in the invention of new societies. No matter that many of these experimental settlements would actually diminish autonomy, the dynamic which sought individual salvation demanded these kinds of inventions.

Chapter 4

Generative Inventions

I have focused thus far on the similarities among inventions. But there are obviously different kinds of inventions in terms of scope and impact. The paper clip and the telephone are both inventions, but despite its ubiquitous appearance, the fastener is not an invention of the same caliber as the phone. Swift's refrigerated railroad car was largely an engineering innovation, but it allegedly created the city of Chicago. Similar distinctions can be made in regard to social, political, and economic institutions.

It can be helpful, I think, to speak in terms of three kinds of inventions: generative, supporting, and transitional. But we must not regard these three categories as exclusive ones. The telephone, our archetypal example of technological invention, is fundamentally a generative institution. But in many areas it functions as a supportive one and, depending upon further developments, may exhibit the characteristics of a transitional invention. What appears as the most minor supportive invention may, on closer examination, reveal hidden generative capacities. Moreover, because generative inventions themselves are especially prone to producing associated inventions, it is not always easy to determine how these clusters fit together. Despite these qualifications, this distinction among three types can illustrate the complex kinds of changes inventions create in our lives.

There are some inventions that change our lives in momentous ways. They do so because they radically refashion our everyday existence, because they "generate" whole sets of supporting institutions, and because they reorient systems of thought. If we take a wide anthropological perspective, we can approach this category very broadly and identify the basic institutions of human culture as generative inventions. The origins of family forms and religions could, for instance, be seen as generative institutions whose inventors are lost in primitive history. In fact, Sigmund Freud approached the question of the origin of exogamy as an exercise in invention analysis. Freud posited the existence of a primal father who ruled over a horde of men and women, keeping all females to hemself and driving away pubescent sons. One day the expelled sons joined forces, slew and ate the father, and thus put an end to the father horde. But without the primal father, the new brother clan was an ineffective organization. Every brother sought to be the "father" and was the others' rival among women. After many difficult experiences, the brothers invented the incest prohibition "through which they equally renounced the women whom they desired, and on account of whom they had removed the father in the first place." For Freud the family was a generative invention of tremendous consequence; it was the origin of "social organization, moral restrictions and religion."

Fortunately, for our purposes we need not accept Freud's account of the family as a generative institution. Nor is it necessary for us here to establish the origins and nature of the great inventions of human culture. But these primal creations may in fact be thought of as inventions in a broad metaphysical sense, as Freud himself did in his construction of what he called his "fantastic hypothesis." Nisbet's examples of the walled town, the manor, and the university, while not of the significance of the invention of primordial family forms, are generative inventions. They spawned new institutions themselves and became the major units into which successive generations would organize their lives. More recent examples of generative inventions would include that of a legislature and the complex of institutions that were eventually to surround it (different systems of election, representation, and rule-making), as well as the changes that it brought about throughout the whole society. Another example would be the Marxist-Leninist invention of the Party, as mentioned in the first chapter.

Telephonic Communities

It is always easier to establish the generative power of technological inventions, not because they emerge so quickly, but because technology is so readily identified as a dependent variable

resting outside our behavior. The immediate revolutionary character of the phone can be seen from the nature of the instrument
itself. The telephone, in the words of Ithiel de Sola Pool, "transformed what previously seemed an eternal aspect of space and
time." Audiences at Bell's demonstrations may not have grasped this
aspect of universal use, but they were no less awed by the experience
of voice transmission.

The greatest impact of the telephone lies with this transformation of space and time. Edward Ackermann has defined the telephone as a "space adjusting" invention; Jean Gottman has spoken
of the role of the phone in making geographic space "fungible."[1] As
a generative invention, the telephone is itself an invention producer
as well as a model of imitation. We have already noted that successful inventions have some replication procedure as well as an
invention linkage system. But the telephone also transformed aspects of society in other ways. Generative inventions are like explo-
sions in this respect: they alter our environment in a varied and
unpredictable manner. When one attempts to assess the changes the
telephone brought to the American city, for instance, one finds a
variety of contradictory developments wrought by this fundamental alteration of space and time. It is generally thought, for example,
that the telephone helped disperse the downtown business district.
As Ithiel de Sola Pool notes, before the phone, businessmen needed
to locate close to their business contacts: "Every city had a furrier's
neighborhood, a hatter's neighborhood, a financial district, a ship-
per's district, and many others. Businessmen would pay mightily for
an office within a few blocks of their trade center; they did business
by walking up and down the block and dropping in on the places
where they might buy and sell. For lunch or coffee, they might stop
by the corner restaurant or tavern where their colleagues congre-
gated."[2] The telephone changed this configuration. Merchants and
financiers could be geographically separate from one another but
still participate in a communications network for necessary business transactions. Individual businesses were also dispersed by the
invention of the telephone. P. W. Daniels has recorded the geographic separation of office work from other portions of business
operation such as production and shipping as being a result of the
phone.[3]

But, paradoxically, the phone has been a major force in the
concentration of urban areas as well. John J. Carty, an AT&T en-

gineering executive, was an early interpreter of this aspect of telephonic change: "It may sound ridiculous to say that Bell and his successors were the fathers of modern commercial architecture—of the skyscrapers. . . . But wait a minute. How many messages do you suppose go in and out of those buildings every day? Suppose there was no telephone and every message had to be carried by a personal messenger. How much room do you think the necessary elevators would leave for offices? Such structures would be an economic impossibility."[4]

Thus the telephone pushed cities outward and upward. The debate over whether the phone is a centralizing or decentralizing invention with respect to cities in some ways misses the point. The telephone has *transformed* the city. Ronald Abler has focused upon this transformation, noting that, as the telephone "conquered distance as no other technology has, it has helped create an "information economy." "A labor force," he contends, "in which half the workers earn their living by reading, writing, talking, calculating, and deciding would be unthinkable without the telephone's information-carrying capacity."[5] Thus, for Abler, the telephone was the inventive base for the post-industrial society.

This telephonically induced social change is still not completed. The linkage of the telephone to new inventions that we described in the last chapter may create even more transformations. Some analysts have contended that telephone linkages (computers, telex, television, video, etc.) may totally eliminate the need for a physical presence "at work." Peter Cowne's study of English offices led him to conclude that "office work may become a cottage industry." Nicholas Johnson, a former FCC Commissioner, has spoken in utopian terms of a "home communication center where a person works, learns, and is entertained and contributes to his society by way of communications techniques we have not yet imagined, incidentally solving commuter traffic jams and much of their air pollution problems in the process."[6] If we do end up "communicating to work," current patterns of concentration/dispersal created by the telephone will be simply a transitional stage of telephonic development.

Of course, if we do begin to be what Suzanne Keller has called "stationary nomads" or "species of exotic insects . . . going everywhere without moving from a spot, in instant contact with any and everyone, armed solely with ourselves, our personal computers and

our portable telephones," our conceptions of home and work will
be radically transformed.[7] There may now be a severe alienation
between work and home, public and private, but the new telephonic cottage industry may not recreate the village or family farm.
Informational cottage industries will bring work into the home in a
way that has never been experienced. The connection with the
outside world will be so complete and so instantaneous that privacy
may have no viable function.

The telephone's alteration of space has not only transformed
economic relationships; it has also transformed social ones. Here
the present impact of the telephone may also be a transitional one,
for the telephone has been the impetus for the formation of new and
revolutionary conceptions of community. A brief look at the nature
of telephone conversation can illustrate how it has altered social
relationships.

It is intriguing to imagine precisely how early users picked up the
telephone. Did the body jerk at the ring? Did the user run to the
phone or leisurely advance as one would to a request from someone
in the house? How was the receiver picked up? Was it cautiously or
with practiced movement? How did people talk over this new instrument? And perhaps more importantly, what image appeared
before the user as the phone rang? We have anecdotal information
to answer some of these questions. It was apparently common for a
caller to ask, "Are you there?" When the answer was affirmative, so
the joke went, the caller would say, "I will come right over. I want to
talk with you!" In 1880, *The New York World* admonished its
readers about telephone manners: "There seems to be a popular
misconception about conversing through the telephone. . . . It is
not necessary to roar into the instrument so that you can be heard
eight blocks away . . . the telephone is not deaf."[8] The ring elicited
the most significant psychological reactions. It still does. Robert
Louis Stevenson complained that the phone "bleated like a deserted
infant." More recently, Marshall McLuhan asked "Why does a
phone ringing on stage create instant tension?"[9]

Our relationship to the telephone is now habitual, although not
as casual as we often think. The telephone still has three very important characteristics as a medium of social exchange. First, it is a
form of social intercourse that is blind. The absence of vision places
an enormous strain upon social relationships. We must identify a
caller by voice and/or introduction. Human beings communicate

with one another in part through visual patterns. In the absence of these additional demands are placed on voice intonations, delays in response, hesitations. Proust captures this feature so perfectly when he has Marcel wonder why modern artists, instead of painting scenes of everyday life like "The Letter" and "The Harpsichord," don't compose a portrait entitled "At the Telephone," in which "there would come spontaneously to the lips of the listener a smile all the more genuine in that it is conscious of being unobserved."

Second, the telephone permits social interactions which otherwise may never occur. The "a stranger calls" phenomenon is recognized by every phone user, and the obscene phone call is the epitome of social violation by strangers. In a public setting, there are innumerable ways in which one can avoid unwelcome conversation. One can lower one's eyes, look sideways or upwards, or turn away. We are often protected from intrusion by strangers in our public lives by receptionists, security guards, and even modern architecture itself. The telephone explodes this insulation with its ring. Of course, one can refuse to answer, but few experiences are more unnerving than a continuing telephone ring. Ironically there are telephonic solutions to the phenomenon of a stranger calling. Receptionists and secretaries who intercept phone calls, recording instruments, along with the ubiquitous pink "while you were out" slips, are all efforts to avoid intrusion. They are used with the same subtlety as the downward look.

Third, the telephone requires instantaneous social interaction. Preparation is not always possible. The "blind" character of the phone does not allow for gradual social interaction. Silence cannot be surrounded by body language. McLuhan's observation on the reaction to the ringing stage phone reveals the source of audience anxiety. For the phone demands a partner with all the "intensity of electric polarity."[10]

We have developed numerous ways to deal with these jarring features of the telephone. The sociologist Emmanuel Schesloff has observed complex systems of verbal behavior employed to cope with the "stranger call" problem, as well as with the phenomenon of "blind" conversation.[11] Telephone conversation does not, in Schesloff's view, permit what he calls a "prebeginning" sequence of visual interaction. Thus, "when personal recognition of another occurs, and especially when it is potentially reciprocal, a subtle or elaborate display of its accomplishment is made and constitutes a "social" rather than a "cognitive" event. Schesloff has discovered that the first few seconds of a telephone conversation are very significant for subsequent interaction. An identification/recognition sequence procedure must be worked through quickly and as smoothly as possible. Two "Hi"'s separated by only a second are examples of greetings used for reciprocal recognition. A delay of another second, or a noncommittal "Hi" indicates a second turn is necessary, one which requires explicit introduction or an alternate greeting ("How are you?") to allow another chance of voice recognition. An "Oh, hi!" or "long time, no see!" or the more direct "I didn't recognize your voice" can establish contact and the conversation can proceed. We must undertake these rituals every day. Children often have great difficulty acquiring them. They are frequently speechless after picking up the phone and require explicit instruction in telephone etiquette (ask who it is, take a message, don't give out the number, etc). Schesloff wryly observes that what was associated in the Western mythic past with heroes and elders such as Odysseus and Isaac—recognition when identity is partially masked—has become democratized. Writ incomparably smaller, "it has become anyone's everyday test."

Of course, social exchange as dialogue is not community. It is, however, a precondition for one, and it is important to ask how the telephone has altered our conception of community. One way in which we can begin to understand the relationship between the two is by looking at some studies of telephone usage. Again we will discover the transforming nature of the phone.

In some respects, the telephone has served as a relatively neutral adjunct to existing community. It has functioned as a supporting institution for communities. Nowhere was the telephone more enthusiastically received than in America's rural communities. Not only did the phone provide a communications system that could save lives (one such widely publicized incident is generally regarded as essential to the phone's early expansion), but it helped maintain social networks among families. In 1907, the number of rural telephones had increased to over 1.5 million from 267,000 in 1902. The densest telephone concentrations appeared in Iowa, Nebraska, Washington, California, and Nevada. Here, one in ten people had a telephone, as compared to the eastern states in which the ratio was between ten and thirty per phone. In fact, rural communities seem to have appreciated the social aspect of the phone early. Farmers often set up their own "private" systems of ten to fifteen families, constructing telephone poles communally in the manner of barn-raisings.

But the telephone transformed existing communities as well. Had rural communities been only internally connected by home-made systems, the impact of the phone would have been different. As it happened, the telephone represented the penetration of the town by national influences. One glimpse at this change in an urban neighborhood has been offered by Alan H. Wurtzel and Colin Turner in their study of a 23-day telephone black-out caused by a fire in a Manhattan switching center in the winter of 1975.[12] Almost universally, respondents to the study felt "uneasy" and "isolated" and "in less control" from the absence of a telephone. The one major positive feeling was the blackout's removal of the "stranger calls" fear; 42 percent of respondents noted that they "enjoyed the feeling of knowing that no one could intrude on me by phone." The types of calls most missed were overwhelmingly those to and from primary groups. Over 67 percent missed the ability to make calls to friends and family; over 80 percent missed the opportunity to receive such calls. When asked how they compensated during the blackout period, 34 percent answered that they visited more. Another 31 percent observed that they found themselves "using more media than usual," especially television.

Several intriguing conclusions emerge from this study. The telephone is used as a major instrument of primary social interaction. Wurtzel and Turner refer to the telephone as a creator of "psychological neighborhoods." A person's "psychological neighborhood" is "not just a mental landscape beginning at the borders of his actual neighborhood, but one that superimposes itself upon his immediate environs, drawing him into a home-based telephonic web. . . . Many urban neighborhoods have been shattered by migratory waves and economic dislocations. This telephonic neighborhood, overlaid upon the geographic one, at once facilitates dispersion and protects intimacy."[13]

What Wurtzel and Turner refer to as the telephone's promise of "imminent connectedness" and "symbolic proximity" do constitute immediate socialization. It is especially interesting that so many telephonically blacked-out respondents turned to the television. What stations did they watch? Did they crave "mediated" conversation? Or were they simply filling in for loss of social time?

Would visiting have increased gradually had the blackout lasted longer? Would the psychological neighborhood have shrunken and the geographical one have expanded? Wurtzel and Turner also won- der: "The image of people turning from a disconnected source of personal exchange to the unresponding faces, voices, and the printed words of our mass informers and entertainers suggests a certain mutability among our communicative needs; that is an area for future investigation."

It is difficult to imagine pure telephonic communities, communities composed of people who have never talked face-to-face, or shared a meal or some "unmediated" experience. A society composed entirely of these kinds of communities would indeed resemble Suzanne Keller's species of exotic electronic insects. But a question also worth posing is this: How has the telephone as the space and time adjuster we have discussed fundamentally altered our conception of community in general? When we try to build communities, do we implicitly assume "fungible" space? Do we entertain some principle of immediate interaction like Schesloff's conversations? Are we waiting for the stranger to call?

The Penitentiary and the Free World

The telephone's characteristics as a generative invention, its explosive and transforming nature, its capacity to generate new invention, its power of imitation, all are also shared by the modern prison. As we noted, the penitentiary was America's first total institution, and the society has still not abandoned its obsession with the prison as an institution. Today there are over 200,000 inmates in American penitentiaries, about 10 percent of which are under federal jurisdiction. The prison as an institution still rests upon the four pillars of the Pennsylvania and Auburn models: deterrence, rehabilitation, retribution, and protection.

Penologists have long known that these elements are in basic contradiction. But this logical inconsistency has proved to be part of the prison's strength as an institution. If faith in the possibility of rehabilitation should decline, the prison could still be defended as an agency of deterrence or retribution. As a last defense, the prison could always be promoted as an institution which protected society from danger. Thus Norval Morris in *The Future of Punishment* writes, "Prisons have other purposes [than rehabilitation]—to punish, to deter, to banish—which assure their continued survival."[14] Or William G. Nagel in his *The New Red Barn: A Critical Look at the Modern Prison:* "Until we invent an acceptable substitute for prisons in which to hold the relatively small numbers of intractable criminals among us, we will, in time, have to build better facilities."[15] In truth, despite the current absence of zeal for the prison, the inmate population in the last ten years has not declined. In fact, until very recently, the number of inmates per 100,000 population has remained quite stable. Between 1950 and 1970, it has averaged about 110. There have been shorter periods, however, in which the rate has jumped precipitously.[16]

For whatever philosophical reasons, the existence of this numerically stable population throughout history also forms the basis for continued invention. The four pillars need not presuppose the maintenance of total institutions. Yet penology has always been infected by the totalistic premise of the original invention. It is this fascination with the totalistic possibilities of the prison, despite some strident objections, that gives the prison its generative capacities. In an 1829 report, the Reverend Louis Dwight, founder of the reformist Prison Discipline Society and ardent supporter of the Auburn system, wrote that the penitentiary was a model for all society. The principle of solitary quartering at night "would be useful, in all establishments, where large numbers of youth of both sexes are assembled and exposed to youthful lust . . . it would greatly promote order, seriousness, and purity in large families, male and female boarding schools, and colleges." Dwight recommended to a Massachusetts school a plan in which bedrooms would be placed in galleries so that they could be available to surveillance from a central location. The general principle of "increasing vigilance" could be extended and adapted to "families, schools, academies, colleges, factories, mechanic's shops."[17]

There is a tendency in American social science, especially that driven by radical perspectives, to see the factory as the generative invention of order and discipline. Certainly, one can make this case, but in a sense the search for a single source of transformations so complex is probably futile. New institutions and techniques of order occur at various and numerous points, especially in American social structure. They interact with one another. But if one could identify some major generator of order and discipline in American

society, it would not be outlandish to name the prison. For no
matter how regimented the factory, it is but a faint imitation of
prison. The casually whispered remark that one often hears when
entering some institution—"This looks like a prison!"—is evidence of its awesome nature.

Michael Foucault, in his *Discipline and Punish,* has made the
most compelling argument for the imitative power of the prison.
After surveying early American penology, he writes:

> A whole series of different conflicts stemmed from the opposition
> between these two models. . . . But at the heart of the debate, and
> making it possible, was this primary objective of carceral action: coer-
> cive individualization, by the termination of any relation that is not
> surpervised by authority or arranged according to hierarchy.

The idea of complete "coercive individualization" is the key to
the generative character of the modern prison. Of course, the idea of
a total institution will hold different possibilities in different
cultures and political systems. But in America, as a liberal society, it
advances a unique set of possibilities. In an earlier chapter we
quoted Tocqueville's remark that, in a land of the "most extended
liberty," the prison is a "spectacle of the most complete despotism."
The prison represents both the antithesis of liberal individualism as
well as one consequence of it. For the penitentiary is the ultimate
atomistic society. The difference, of course, is that in prison no
relationship is permitted that is not supervised by authority. The
prison is a Hobbesian state in which all consent given arises from
fear. But the prison is also a state of nature in which, in Hobbes'
words, "there is a war of all against all," and life is "nasty, solitary,
brutish and short."

Donald Clemmer's classic 1940 study, *The Prison Community*
and Gresham M. Sykes' *The Society of Captives* offer us glimpses
into the world of the "intimate subculture" in which a prison argot
classifies inmates into "social" roles.[19] This terminology is vividly
brutal and focuses heavily upon sexual and violent behavior: "rat"
(informer), "real man" (unviolated and uncomplaining inmate),
"gorilla" (one who forcefully expropriates cigarettes and food),
"wolf" or "jocker" (one who takes an inserter role in sexual encounter), "punk" (insertee role). The transformation of sexuality,
particularly in male prisons, so fits Hobbes' treatment as to make it
appear to be prophetic. Hobbes described sexual behavior in the

state of nature as based upon a "natural lust" in which men use "violence to make themselves Masters of other men's persons." Here is Jack Henry Abbott's commentary in *In the Belly of the Beast: Letters from Prison:*

> . . . There is no camaraderie among prisoners as a whole any more; there is a system, a network of ties between all the tips (prison cliques) in the prisons, and it's this that resembles "comradeship" in general. Most prisoners fear almost every other prisoner around them. . . .
>
> One of the first things that takes place in a prison riot is this: guards are sexually dominated, usually sodomized. . . .
>
> Only once or twice in my life have I seen (in) any prison two men demonstrate sexual affection by kissing or otherwise touching each other.[20]

All of this is not to say that there are never fraternal relationships in prison. No human institution will ever more than approximate the "purity" of Hobbes' model. But it is this peculiar combination of authority and anarchy, total management and brutal, personal and "hidden" subculture that, I believe, so fascinates the American mind. Prison autobiographies have always been extremely popular in America. It may be true that the comfortable bourgeois reading the memoirs of George Jackson or Caryl Chessman can never really understand prison life. But at one level, an understanding is there, all right. The American can see the possibilities of total management from his own work as he can see the potential for social atomization in his family and community life as well. Most prison memoirs contain within them a conversion narrative, some experience that transforms the prisoner by reintegrating his disintegrated personality. Sometimes it is a political conversion such as that offered by Malcolm X; more often it is a religious one. The conversion narrative is the romance of the prison memoir, for it insists that real individual control can be asserted even in this environment. This, too, the American can understand because he hopes for just such an experience.

I do not want to make some jeremiadic indictment. America is not a prison or "like a prison" in any direct sense. But the prison stands out so clearly as a cultural possibility that it maintains a powerful psychic hold on our imaginations. As such, it may well be a deterrent for the middle classes. For those whose lives already closely approximate the Hobbesian state of nature, the prison is less

a threat. There may be, then, more than a rational frustration among those who complain that prisons "do not work." For if a radical inversion of the liberal vision causes no basic rehabilitation, then there is no real social control available.

The prison evokes more than a psychic imitation. The pattern of "coercive atomization" does appear in all our major institutions. The hospital, factory, school, and even, to a certain extent, the modern family itself all contain some features of total management and half-hidden asocial subcultures. Again, it is essential to point out that none of these institutions lacks a firm base of genuine social cooperation and affection. But still the prison stands as a historical alternative to present organization. Perhaps we should be thankful that the prison is perceived as "not working." If it did, we might see the direct application of Lewis Dwight's recommendations.[21]

This core aspect of the prison in American society also explains the continued inventiveness associated with the penitentiary. The prison itself has been a laboratory of invention in a very literal sense. We saw how the two prototype prisons, Pennsylvania and Auburn, approached the question of rehabilitation in an atomsphere of experimentation. Today, this same spirit of inquiry exists, but now on a more generalized, complex and bureaucratic level. James V. Bennett, former director of the U.S. Bureau of Prisons asks in his book *I Chose Prison*, "What will the prisons of 2000 A.D. be like?" He answers: "In my judgment the prison system will increasingly be valued, and used, as a laboratory and workshop of social change."[22]

The prison as a laboratory for new inventions consists of interlocking sectors of state and federal government as granting agencies, social and medical scientists, the corrections professionals, and private corporations and foundations. One set of experiments centers around the use of inmates as volunteers in medical and drug programs. Another involves the experimental application of techniques of social control and rehabilitation. The first has nothing to do with any of the four pillars of punishment, at least not directly: the prison is simply used as a laboratory for general and applied scientific research. The second experimental approach is more directly related to the prison as an institution. Researchers attempt to find and test new techniques that will make the prison a better rehabilitative institution. Of course, these two lines of experimentation do cross, as in the experimental use of drugs as "behavior modifiers."

Medical research on prisoners is almost as old as the penitentiary itself, but the FDA requirement that new drugs be tested on humans has created a large set of supporting institutions around the prison. For instance, in the 1960s, Upjohn and Parke Davis acquired exclusive rights at Jackson State Prison in Michigan. The two firms invested $500,000 in laboratories and a forty-bed hospital on the premises. Over one fourth of Jackson's inmates were participants in the research programs at any given time. In 1963 the companies donated the facilities to the state of Michigan. Jessica Mitford, a strident critic of prison medical experimentation, reported that during 1971–73, research programs were being conducted in fifty state and federal prisons in twenty-five states.[23]

Medical experimentation has been historically scandal-ridden. Reports of poorly conceived, scientifically unnecessary, and life-threatening experiments occur periodically. One of the most outrageous involved the work of Dr. Austin R. Strough, who from 1963 to 1969 conducted over 130 studies in several states for 37 drug firms including Bristol-Meyers, Squibb, Merck, Sharp & Dohne and Upjohn. Strough also collected plasma donations from prison populations. Inmates died from his experiments; hepatitis epidemics abounded. As the *New York Times* unraveled the doctor's activities, the inadequacies of the prison medical experimentation systems were clearly exposed. The pharmaceutical firms stood by their man. The FDA admitted that it was its responsibility to evaluate data, but not to directly supervise drug investigations. The Alabama State Health Department declared that it had no jurisdiction over prisons.[24]

Various agencies and organizations have developed guidelines for medical experimentation with human subjects. Each includes the following basic principles: all human experimentation must be based upon prior laboratory work on animals; all subjects must give informed and voluntary consent; experiments must have scientific value; subjects must not be subject to unnecessary pain or risk. But even these guidelines are difficult to enforce. Reports on drug testing are limited by the Trade Secret Act, scarcity of FDA personnel, and reluctance to question the professional status of the grant holder. Even more disturbing, however, is the basic contradiction between the assumptions of volunteerism and rational choice on the one hand and the fact of participants' captivity on the other. Dr. Robert E. Hodges may contend that inmate subjects are "our companions in medical science and adventure," but the desire for parole and/or pocket money seems more likely to provide compelling motives.[25]

As we noted in the last chapter, the search for an ideal architectural solution for the prison continues; so too do attempts to find the perfect method for behavioral transformation. The reader will recall that the Philadelphia reformers thought that only a radical solution would jar the criminal into a new state of grace and therefore adopted the principle of solitary confinement as both a penance and a rehabilitative technique. In 1962 Edgar H. Schein, a psychologist, repeated the basic assumption of the Philadelphia reformers: ". . . in order to produce marked change of behavior and/or attitude, it is necessary to weaken, undermine, or remove the supports to the old patterns of behavior and the old attitudes." Such a "deliberate changing of human behavior and the old attitudes" requires "relatively complete control over the environment in which the captive population lives."[26] One of the most intriguing aspects of the prison as an inventive environment is that new techniques of social control and rehabilitation arise in periods both of penological reform and of retrenchment. It is especially during the latter that the most radical alternatives are often explored. James V. Bennett's reaction to the use of Anectine, a muscle relaxant used in "aversion therapy" in California in the 1960s, is informative: "If it could be shown empirically that hitting an inmate on the head with a hammer would cure him, I'd do it."[27]

In recent years every new approach to social control developed by behavioral social scientists has been tried on prison populations: behavior modification, reality therapy, transactional analysis, responsibility therapy, moral development therapy. The use of drug therapy is, however, the most controversial. Sensory deprivation was the foundation of the Pennsylvania model: drug therapy is its modern equivalent. It is also a fascinating cultural statement when one considers that mind-altering drugs were offered with the same enthusiasm by counterculturists of the 1960s as a basis for liberation.

A stunning popularization of the promise of drug therapy appeared in *Psychology Today* in 1970. James V. McConnell, whose research involved the training of worms to respond to maze instructions by electric shocks, wrote: "I believe that the day has come when we can combine sensory deprivation with drugs, hypnosis, and astute manipulation of reward and punishment to gain almost absolute control over an individual's behavior." Felonious acts, argued McConnell, indicate such "full-blown social neurosis" that cure, not punishment, is necessary. In order to effect a cure "we'd probably have to restructure [the animal's] entire personality."[28]

As of May 1982, the American prison population reached record levels. Every state except Michigan recorded significant increases. The ratio of prisoners sentenced to greater than one-year terms was 154 per 100,000. Despite these increases, the prison is not an invention in ascendancy. As we have suggested, discouragement often leads to more vigorous attempts to re-invent the prison. But there is some evidence to indicate that current opposition is more fundamental, that we may be witnessing a movement with the most difficult set of goals—the "de-invention" of a major institution.

De-invention requires much the same set of factors described in the chapter on the invention matrix. Crucial to this process is the existence of dedicated and coordinated promotion groups. The *National Prison Directory* lists over three hundred organizations devoted to prison reform in America. Many are reformist and/or multi-purpose groups such as the ADA and the ACLU. Others are service organizations, such as the new prisoners' unions. But among this network are local and national groups advocating the "abolition" of the prison. One of the largest of the abolitionist organizations is the National Council on Crime and Delinquency (NCCD). It recommends that no "non-dangerous" offenders be incarcerated. "Non-dangerous" is defined as those who do not show persistent records of violence and evidence of mental disorder. The NCCD claims that only 10 to 20 percent of the current prison population would thus qualify for imprisonment. Other abolitionist groups offer similar estimates. The Fortune Society, an ex-offender group, contends that 85 percent of prisoners could be released without negative consequences. Robert Summer, writing in *The End of Imprisonment* argues that 25 percent of inmates could be released immediately without threatening public safety.[29] As part of its program, the NCCD has sponsored a National Moratorium on Prison Construction. Since a prison can last more than one hundred years, moratorium proponents argue that no new prisons be constructed until alternatives are fully explored.

De-invention not only requires new promotional groups, but a
redefinition of a use community, and alternative inventions with
promising appropriate invention linkages as well. The abolitionist
movement has focused upon community-based correctional centers
as an alternative to the prison. An offender is placed on probation
and is required to live in a group home or report to a nonresidential
center. The National Advisory Commission on Criminal Justice
Standards and Goals has provided a set of principles which are
congenial to the abolitionist program. Some states have fused the
community correctional model with the goal of restitution either in
a general sense, as through community service (hospital janitors
and street cleaning), or in a more personal way, as a "pay-back" of
income to the victim through a probation supervisor.

Minnesota's experimental program (Property Offenders Program) funded by LEEA showed one hundred offenders repaying
sums to about three hundred victims in its first three years. Also
prominent in the abolitionist approach is an attempt to create a new
use community through the widespread use of volunteers in corrections. The NCCD's Volunteers in Probation (VIP) list over thirty
thousand volunteers in correctional centers.

But ever since the invention of the prison, innovation has straddled a fine line between soft and hard reform. The recent dissatisfaction with the prison shows this same set of reactions. Abolitionists
view the prison so critically they are seeking to invent alternative
institutions. Another set of reformers, "pragmatists" in penological
lexicon, are moving in a different direction. In general, they too have
lost faith in the capacity of prisons to rehabilitate. They also share a
moral revulsion against certain modern therapeutic techniques
and, as well, a recognition that the prison is a savage institution.
But, while their remedies may vary, their approach is different from
that of the "soft" reformers. David Fogel, an experienced corrections official, had developed the "Justice Model" of correction.[30]
He too supports a community corrections approach. But for those
offenders whose crimes require prisons, he recommends the abolition of therapeutic programs, parole, and indeterminate sentences
and their replacement by relatively short "flat sentences" without
parole and only "voluntary" rehabilitation therapy. Fogel has also
proposed a precise schedule of sentences by grouping felonies into
five categories. Murder is a separate category and would require
that a judge give an offender a sentence of from twenty-five years to

death. Class one felonies would carry an eight-year sentence; class two, five years; class three, three years; and class four, two years. This "2, 3, 5, 8" schedule corresponds to an enhanced "5, 6, 9, 15" schedule for repeat and dangerous offenders.

While Fogel insists he favors the abolition of the prison: "I have no illusions about reforming the fortress prison. It has to go. Rather my intention is to help make it a safe and sane work and living environment (until we can quickly get out of it). . . ."[31] But the de-inventors are not convinced. They worry that the Justice Model, if widely adopted, will increase the flat sentences and create new demands for more prisons.

Robert Martinson proceeds from similar premises.[32] He made an exhaustive review of rehabilitation programs, concluding that none of these efforts has a major effect on recidivism. Martinson focuses upon altering the parole system to make it kind of a person-al and extensive surveillance system. An offender would be given a fixed sentence to be served partly in prison and partly under super-vision. The parole officer ("community-restraint" officer under Martinson's system) would serve more as a policeperson. Since Martinson believes that the prison population can be reduced by 90 percent under this arrangement, one community restraint officer per six offenders would still result in savings.

There is, in Martinson's proposal, a whiff of the police state. The prison may be abolished or significantly reduced, but the prison is carried out to the world in the form of fifty thousand community restraint officers. Presumably, an offender's associates would be in-directly under surveillance as well.

Although confidence in the prison has faded dramatically, an Auburnesque style of reform can be seen in other recent proposals. Walter Berns has blamed both the invention of the prison and the opposition to the death penalty upon the reformer's preoccupation with the rehabilitation ideal.[33] As a result, compassion has incor-rectly focused upon the criminal, making it "more difficult to ap-prehend, convict and punish criminals," and, therefore, contribut-ing to the increase in the number of crimes, including murders, being committed. If the prison is not a deterrent to crime, the death penalty is: some proportion of people "might be deterred by the threat of truly ruthless punishment summarily imposed."[34] Berns considers, in a philosophical mood to be sure, the impact on shop-lifting should supermarket check-out clerks be "authorized summarily (perhaps with small-scale guillotines conveniently located next to their cash registers) to chop off the hands of everyone apprehended in the act of stealing from the store."[35] He notes, however, that a cultural restraint in America is unlikely to support such measures without a trial. In any case, "American juries, civilized or softened by their life in the commercial or bourgeois society, would simply refuse to convict anyone of shoplifting if the crime carried a mandatory punishment of this order of severity."[36] Berns does, however, strongly support the death penalty as a retributive as well as a deterrent act. It is, he argues, a proper response of moral indignation and anger, and he proposes a return, in limited form, to public executions.

Ernest van den Haag, in his *Punishing Criminals*, recommends prisons for only a relatively small group of offenders.[37] He also reconsiders all the pre-Enlightenment forms of punishment. "Is," he asks, "a thief better off incarcerated for two years than receiving sixty lashes?" For van der Haag, the question is an open one. The reason we find such measures "cruel and unusual" is that we have come to regard corporal punishment as a form of sexuality. While this "sexualization of punishment helps explain its abandonment," it does not tell us whether this abandonment is right. He also explores the viability of a return to fines, exile, and penal colonies.

Will the prison be transformed or abandoned (de-invented) or be subject to only minor adjustments? A recent criminal justice text offers a sober prediction:

> Prisons will be relics of the past. Institutionalization of any kind will be reserved for the most extreme cases. The remaining institutions will have the same character as that of schools and hospitals, and the re-socialization methods will include those developed in schools and hospitals. *The only institutionalized public offenders will be those deemed dangerous to society*—not in the political sense, but in the sense of exhibiting uncontrollable violence. Those persons will be treated primarily through a combination of drugs and hormone therapy and behavioral change programs, primarily based on the Skinnerian model and new models that have emerged [italics added].[38]

I believe that the authors wrote this prediction with a sense of optimism and relief in their expectation of the demise of the prison. But two considerations need to be addressed with regard to the future generative capacities of the prison. First, if indeed the prison is (almost) de-invented and only twenty to thirty thousand of the most stigmatized and dangerous offenders remain, those whom society has truly marked off, what new invention will this new "elite" prison produce and how will our contemplation of its existence infect our general cultural dispositions? The authors quoted above unwittingly suggest an answer: radical therapy and "new models" will be employed. Second, will the abolition of the prison be a major step in bringing the techniques and structure of the prison to the "outside" society? The authors note that "remaining institutions" will use the resocialization methods already developed in schools and hospitals. The age of the prison as a generative invention is not over.

Chapter 5

Supporting Inventions

Although they animate the vision of the revolutionary, the actual invention of generative institutions occurs rarely. Many inventions function in support of the goals of broader, existing institutions. The quilting bee met and helped sustain the needs of the frontier settlements both by providing a necessary service and by fostering an arena for the development of sorority among transplanted women. Other institutions also performed this task (house-raisings, festivals, house-warmings), and together they helped establish a particular kind of community. The loss of any one of these would not challenge the existence of the community among frontier settlements. Supporting inventions are common inventions, thrown off, so to speak, by generative inventions. They often form a constellation which surrounds the parent invention.

But we must not fall into a simple functional perspective in regard to supporting inventions. A supporting invention can itself develop generative capacities. The relationship between a supporting and generative invention is often very complex, sometimes it is remote, sometimes intimate, and sometimes alternating between both. Supporting institutions can become dependent upon new generative inventions and be transformed in the process.

Motel Sex

The complexity of the supporting invention is evident in the case of the motel. The motel was clearly an inventive response to the automobile. But, as we noted, while the motel was rapidly introduced into American society, it was itself only one invention in a whole string of innovations which attempted to meet the needs of the auto traveler. We have suggested that other inventions may supersede the motel, just as the motel replaced the autocamp. The auto industry itself has not been a kindly parent; it has introduced the trailer and the van as competing, mobile motels. The motel also began as an ideal supporting invention for American cottage industry, but, as is common in other areas of economic invention, it became a supporting invention for corporate enterprise.

The motel served as a supporting institution in an additional respect. It has supported a "sexual revolution," a series of behavioral changes beginning in the 1920s and, with some ebb and flow, continuing to the present moment. It is these changes in sexual behavior, and the role of the motel in promoting them, that I would like to focus on this chapter as an analysis of supporting invention.

To a significant extent the American sexual revolution has been technologically driven. The auto, the movie theater, the radio, the television, and advances in gynecology have all in different ways supported changes in sexual behavior. But the impact of these developments can be overemphasized: Technological invention has merely expanded long-existing cultural dispositions toward individualization. The automobile has been perhaps the major invention in altering sexual behavior. It was an invention which altered space and therefore destroyed the insularity necessary to regulate behavior. It also introduced a new kind of privacy. In Daniel Bell's words, "the car became the *cabinet particular* of the middle classes, the place where adventurous young people shed their sexual inhibitions and broke the old taboos."[1] Of course, pre-automobile societies, even the most vigilant, permitted (or were unable to prevent) the isolation of couples. But the car offered two distinct major advantages for assignations: it could quickly carry a couple *far* away from the watchful community, and it provided a mobile and enclosed space. In the 1920s the Lynds confirmed the use of the car as an agency of escape and sexual liberation.[2] Young Middletowners regularly drove twenty miles away to dance at a roadhouse café.

Of course, the motel was not invented *as* a supporting sexual institution. As we reported, the motel was a response to the new form of travel. While users playfully toyed with a gypsy motif, they traveled *en famille*. It appears, however, that the role of the motel as a sexual institution emerged quite early. Norman Hayner, writing

in *Hotel Life* in 1936, spoke of the use of the motel as an occasion
for a "moral holiday."[3] A business slang emerged to describe this
alternate economy. Motel owners spoke of a "hot pillow" and a
"bounce-in-the-bed" business and the "no-tell motel."

J. Edgar Hoover launched a major attack against the new institution in 1940, a period in which the motel was not yet firmly established. In "Camps of Crime" Hoover said that most motels were
"dens of vice and corruption" catering to criminals, prostitutes, and
promiscuous youth.[4] The motel industry was in something of a
bind. The motel as sexual institution was profitable, but it did
threaten the institution's image as an alternative for the traveling
middle-class family. Some motels added signs like "No locals"
(which obviously did not limit sexual adventure for the nomadic)
and adopted more extensive registration procedures. The *Tourist
Court Journal* denied that the motel was primarily a supporting
sexual institution: "The truth, 'sin is where you find it', applies
equally to every branch of the tourist trade . . . story writers are
constantly in search of the new locale for an old plot . . . and it is
flattering to the tourist court that even the best writers are aware of
this tremendous industry still in its teens."[5]

I think the role of the motel as a supporting sexual institution can
tell much about modern American supporting institutions in general. It is correct to argue that the objective character of the motel
permitted its being adapted to such a use. The motel provided
cheap, short-term, anonymous lodging. Naturally it would be used
for sexual purposes. The booster's worldly concession, "sin is
where you find it," can be applied to the automobile as well. In this
respect, and contrary to Hoover's analysis, the motel as an institution is not analogous to the adult bookstore. The motel is not a
specialized institution. One may patronize it for a variety of reasons, but one does not walk into an adult bookstore for purposes
other than sexual titillation. It is *like* a general bookstore only in the
sense that it sells books.

Yet the motel is a multiple-use supporting institution that came
to include the specialized use of sexual encounter can be explained
by more than its having simply provided enclosure. For the motel
itself represented a major departure from the norms of early auto
travel. The motoring gypsies described by Warren Belasco saw vacationers differently than their railroad counterparts. First, travel it-

self was to be part of the vacation experience. Second, the vacation was conceived as an adventure. Third, the traveler, by playing a bohemian persona, emphasized free and casual behavior. The auto-camps captured this self-conscious fantasy. They represented a "de-centralized" vacation as opposed to the "herded" life of the large hotel. The camp, however, straddled a very thin line between social democracy and anomic freedom.

The camp was touted as an "absolute democracy" where open, classless friendship flourished. Belasco has observed that "cele-brants hoped that, by coming together in a new relaxed environ-ment, tourists might rediscover a common thread broken in every-day life."[6] The *Saturday Evening Post* proclaimed that a "new American democracy" was forming in the auto camps.[7] And the camps did indeed represent an intermingling of the broad and swollen American middle class. Businessmen, teachers, farmers, students, lawyers, clerks, and retirees learned that they were all "just folks."

But at the same time, this comradeship was purposefully quite limited. A 1924 *Literary Digest* article aptly conveyed the essence of this new friendship. It was entitled "Neighbors for a Night in Yel-lowstone Park." Most informative is a contemporary account that reveals the practiced anonymity of the camps: "We chatted daily with people who knew the salient facts of our history, and told us in return the stories of their lives, but in very few cases did we learn their names, or they ours." Campers assumed *noms de tour*. Identi-fication was derived from physical characteristics: ("The Blond") or license plate ("the New Yorker"). This anonymity and brevity of contact appears to have been prized and savored. "You seem to dip into other people's lives at odd moments, as if you opened a book at random."[7]

The invention of the motel represented a retreat from even this conception of community. Again, it is true that the motel offered basic objective advantages over the camps. They were enclosed, thus providing shelter from summer showers. They offered certain amenities like bedding that made travel less cumbersome and more comfortable. But still it is the peculiar community of the camp that provides the key to the cultural significance of the motel. True the motel represented a withdrawal from the democracy of the camp, a process that began with the introduction of fees in the 1920s. But if

the nomadic community of the camp was abandoned, its atmosphere of adventure, informality, anonymity, and privacy was not.
Early motels had no registration or reservations, a practice which
obviously upset the FBI Director. They were set in relatively remote
places. Moreover, the motel itself, especially in its architecture,
seemed to celebrate impermanence. It eschewed the aura of stability
that surrounded the old hotel. (The early chains made only a single
concession of this regard: In recognition of the need for easy market
recognition, they often used a permanent trademark. Thus Howard
Johnson's adopted the orange roof which could be quickly identified from the road.) But when motels did not use simple, utilitarian
cabin construction, they adopted an architecture that openly and
often garishly, suggested transience. Motels were made to look like
teepees or missions or Tudor cottages. The replicas were never
accurate. Too small, too crowded, too eclectic, these motels showed
less an effort at pretension than an attempt to convey an openly
admitted pseudo-reality. Eventually, of course, the motel would
develop a sleek, utilitarian architecture. But theatrical elements still
grace the motel: dining areas decorated as country inns (with for-
mica beams), lobbies adorned with plastic chandeliers and gold
paint as trim.

Therefore, the motel as cultural symbol and supporting invention represents something more than "sin is where you find it." It
represents the union of a utilitarian consumption-economy and
sexuality. In the words of Nabokov's Professor Humbert, who
"grew to prefer the Functional Motel," the American invention
offered "clean, neat, safe nooks, ideal places for sleep, argument,
reconciliation, insatiable illicit love."[8] No sociological study can
reveal this aspect of the motel more fully than Nabokov's account of
Humbert's journeys with Lolita:

> We came to know—*nous connumes*, to use a Flaubertain intona-
> tion—the stone cottages under enormous Chateaubriandesque trees,
> the brick unit, the adobe unit, the stucco court . . .
>
> Nous connumes . . . the would-be enticements of their repetitious
> names—all those Sunset Motels, U-Beam Cottages, Hillcrest Courts,
> Pine View Courts, Mountain View Courts, Skyline Courts, Park Plaza
> Courts, Green Acres, Mac's Courts. . . . the baths were mostly tiled
> showers, with an endless variety of spouting mechanisms. . . . Some
> motels had instructions pasted above the toilet (on whose tank the

towels were unygienically heaped) asking guests not to throw into its bowl garbage, beer cans, cartons, stillborn babies; others had special notices under glass, such as Things to do. . . .[9]

The phrase "we came to know" is especially accurate. For Nabokov managed to include in it both carnal and consumer knowledge.

A generation earlier, as the transition from the auto camp to the motel was just being appreciated, the elements of Nabokov's portrayal are already evident but more sketchily drawn, less ripe. We can see evidence of this in items from popular culture such as Frank Capra's film *It Happened One Night,* based upon a Samuel Hopkins Adams short story. This romance revolves around the themes of anonymity, happiness, liberation and, of course, sexuality. Claudette Colbert, millionairess daughter, runs away because her overprotective father threatens to have her recent marriage annulled. Clark Gable, a reporter, agrees to help her in return for a story. The couple banter over class differences as they board a bus traveling from Miami to New York. The first of three motel scenes follows shortly. The first, and by far the most electric, occurs on the first leg of the trek when Gable and Colbert are still strangers. The busdriver stops and yells, "auto camp!" For reasons of economy Gable takes a single room for both under a false name at the rate of two dollars. Colbert is enthralled with the homeyness and compactness of the room, "How clever," she exclaims. But then, as the sexuality implicit in the situation dawns on her, she threatens to leave. Gable rigs a blanket over a clothesline between the two beds, which he refers to as the "walls of Jericho". Colbert replies, "I suppose that makes everything alright." The immediate reference is clear, but one can imagine its implication in the context of the whole scene for the potential of this new institution: Does the privacy and anonymity of the motel legitimatize sexual behavior?

Gable announces that he is going to bed and suggests Colbert retreat to the other side of the wall. Confused, almost transfixed by the situation, Colbert remains. The following sequence transfixed a generation of moviegoers as well. Gable, promising carnal knowledge, delivers a lecture: "Perhaps you'd like to know how a man undresses." As he strips (to reveal the absence of an undershirt), he never stops talking; "there is a 'science' to disrobing, some men remove their shoes first, I however . . ." Colbert looks properly shocked; when Gable hesitates just a second (now come the pants), she runs to "her" bed behind the wall. But during the entire scene her eyes never leave Gable's body. Again, the knowledge (or at least some of it) is conveyed, despite the absence of a physical act. But the film's exploration of the possibilities of the motel as an agency of sexual freedom continues. Colbert undresses behind the blanket. This time it is Gable who watches. The "wall" undulates erratically (erotically?) as Colbert undresses. Nylons and lingerie fly across the blanket. A plaintive request: "I wish you'd take those things off the wall of Jericho." Colbert mumbles, with a sudden appreciation for male sexual longing, "Oh, of course!" An act of consideration for unspent sexuality? The next shots, however, seem post-coital. Gable lies in bed smoking a cigarette. Colbert, in men's pajamas (she had arrived sans suitcase) asks the prototypical question of anonymous promiscuity, "By the way, what's your name?" Post-coital this is not, however, and Gable playfully begins a seductive monologue: "my name is the whipoorwill"; I am the "soft breeze that caresses your face." But he then abruptly alters the mood and tone to one of cynicism and illicit sexuality between strangers: real names don't matter anyway—he had registered under false pretenses.

The following morning the couple shows a liberation from gender roles. What a difference a night in the motel makes! Gable has a table set for breakfast. Colbert awakes late. She is cheerful and ravenously hungry. (The result of sexual release—metaphysical, of course). Between gulps of coffee she proclaims: "last night was the first time I've ever been alone with a man!" Gable continues his teaching, however, this time showing how to dunk doughnuts.

The characters Gable and Colbert play are public figures. She is the subject of news and he is a seeker. Unlike Humbert and Lolita, they travel by bus. No privacy here. There is a genial and comradely atmosphere on board, illustrated by card playing and singing. But the public character of the bus threatens anonymity. A man doesn't think the couple look like husband and wife (a suspicion also raised by each mom-and-pop motel owner). A newspaper displays the heiress's picture and threatens to expose the charade. Only in the motel can Gable and Colbert pursue authenticity. The next stop at a motel is engineered by Colbert. It is only three hours to New York, but who wants to arrive in the middle of the night? This scene is visually more frank. The camera switches back and forth across the "wall" as each undresses more casually now. Has carnal knowledge, contrary to the Biblical tradition, erased modesty? The focus here, however, has shifted. Gable confesses. He would like to be married, but only to "the right sort of girl." Not a girl, chaste like his sister or mother, but "someone, that's real, that's alive." He would take her to "an island of paradise, to a place where the moon and the water and a couple could become one . . . big and marvelous." Gable yearns not for sex, as he did on the first night, but for the unity of dyadic love, what Freud had called the most sublime form of community. Colbert is touched. In tears, she comes from behind the blanket. Gable sends her back: he has fallen in love. The next morning he leaves to "go public" by telling his editor about the "best story he ever wrote." A series of misunderstandings follow, but boy does get girl. The final scene is set in a motel. This time the audience only overhears the mom-and-pop motel keepers gossip about the couple. They had asked for a clothesline, says the grandfatherly figure, and "made me buy a toy trumpet."

The conventional ending of "*It Happened One Night*" keeps the presentation of the possibilities of the motel within safe bounds. But the explosive capacity of this institution has never been more clearly outlined: the "opening up" of privacy as a liberating experience and the subsequent problems confronted by strangers who covet both sexual anonymity and community. But Colbert's character was a public figure, the object of attention, and Gable's reporter was the recorder of public events. The motel scenes, themselves focused upon watching, disrobing, and anticipating reactions, with both characters vaguely hoping that the shedding of clothes and of public pretension would reveal real selves with common understanding. In the romance, this private watching begat an authentic relationship.

Today the motel does not represent this union of sexuality and consumption in such sharp focus. One could not recapture today the intense sexual tension of the motel as developed in Frank Capra's 1934 *It Happened One Night,* or the naivité of Claudette Colbert's character, as fascinated with the conveniences of the motel as she was upset and attracted to its sexual potential. New supporting sexual institutions have now been invented: the singles bar, the adult bookstore, "swingers" networks, even the "adult motel." Of course, the motel continues to fulfill a supporting sexual function, but by now the surrounding society itself has absorbed the ambiance of the motel.

I have suggested that the invention of the pieced quilt as well as the invention of the social tradition surrounding it fell into disuse because of the decline of the household economy. But the decline of quilting can be more fully understood by reviewing the nature of quilting as a supporting institution.

As noted, the modern image of the craft of quilting is one of a stable and ordered practicality, an image evoked by many of the quilt designs themselves. But this image of simplicity and stability, like those attached to "Vermont maple sugar" or "split rail fences," is itself an invention. In fact, the quilt is part of a broad and complex cultural invention by which America has reconstructed its own past. This invention is not even a recent one. We can find it in Harriet Beecher Stowe's *The Minister's Wooing*.

> "Girls ain't what they used to be in my day," sententiously remarked an elderly lady. "I remember my mother told me when she was thirteen she could knit a long cotton stocking in a day."
>
> "I haven't much faith in these stories of old times—have you, girls?" said Cerinthy, appealing to the younger members at the frame.
>
> "At any rate," Mrs. Twitchel, "our minister's wife will be a pattern; I don' know anybody that goes beyond her either in spinning or fine stitching."
>
> Thus the day was spent in friendly gossip as they quilted and rolled and talked and laughed, and as the afternoon sun cast lengthening shadows on the grass, Mary and Miss Marvin went into the great kitchen, where a long table stood exhibiting all that plentitude of provision which the immortal description of Washington Irving has saved us the trouble of recapitulating in detail.
>
> The husbands, brothers, and lovers had come in, and the scene was redolent of gayety. When Mary made her appearance, there was a moment's pause, till she was conducted to the side of the Doctor; when, raising his hand, he invoked a grace upon the loaded board.
>
> Unrestrained gayeties followed. Groups of young men and maidens chatted together, and all the gallantries of the times were enacted. Serious matrons commented on the cake, and particular secrets in the culinary art, which they drew from remote family archives. One might have learned in that instructive assembly how best to keep moths out of blankets; how to make fritters of Indian corn undistinguishable from oysters; how to bring up babies by hand; how to mend a cracked teapot; how to take out grease from a brocade; how to reconcile absolute decrees with free will; how to make five yards of cloth answer the purpose

of six; and how to put down the Democratic party. All were busy, earnest, and certain, just as a swarm of men and women, old and young, are in 1859.[10]

I am not suggesting that Stowe's account of sorority is a fabrication. Its sense of detail confirms its authenticity, as do other descriptions from this period. What is invention is the nostalgic implication in Stowe's narrative that a placid insularity reigned in the era she is describing. A few other scraps of evidence can help make our point. Perhaps the most revealing symbol of the American quilt as a supporting institution is a design called the "Rocky Road to Kansas." It was named after other states as well. In one quilt, the road is composed of four-pointed stars. Their ends touch so that open diamond spaces rest between the stars. Here is one woman's musings on its theme:

> I guess they named it that for a purpose. People thought a lot about roads in the old days. Specially when they didn't have any. Seems the road got important enough to name a quilt after anyways. When you was in a wagon train and didn't have no road to follow. . . . now that rocky road meant hard times to Kansas. But in them days when you made a road, the thing you remembered most about it was the rocks you had to move. Rocky Road to Oklahoma they sometimes call it too. Making new roads through the rocks.[11]

Let me offer another fragment about the pieced quilt. Christiana Tillson in her autobiography *A Woman's Story of Pioneer Illinois,* tells of her experience of making a quilt. She was able to find some bales of cotton:

> I then commenced the ardous task of separating the cotton from the seed, and after much labor and wear and tear of fingers I succeeded in getting enough to fill a comfortable. It had to be carded and made into bats before it could be used, and fortunately my maid-of-all-work knew how to card. But the cards: where were they to be found? After much inquiry I heard someone who was willing to lend her "kairds" to a Yankee woman. So the cotton was carded, after about a week's labor by Joey, and meanwhile Loomis had made a quilting frame and the great affair of making a comfortable was accomplished. The neighbors came in to see it. They had "heirn" that Tillson's wife had borrowed kairds, "but reckoned she didn't know how to spin a draw" and "couldn't think what she could do with kairds."[12]

Tillson breaks her quilting narrative at this point and discusses her plans to add a chimney and a window to their cabin. One recent book on quilting cites this autobiography as evidence of women eagerly exchanging opinions, ideas, and organizing community projects.[13] *A Woman's Story* does contain episodes of this sort; Tillson, a native of Massachusetts, is genuinely impressed by the "hospitality" of frontier families. But if one looks more closely at the narrative we have quoted, there is evidence for a contradictory image: the frontier may also be considered a temporary and fragile community of suspicious strangers. Tillson casually notes that she finally found a woman willing to lend her kairds to a Yankee. Regional hostilities traveled across the frontier and, in this case, represented more than political differences. Tillson regarded pioneers from the South as ignorant and slothful. While Stowe fondly reproduces dialect, Tillson ridicules it. In turn, these neighbors seemed to have doubted Yankee abilities. But they did come to visit and quilt. A 1919 introduction to Tillson's autobiography carefully notes that "only by the exercise of much patience and forbearance was it possible for the two elements to associate on terms of neighborly equality."[14]

Let us offer one final example about another practice recalled by Hamlin Garland, a writer not at all adverse to constructing a frontier romance. Neighbors have just arrived to celebrate the family's departure:

> It was a very touching and beautiful moment to me, for as I looked around upon that little group of men and women, rough-handed, bent and worn with toil, silent and shadowed with the sorrow of parting, I realized as never before the high place my parents had won in the estimation of their neighbors. It affected me still more deeply to see my father stammer and flush with uncontrollable emotion. I had thought the event deeply important before, but I now perceived that our going was all of a piece with the West's elemental restlessness. I could not express what I felt then, and I can recover but little of it now, but the pain which filled my throat comes back to me mixed with a singular longing to relive it.
>
> There, on a low mound in the midst of the prairie, in the shadow of the house we had built, beneath the slender trees we had planted, we were bidding farewell to one cycle of emigration and entering upon another. The border line had moved on, and my indomitable Dad was moving with it. I shivered with dread of the irrevocable decision thus forced upon me. I heard a clanging as of great gates behind me and the field of the future was wide and wan.

From this spot we had seen the wild prairies disappear. On every hand wheat and corn and clover had taken the place of the wild oat, the hazelbush and the rose. Our house, a commonplace farm cabin, took on grace. Here Hattie had died. Our yard was ugly, but there Jessie's small feet had worn a slender path. Each of our lives was knit into these hedges and rooted in these fields and yet, notwithstanding all this, in response to some powerful yearning call, my father was about to set out for the fifth time into the still more remote and untrodden west. Small wonder that my mother sat with bowed head and tear-blinded eyes, while these good and faithful friends crowded around her to say goodbye.[15]

Garland's affection-laden memory then sours. He asks: "Why should this suffering be? Why should mother be wrenched from all her dearest friends and forced to move away to a strange land?"[16]

I do not wish to necessarily support the view of the frontier as a society of greedy speculators, or crude and slovenly marginals, but I only wish to emphasize the history of the invention of the quilt as a supporting institution for a restless and mobile population, an invention of a series of immigrant communities extending historically from the New England "city on the hill" to Ohio pioneer towns to prairie junctions. Only in New England was there a sustained conscious effort to create a model town of tightly knit homes surrounding a common. But then these Yankees did leave, and leave in tremendous numbers, to Western New York and Ohio. In 1643, William Bradford compared the Plymouth Colony to an "ancient mother" who had "grown old, and forsaken by her children (though not in her affections)."[17] The Western Reserve saw attempts to replicate the New England town, but here too the communal idea collapsed in the face of speculation, regional and ethnic heterogeneity and, again, the brute fact of American history—space. One traveler saw the tasks of farmer and speculator conflated: "If you accost a farmer in these parts, before he returns your civilities he draws from his pocket a lithographic city, and asks you to take a few building lots at one-half their value . . . as a personal favor conferred on you."[18] Towns were created with a nonchalance that horrifies the Burkean mind. Eliza Farnham's *Life in Prarie Land* (1847) expresses affection for these town jobbers. She looks over "the picture of this little town, or rather the spot selected for it; for no town is yet there" and speaks of its founder as an "extrodinary genius" who is now a "gentleman of leisure." "The advantageous sale of his property enables him to spend his time and as his tastes and pleasures lead him."[19]

The rates of geographic mobility in the nineteenth century are startling. Merle Curti's study of a Wisconsin county from 1850 to 1880 shows that in none of the occupational and ethnic groups studied did as many as half the inhabitants remain in the county a decade. The average rate of *those who remained* was 25 percent from 1860–70 and 29 percent from 1870–80.[20] Richard Lingeman writes appreciatively of this paradox: "Americans were constantly exchanging realized settled communities back east, or in the old world, for the assertion of individual interests to better themselves. Most of them, as soon as they arrived in the new place formed new communities—settlements, rural neighborhoods, villages, towns."[21]

The pieced quilt as a supporting institution is all the more important (and poignant) when seen as being an invention of transients. For the quilt represented concrete evidence of memory of past communities as well as the basis of an attempt to form new communities. That quilting bee, so deeply imprinted in the American collective memory, was an invention designed to support a claim for instant community. And, after all the romance in American literature and oral tradition is accounted for, this is the kind of community that Americans have empirically chosen. The quilting bee brought women together quickly and efficiently. In some accounts women mention the receipt of four, five, and six friendship quilts, which were pieced for them when they arrived in new communities. The rapidly changing, bold and explosive designs of the American pieced quilt were a pleasant and, in many cases, magnificent, unintended consequence of this supporting invention. Memory selectively emphasizes the tranquility of quilting and the gregariousness of the bee. These recollections, of course, nurture the romance of the quilt, so when a student such as Kathryne Travis witnesses their shoddy treatment, she sees it as a kind of desecration. Here is one of her accounts written in 1930:

> "Stop the car. Did you see that 'Drunkard's Path' on the line?"
> A row of heads could be seen at the edge of the door; a hound began to bark, two small children ran behind the smokehouse and peered from their hiding place. "Hello," I called. A tall, gangling woman came slowly

forward into the light. Behind her, clinging and hiding, were four small, dirty, ragged children. "May I get a drink of water here?" I asked. "Yes, I reckon so. Hey, you Hennery, run down yander to the spring and tote up a bucket of fresh water fur the lady." Henry emerged from behind the smokehouse, and keeping his eye on me, he picked up a lard bucket and slowly vanished. "That's a bright quilt you have on the line," I said. "Did you make it?" "No'am, my old man's ma made hit. The children's been usin' hit fur a pallet here on the porch, and out in the field to put the baby on." Three chickens wandered out of the house and jumped off the porch. "Hit rained last night and everything got wet; I jes' hung it out to dry." I looked through the door; the floor was half gone and the roof full of holes.

"Have you any more quilts as pretty as that?" I asked. "No, we useter have a lot, but they's all been used up. My old man's ma was a hand at makin' quilts. She made one with over six thousand pieces in hit, but the young uns done tore hit up." I then saw an ironing board leaning against the wall. It was covered with the remains of a quilt scorched and browned almost beyond recognition; it was the "Tree of Paradise" design. I mangaed to find a complete block visible, in which I counted one hundred sixty-five pieces. I later estimated the quilt to contain twenty blocks, making four thousand one hundred and twenty-five pieces in the quilt. It was a master-piece of intricate quilting. Was this the end of patience and love of the beautiful in this family? Or was it patience of another kind—patience with shiftlessness?[22]

When she is so moved as to ask "was this the end of patience and love of the beautiful in this family?" does she reveal the cultural power of this invention, one which grows despite (or even because of) its disuse? For the quilt in individual and collective cultural memory represents moments of community within a dominant historical pattern of restless movement. The strips of forsaken community are forgotten, and the romance is treasured. Travis is at least able to retrieve a single block not ruined by the iron. It was appropriately named "Tree of Paradise."

It was, I think, not just the sewing machine or the factory, that brought the quilt to disuse, but the fact that other inventions were offered which could more easily serve as supporting institutions for instant community: the telephone, the automobile, the motel, the computer, the television. Americans would become rapturous about these as well.

Chapter 6

Transitional Inventions

If some inventions create new social forms and others sustain them, there are also others that alter both. They may themselves die out, or they may continue as supporting institutions for different forms. Transitional inventions are like meteors. Of short but spectacular duration, they shatter and change all objects in their path.

The revival camp is such an invention. In fact, it is a variation of a primal human invention: the large meeting. The large meeting, whether a political rally, festival, or religious gathering, is an antibureaucratic social form, one which celebrates contagion and enthusiasm as a basis for action. To be sure, the large meeting has its manipulative leaders who hope to direct its outcomes. But even routinized versions always threaten to break away from this sort of control. This is the case, for instance, with the American presidential nominating convention. But if elites sometimes overestimate their ability to manage this form, the rank and file often fail to recognize that the large meeting cannot be an ongoing social structure without elite management. Woodstock Nation, for example, had its significance, but it still must be counted as effusion rather than imminent institution.

I have tried to show how the American revival camp eventually succumbed to bureaucratization, and also how, in this process, it radically altered American religion. In this section, as an illustration of the nature of transitional invention, I would like to review how meteorlike were the changes it wrought.

The revival camp was an institutional invention of American Protestantism design to cope with a new and highly competitive religious atmosphere. In this respect, the camp can be seen as an invention of elite control. But we saw how unmanageable the camp proved to be in this regard: By its nature, it afforded none of the stability of the reform societies created as part of the "benevolent empire" of American Protestantism and was not easily subject to bureaucratic control. The reform organizations could function well as interdenominational front groups for particular religions, but the interdenominationalism of the camp was more genuine and more unstable. The camp fostered a kind of free-floating entrepreneurial leadership sometimes only loosely attached to a denomination. The Methodists were especially adept at dealing with this "problem." The circuit-rider system provided both bureaucratic control and entrepreneurial initiative. But even here full control was not assured. Peter Cartwright tells us in his autobiography that while the Methodists had "excellent preachers to steer and guide the flock," some still "ran wild, and indulged in extravagancies that were hard to control."[1]

Social Transformations

The instability of the camp as an agency of political control can, or course, be traced to the emotional atmosphere of the meetings themselves. A good part of this instability can also be attributed to the basic character of the meeting. For the camp meeting was, in its essence, a social institution. It placed a great value on communicative skills. The effects of persuasion and exhortation were purposely heightened by the relative isolation created by the camp. The Eastern variant of the protracted meeting was designed to transform the town (momentarily to be sure) from a multidimensional environment to a single institution devoted exclusively to talk. When such a structural change occurred, the skills of a local elite may or may not have been appropriate to this new temporary "society." The received rules for establishing power and status no longer automatically obtain. Even the authority of the local pastor was now divided and subject to comparison to other preachers. The unconverted businessman found that church attendance no longer supplemented community prominence. Moreover, the established elite discovered that they had to publicly submit to the indignities of religious rebirth. Charles Finney provided us with one such example which occurred at his revival in Utica, New York, in 1825. He speaks of an "energetic, highly cultivated" woman who at first

opposed the protracted meeting. But her opposition faded and was
replaced by an intense concern for her salvation. Finney visited her
frequently during her long ordeal and after a series of conversations
saw that she was "ready to sink under the ripened conviction":

> Her contenence waxed pale, in a moment after she threw up her hands
> and shrieked, and then fell forward upon the arm of the sofa, and let her
> heart break. I think she had not wept at all before.[2]

As community leaders underwent status changes, so did the
mass of people who attended the revival meetings. Contemporaries
of the revivals as well as modern scholars have argued that the
attraction of the meetings could be traced to the boredom of frontier
and small-town life. On this interpretation the revival can be compared to the circus, or more charitably, to the large social gathering.
There is truth to this assertion, but it misses the essential point of
the camp and protracted meetings. Many of those who converted
underwent an immediate elevation in power and status. Both the
semiliterate preachers who so horrified established denominations
and the "little bands of sisters" enjoyed the kind of social transformation that can only occur under special conditions.

The camps altered everyday lives in more subtle ways. We tend to
focus exclusively on its manipulation by elites and thus ignore
important changes created by the camp meeting. Again, Finney
offers us an example. He recalls the following practice at conventional prayer meetings:

> . . . every professor of religion felt it a duty to testify for Christ. They
> must "take up the cross" and say something in the meeting. One would
> rise and say in substance: "I have a duty to perform which no one can
> perform for me. I arise to testify that religion is good; though I must
> confess that I do not enjoy it at present. I have nothing particular to say,
> only to bear my testimony; and I hope you will all pray for me." This
> concluded, that person would sit down and another would rise and say,
> about to the same effect: Religion is good; I do not enjoy it; I have
> nothing else to say, but I must do my duty. I hope you will all pray for
> me." Thus the time would be occupied, and the meeting would pass off
> with very little that was more interesting than such remarks as these. Of
> course the ungodly would make sport of this.[3]

Finney found these prayer meetings "silly," even "ridiculous and
repulsive." In their place he invented a new form, one which was a
combination of prayer and preaching. These meetings had a So-

cratic and seminar quality about them. Finney would deliver a short sermon, pray himself, select a text and interpret it briefly; "Then, when I saw that an impression was made, I would stop and ask one or two to pray that the Lord might fasten on their minds. I would then proceed with my talk, and after a little stop again and ask some one or two to pray."[4] Finney was, in fact, teaching communicative skills. The object was a narrow one of seeking conversion, but as a by-product, the audience learned new modes of thinking and expression. We can see how successful this aspect of the protracted meeting was by following his reports of conversions. Instead of the stunted response, "religion is good," converts spoke in poignant and lilting metaphor.

These patterns of activity caused by the revival bear striking similarities to revolutionary change. The rapid alteration of power and status, the proliferation of pamphleteering, the sudden and massive increases in participation, and the adult socialization are all characteristics of major modern revolutions. But it must be remembered that while the Great Revival was like a revolution, it still was not one. Much the same assessment can be made in regard to inventive outbursts in other periods of American history. The "cultural revolution" of the 1960s is an obvious example. Genuine revolutions do, of course, produce transitional inventions. But they also invent generative ones which fundamentally and permanently close off some alternatives and open new ones. The revival camp and the protracted meeting, as well as sit-ins and teach-ins, still permitted egress to conventional structure. The eastern businesman could rebuild status when the protracted meeting gave way to spring; the western farmer returned, certainly as a changed person, to the homestead.

This is not to say that the camp had only a trivial impact on society. The cliché of the converted drunk or prostitute who shortly returns to old habits is not an accurate assessment of the revival camp. As we indicated with respect to other American inventions, it is often difficult to trace consequences. The revival camp did democratize American Protestantism. But it did not represent part of some general process of universalism and secularization. In fact, the camp produced quite the opposite effect. As an invention it was used to savagely attack the new modernist religious forms of Unitarianism and Universalism. Yet its very structure implied a repudiation of

Calvinism. Historians have an equally difficult time establishing the relationship between revival and Jacksonian reform.[5]

One way to understand the kind of change which was fostered by revivalism is to focus on its impact on the structure of American Protestantism. The Great Revival did serve as a basis for recruitment for American denominantions. Some church memberships declined, others enjoyed dramatic increases. But the camps also produced an enormous number of new religious divisions which stunned even the most ardent supporters of the revival. Protestantism is in general prone to schismatic behavior. But the Great Revival created a truly incredible profusion of sects. The camp meeting exacerbated old European quarrels. It reinstigated disputes which had arisen during the Great Awakening. Even more radical anti-Calvinist churches found themselves subjected to reevaluation and scorn as new groupings challenged their authority. As Presbyterians debated the predestination question, schisms over Old and New Light sects multiplied. The decentralized structure of the Baptist church produced a dizzying and nearly uncountable array of sects. Anti-Mission Baptists, Two-in-the-Seed Baptists, Free Will Baptists, Duck River Baptists, Dunkers, General Baptists, Separate Baptists, Seventh Day Baptists, and Christadelphians were all part of this schismatic swirl. The Methodists, with their new theology and centralized organization, worked hard to maintain unity. But they, too, eventually fell to sectarian division over the issue of the episcopacy. As this sectarian behavior increased, the ad hoc coalitions necessary for interdenominational meetings proved more difficult to maintain. Finney warned converts not "to dwell upon sectarian distinctions, or to be sticklish about sectarian points."[6]

Not only did the revival camp meeting encourage sectarian division, it also provided an atmosphere fostering the invention of new religions. In 1828, William Miller, himself a convert of a local revival, announced at a camp meeting his "call" to tell the world of his discovery that the world would end in 1843. Miller became an exceptionally popular revivalist. He picked up converts who also became itineratnt speakers. Millerites awaited the last "year of time" with increasing anxiety. Farmers left crops unharvested, sold their houses and possessions.

Alice Tyler summarizes some of their activities on the prophesied day:

Plans were made among the Millerites to meet the long-awaited day in groups. Tents were put up outside cities, preferably on hilltops, and hundreds of people assembled on the night of October 21 to keep vigil together. No provision was made for food or rest, and as the night passed and then the day and the next night wore on, the tension was intolerable. In some sections severe storms and heavy rainfall added to the alarm and suffering. The plight of the children in these camps was piteous, but many of their elders succumbed more completely to the nervous strain. There were several suicides, and as the dawn of October 23 served notice that "time continued" regardless of prophecy, some heart-broken Millennialists were led away, insane.[7]

William Miller insisted he had only made an error in his calculations, but his followers disbanded.

The Millerites were not the only new adventist group to be formed as a result of the revivals. The most extraordinary development of this kind was the creation of the Church of the Latter Day Saints by Joseph Smith after a revival in Palmyra, New York. The Smith family had recently converted to Presbyterianism when Joseph experienced a series of visions in which he was told that all existing religious beliefs were false. Shortly later he was said to have been led into the woods by a group of angels who, with the aid of a special instrument, showed him a history of the world. In 1830 an account of the contents of these "plates" was published. It was to become the Mormon bible. With a growing number of converts Smith moved to Ohio, then to Missouri, and on to Navoo, Illinois, where he formed a mini-state and announced his revelation of the justification for polgamy. He was murdered in jail by a mob in 1844. The Church of the Latter Day Saints survived, breaking up into several sects. One journeyed to Iowa, another to Wisconsin. A third, under the leadership of Brigham Young, traveled west outside the authority of the United States government. Today Mormonism is an established and venerable institution.

Inventing Little Societies: The Communes

The revival camp meeting also spawned another series of inventions, the communes. The commune as an organizational form was not new to America. Moreover, there were communal experiments in America before the Great Revival. But the camp meetings

did provide a basis, both directly and indirectly, for a particular
kind of communal experimentation. They are an example of inventions created by transitional institutions.

The Shakers, founded by Ann Lee, daughter of a Manchester
blacksmith, were a small celibate religious sect until the Great
Awakening provided new converts. The Western Revival created
even more opportunities for recruitment. Shakers sent representatives to the camp meetings. Finney recounts reports of Shakers
ominously waiting on the edges of camp grounds for converts. A
contemporary historian claims that a pattern soon developed during the revival in which Shakers gathered in men and women who,
"jarred from their spiritual moorings," had been "awakened by
evangelical preaching but not satisfied by it."[8]

As the meeting declined, communal experiments flourished. In
New York's burnt-over district scores of communes appeared in the
1840s. Towns which had earlier been given over to winter protracted meetings now formed conventions and societies devoted to
a sympathetic examination of communes. These communes varied
greatly in their social and economic practices and in their religious
doctrines, but they all had one element in common: a fervently held
belief in the possibility of reorganizing society into "perfect" little
communities.

Two examples can illustrate the relationship of the commune to
the camp and the inventive power of the commune itself. The
Oneida Perfectionists and the Shakers attempted to transform the
theological tenets of the camp into principles of permanent social
order. Both avoided the organizational weakness of radical adven-
tism by declaring that the millennium had already arrived.

The Oneida commune movement had its origin in the Great
Revival. John Noyes, a young law clerk recently graduated from
Dartmouth, reluctantly attended a protracted meeting at his mother's request. Noyes wrote in his diary that he had "looked on religion as a sort of phrenzy to which we are all liable" and had
explained to his mother that she "would be disappointed" with his
reaction. To his surprise, Noyes was immediately converted at the
meeting. For four days he struggled until "light gleamed upon his
soul." Noyes pledged to devote his life to the service of God, vowing
to live in the "revival spirit and be a young convert forever."[9]

Noyes was disappointed by the "professional spirit" of the staff
and students at the Andover Seminary, however, and transferred to

Yale, where he studied under Nathaniel Taylor, a popular teacher with perfectionist inclinations. New Haven was itself undergoing a revival and Noyes quickly drew out its possibilities, which were in fact already being considered by many revivalists. If conversion, and hence salvation, were available to all, then was sin itself avoidable? Noyes, as did all the perfectionists he gathered around him, confessed "sinlessness." The second advent of Christ must already have occurred; the Gospel itself could provide for complete salvation from sin. When Charles Nordoff asked members of the Oneida commune for the bare doctrine of Perfectionism, they replied: "As the doctrine of temperance is total abstinence from all alcholic drinks, and the doctrine of anti-slavery is immediate abolition of human bondage, so the doctrine of Perfectionism is immediate and total cessation from sin."[10]

The Shakers developed a heretical position that also met the adventist problem. Divine history was divided into four epochs: the first ended with Noah, the second with Jesus, the third with Ann Lee, the fourth was in the process of formation. The Shakers believed theirs was the "Church of the Last Dispensation." The completion of the Godhead had already occurred with the worldly appearance of Ann Lee. The Shakers offered a kind of feminization of religion. They expanded the Trinity to read Father-Son-Holy Mother-Wisdom Daughter. The masculine/feminine principle was implemented throughout Shaker administration. Elders and elderesses, deacons and caretakers (child-minders) were all composed of two sets of people equally apportioned between the sexes. In a sense, then, the Shakers had institutionalized the gender transformations created by the protracted meetings.

These communes systematically attempted to invent new social forms which corresponded to the spontaneous radicalism of the camps. The theology of the revival camp promised complete and immediate individual conversion; the commune promised a complete and immediate transformation of social life. The movement to a location *in extremis* represented a firm denial of the possibility for incremental change. Experimentation there was, but it was of a radical and permanent nature. True conversion, argued the communalists, required a concept of individual perfection which was not possible within the confines of society as it was now organized. John Noyes wrote thusly:

[The revival,] if it goes beyond religion, naturally runs first into some form of Socialism. Religious love is a very near neighbour to sexual love, and they always get mixed in the intimacies and social excitements of Revivals. The next thing a man wants, after he has found the salvation of his soul, is to find his Eve and his Paradise. Hence these wild experiments and terrible disasters.

From these facts and principles, quite opposite conclusions may be drawn by different persons. A worldly-wise man might say, they show Revivals are damnable delusions, leading to immorality and disorganisation of society. I should say, they show that Revivals, because they are divine, require for their complement a divine organization of society, which all who love Revivals and the good of mankind should fearlessly seek to discover and inaugurate.[11]

The Shakers and the Perfectionists immediately altered the heart of the social order, inventing new forms of work and of sexual and familial life. The Shakers adopted the principle of celibacy. They organized into "families" of 25 to 150 people. Each "family" lived in a large dormitory governed by elders, deacons, and caretakers. Property was legally owned by the "First Family" at Mount Lebanon, New York, the largest and central commune. In practice, however, each family kept its own accounts and transacted business separately. The celibacy rule was maintained by a strict system of supervision. Even hand-holding was forbidden. Meals and religious services were sexually segregated. Any individual attention between the sexes, colloquially referred to as "sparking," was discouraged. Families entering the society could bring their children, who were cared for communally. The Shakers also adopted orphans, but this practice was later abandoned. The Society experienced great difficulty retaining members as they came of age.

The Shakers spent great effort and ingenuity in the reorganization of work. Not only was property held communally but work was rotated. Manual labor was required by all members. Work for the Shakers was consciously imbued with a religious purpose. The principles of utility and order were meant to give work the quality of ritual. John Meecham, the successor to Ann Lee, explained: "we are not called to labor to excell, or be like the world; but to excell them in order, union and peace, and in good works—works that are truly virtuous and useful to man, in this life. . . . All work in the Church ought to be done plain and decent, according to the order and use of things, neither too high or to low, according to their order and use."[12]

The concepts of order and use, concepts derived from the belief in a perfect society, were responsible for the invention of styles and objects that are stunning in their simplicity. Shaker furniture had an almost hypnotic elegance. Americans avidly bought them (as they did Shaker seeds, applesauce, bonnets, and brooms), and a catalogue was finally issued in 1874. By this time the Shakers had used their functional design to produce specialized chairs that were highly regarded: wagon chairs, dining chairs, slipping chairs, sewing rockers, foot benches.

The Shakers also re-invented household organization. White, pictureless walls featured pegged strips of wood placed at eye level from which chairs, hats, and bookcases gracefully hung. William Dean Howells wrote of the Shaker home: "The first impression of all is cleanliness, with a suggestion of barrenness which is not inconsistent, however, with comfort, and which comes chiefly from the aspect of the unpapered walls, the scrubbed floors hidden only by rugs and strips of carpeting, and the plain flat finish of the woodwork."[13]

Shaker utility did not meet everyone's taste. To Nordhoff, their buildings reminded him of "factories or human hives." But Hepworth Dixon, another observer of the commune, conveys for us a sense of the novelty of Shaker architecture:

> No Dutch town has a neater aspect, no Moravian hamlet a softer hush. The streets are quiet; for here you have no grog-shop, no beer-house, no lock-up, no pound; of the dozen edifices rising about you—workrooms, barns, tabernacle, stables, kitchens, schools, and dormitories—not one is either foul or noisy; and every building, whatever may be its use, has something of the air of a chapel. The paint is all fresh; the planks are all bright; the windows are all clean. A white sheen is on everything; a happy quiet reigns around. Even in what is seen of the eye and heard of the ear. Mount Lebanon strikes you as a place where it is always Sunday. The walls appear as though they had been built only yesterday; a perfume, as from many unguents, floats down the lane; and the curtains and window blinds are of spotless white. Everything in the hamlet looks and smells like household things which have been long laid up in lavender and roseleaves."[14]

One might guess that a conception of work in terms of religious ritual would produce a hostility to change, a spartan and stagnant

aesthetics. In actuality, the Shaker communes were dynamos of
technological invention. In general the Shakers disapproved of patents, but they found them to be a prudent recourse. The following
is only a portion of the list of Shaker innovation: circular saw
(1813), threshing machine (1815), waterwheel with controlling
grates (1831), improved sundial (1836), corn sorting machine
(1857), chair casters (1852), copper vaccum for drying herbs and,
later, milk (1853), washing machine (1858), cast iron fence post
(1859).

The Perfectionists also invented new social forms. Their most
controversial was the system of male continence and complex marriage, inventions of Noyes himself. The Shakers demanded celibacy
as a necessary means to perfection. They insisted that sexual abstinence was the only method to rise above "animal nature." Noyes
had for a time considered this alternative. In his "Confessions" he
supplied this version of what became known as the "Brimfield Affair." During a revival at Brimfield, a doctrinal discussion led by "an
extraordinary group of pretty brilliant young women" assumed a
"social and fanatical form." Noyes' account minimized his role in
the scandal and focused on the culpability of the young women who
had misinterpreted his actions and teachings:

> Several young women who were really leaders of the whole flock, be-
> came partially insane, and began to act strangely. The disorderly doings
> that were reported to me were, first, the case of 'bundling'; and, second,
> a wild night-excursion of two young women to a mountain near the
> village. I had no reason to believe that any act of real licentiousness took
> place; but that the 'bundling' was performed as a bold self-sacrifice for
> the purpose of killing shame and defying public opinion. I confess that I
> sympathised to some extent with the spirit of the first letters that came to
> me about this affair, and sought to shelter rather than condemn the
> young women who appealed to me against storm of scandal which they
> had brought upon themselves. But in the sequel, as the irregularities
> continued and passed on into actual licentiousness, I renounced all
> sympathy with them, and did my best in subsequent years to stamp
> them out, by word and deed, and succeeded.[15]

Noyes admits that he had been in Brimfield a few days before the
incident: "By my position as preacher I was sort of centre, and they
were in a progressive excitement over which I had no control. I
became afraid of them and myself." Noyes had been playing a game
of sexual chicken not uncommon during the revival meetings. One

preacher had boasted that "he could carry a virgin in each hand without the least stir of unholy passion!." Bundling, an old colonial practice, was now used as a test of wills by the young minister and his converts. Whether Noyes came to doubt his own motives or whether he realized the possibility of scandal (or both) is unclear. He does report that he left Brimfield "on foot through snow and cold below zero" to Putney, sixty miles away.[16]

Whether Noyes was a participant at Brimfield is for our purposes a moot point. The revival, and the perfectionist impulse which had emerged from it, had unleased a complex combination of religious and sexual experimentation. The Perfectionists as well as the Shakers had sought to found both experiences on a permanent and systemic basis. Noyes, then, had hardly withdrawn from the sexual question. In fact his communes made it the center of a new society.

In *Male Continence* Noyes considered "three solutions" to the relationship between reproduction and sexuality:

1. Those that seek to prevent the intercourse of the sexes, such as Malthus and the Shakers;
2. Those that seek to prevent the natural effects of the propagative act, the French inventors and Owen;
3. Those that seek to destroy the living results of the propagative act, viz., the abortionists and the child-killers.[17]

The following analysis illustrates the inventive connection made by Noyes between clinical considerations and Perfectionist theory:

We begin by analyzing the act of sexual intercourse. It has a beginning, a middle, and an end. Its beginning and most elementary form is the simple presence of the male organ in the female. Then usually follows a series of reciprocal motions. Finally this exercise brings on a nervous action or ejaculatory crises, which expells seed. Now we insist that this whole process, up to the very moment of emission, is voluntary, entirely under control of the moral faculty, and can be continued or stopped at will, and it is only the final crises of emission that is automatic or uncontrollable.[18]

Noyes appealed to "the memory of every man who has had good sexual experience to say whether, on the whole, the sweetest and the noblest period of intercourse with woman is not the simple presence and effusion, before the muscular exercise begins." Thus the Perfectionists divided sexuality into amative and propagative functions which heretofore had been mistakenly "confounded in the world, both in the theories of physiologists and in universal practice." The former represented a social relationship, "subservient to the spiritual"; the "social office of the sexual organs is their superior function, and that which gives man a positive above brutes."[19]

For Noyes amative sexuality was an act of Christian fellowship. "Let the act stand by itself," he argued, "and sexual intercourse becomes a truly social affair, the same in kind with other modes of kindly communion, differing only by its superior intensity and beauty." He envisioned a society in which sexuality would rank with the fine arts: "Indeed, it will rank above music, painting, sculpture, etc.; for it combines the charms and benefits of them all. There is much room for cultivation of taste and skill in this department as in any."[20]

The new era of communistic love began quietly. In May 1846 Noyes proposed amative intercourse with Mary Cragin, a resident of Putney. She consented. Mrs. Cragin's husband, George, presented the same proposal to Noyes' wife, Harriet. Soon Noyes' sisters and husbands joined the arrangement. All pledged to acknowledge John Noyes as "the father and overseer whom the Holy Ghost has set over the family thus constituted." This central group gradually informed other believers of these exchanges. However, when the people of Putney learned of the practices, Noyes and his band of experimental Perfectionists were forced to flee. Shortly thereafter the commune was formed in Oneida, New York.

Maren Lockwood Carden has examined the personal backgrounds of the 111 members of the Oneida settlement. Most came from small New England or New York towns. Many were farmers; others included a printer, trapmaker, machinery manufacturer, architect, bookeeper, shoemaker, and storekeeper. There were also several teachers, a lawyer, a Methodist minister and a doctor. In short, the commune was a refraction of petit bourgeois America. Members' religous background revealed the battle history of the Great Revival: eleven members had been Baptists and five Presbyterians. From one to three were members of the following groups: Dutch Reform, Millerite, Unitarian, Tobiasite, Universalist, and the Free Church of New Haven.[21]

While the Shakers sought to give work religious expression, the Oneidas appear to have attempted to transcend work. In fact, if the Shakers can be thought of as a religious Sparta, the Oneidans had built an Athens. There was some rotation of work and a commit-

ment to shared labor. But, by 1862, less desirable work was contracted to outsiders.

The Oneidas did some farming. They were adept at centralizing
trade previously performed by itinerant peddlars. The commune
preserved fruit and vegetables, bought pins and knickknacks and
sold them in nearby villages. The mainstay of the Oneida economy
was the Newhouse animal trap, an invention of a founding member.
The Oneidas wore no uniform although the women did devise calf-
length dressed and bobbed their hair, both in the interests of
convenience.

But most of all the Perfectionists talked. The took classes and
music lessons, organized into committees (Oneida had twenty-one
standing committees, ranging from lawn maintenance to photog-
raphy), published journals and circulars, held discussion groups.
Nordoff discovered "an almost fanatical horror of forms" on his
visit to Oneida: "they change their avocations frequently; they remove from Oneida to Willow Place, or to Wallingford, on slight
excuses; they change the order of their evening meetings and amuse-
ments with much care; and have changed even their meal hours."[22]
These Perfectionists had created a permanent protracted meeting.

In fact, the system of "mutal criticism," the central invention of
the Oneida commune, can be seen as an attempt to imbed the
dynamics of the protracted meeting into the social structure. Observers of the Oneidas were often struck by the fact that there were
no formal religious services. But to focus on this apparent absence
misses the essence of the Oneida experiment. If Oneida had indeed
created a society-cum-protracted meeting, separately identifiable
services would have been superfluous.

The mutual criticism sessions were an adaptation of the techniques of the new measures instituted by Finney. Noyes himself had
initiated this system among his fellow students at Andover. The
difference of course, was that mutual criticism was not directed
toward conversion. The Perfectionists had already declared themselves sinless. Moreover, mutual criticism was not offered in the
context of revival. Here badgered merchants could not hope to find
relief in a return to their secular status when spring came. There was
no egress at Oneida short of leaving the commune itself.

Charles Nordhoff attended one of these sessions. Since he regarded mutual criticism such an "important ingenious device" he
supplied a detailed account. A young man, also named Charles, had

agreed to offer himself for criticism. About fifteen people were
present seated on benches arranged along a wall. Charles sat among
them. Noyes entered and took a large rocking chair. When the
doors of the room were closed, Noyes asked Charles if he had
anything to say. Charles responded in general terms. He confessed
some intellectual doubts and difficulties, chiefly, a "tendency to
think religion of small moment." Nordhoff reported some of the
remarks that followed:

> Hereupon a man being called on to speak, remarked that he thought
> Charles had been somewhat hardened by too great good-fortune; that
> his success in certain enterprises had somewhat spoiled him; if he had
> not succeeded so well, he would have been a better man; that he was
> somewhat wise in his own esteem; not given to consult with others, or to
> seek or take advice. One or two other men agreed generally with the
> previous remarks, had noticed these faults in Charles, and that they
> made him disagreeable; and gave examples to show his faults. Another
> concurred in the general testimony, but added that he thought Charles
> had lately made efforts to correct some of his faults, though there was
> still much room for improvement.
>
> A young woman next remarked that Charles was haughty and super-
> cilious, and thought himself better than others with whom he was
> brought into contact; that he was needlessly curt sometimes to those
> with whom he had to speak.
>
> Another young woman added that Charles was a respecter of per-
> sons; that he showed his liking for certain individuals too plainly by
> calling them pet names before people; that he seemed to forget that such
> things were disagreeable and wrong.
>
> Another woman said that Charles was often careless in his language;
> sometimes used slang words, and was apt to give a bad impression to
> strangers. Also that he did not always conduct himself at table, es-
> pecially before visitors, with careful politeness and good manners.
>
> A man concurred in this, and remarked that he had heard Charles
> condemn the beefsteak on a certain occasion as tough; and had made
> other unnecessary remarks about the food on the table while he was
> eating.
>
> A woman remarked that she had on several occasions found Charles
> a respecter of persons.
>
> Another said that Charles, though industrious and faithful in all
> temporalities, and very able man, was not religious at all.
>
> A man remarked that Charles was, as others had said, somewhat
> spoiled by his own success, but that it was a mistake for him to be so, for
> he was certain that Charles's success came mainly from the wisdom and

care with which the society had surrounded him with good advisers, who had guided him; and that Charles ought therefore to be humble, instead of proud and haughty, as one who ought to look outside of himself for the real sources of his success.

Finally, two or three remarked that he had been in a certain transaction insincere toward another young man, saying one thing to his face and another to others; and in this one or two women concurred.[23]

During these remarks Nordhoff saw Charles' face grow pale, "drops of perspiration began to stand on his forehead". Noyes summarized the criticism. He spoke of Charles' abilities as well as his faults and concluded that he thought the young man was earnestly trying to cure himself. It appears that Charles' most grievous failing rested in the charge that he was a "respecter of persons," an Oneidan euphemism for dyadic love. Noyes had reported that Charles had agreed that "he ought to isolate himself entirely" from the woman in question and "let another man take his place at her side." The meeting then ended.[24]

Aside from reacting to "so strong and horrible a view of morals and duty," Nordhoff noticed the extremely" practiced tongues" at the meeting: "The people knew very well how to express themselves. There was no vagueness, no uncertainty. Every point was made; every sentence was a hit—a stab I was going to say, but as the sufferer was a volunteer, I suppose this would be too strong a word."[25]

Finney's new prayer meetings, which had attempted to revitalize discourse and hence consciousness, had succeeded at Oneida. Their direction was vastly different from anything Finney would have conceived or condoned, but Perfectionism, which after all was an ideological consequence of the revival, re-invented the protracted meeting in the form of mutual criticsm. At Oneida mutual criticism transformed the prayer meeting to a new supporting structure.

I have tried to show that communes, themselves examples of inventive responses to the camps and protracted meetings, were anything but static communities. Inventive not only in terms of ideological reformulation and organizational structure, but also in terms of terms of technological change, the communes, despite our image of them as havens from a commercial society, were feverishly creative social forms. But in order to complete our assessment, let us look at two more examples of major internal transformations from the Shakers and Perfectionists.

The Shakers, greatly expanded by the Great Revival, also underwent a revival of their own from 1837 to 1844. At the time Nordhoff visited Mount Lebanon, the Shakers had reinstituted earlier communal patterns and come to regard their own period of enthusiasm as the work of the "Evil one." But for seven years the Shakers had closed themselves off from the world and undergone a revival that superseded Cane Ridge in its intensity.

The Shakers had always professed a special relationship with the "world of spirits." Shaker spiritualism was derived both from their adventist theology and from their pentecostal interpretation of religious experience. Their name had been given them as a description of their visionary activity, which included prophecy and speaking in tongues. But the Shaker revival consumed the commune itself. James Prescott recounted his experience:

"It was in the year 1838, in the latter part of summer, some young sisters were walking together on the bank of the creek, not far from the hemlock grove, west of what is called the Mill Family, where they heard some beautiful singing, which seemed to be in the air just above their heads.

"They were taken by surprise, listened with admiration, and then hastened home to report the phenomenon. Some of them afterwards were chosen mediums for the 'spirits.' We had been informed, by letter, that there was a marvelous work going on in some of the Eastern societies, particularly at Mt. Lebanon, New York, and Watervliet, near Albany. And when it reached us in the West we should all know it, and we did know it; in the progress of the work, every individual, from the least to the greatest, did know that there was a heart-searching God in Israel, who ruled in the armies of heaven, and will yet rule among the inhabitants of earth.

"It commenced among the little girls in the children's order, who were assembled in an upper room, the doors being shut, holding a meeting by themselves, when the invisibles began to make themselves known. It was on the Sabbath-day while engaged in our usual exercises, that a messenger came in and informed the elders in great haste that there was something uncommon going on in the girls' department. The elders brought our meeting to a close as soon as circumstances would admit, and went over to witness the singular and strange phenomena.

"When we entered the apartment, we saw that the girls were under the influence of a power not their own-they were hurried round the room, back and forth as swiftly as if driven by the wind—and no one could stop them. If any attempts were made in that direction, it was found impossible, showing conclusively that there were under a controlling influence that was irresistible. Suddenly they were prostrated upon the floor, apparently unconscious of what was going on around them. With their eyes closed, muscles strained, joints stiff, they were taken up and laid upon beds, mattresses, etc.

"They then began holding converse with their guardian spirits and others, some of whom they once knew in the form, making graceful motions with their hands—talking audibly, so that all in the room could hear and understand, and form some idea of their whereabouts in the spiritual realms they were exploring in the lands of souls. This was only the beginning of a series of 'spirit manifestations,' the most remarkable we ever expected to witness on the earth."[26]

The revival rapidly spread throughout the Shaker settlements. Children were swept into the enthusiasm; mediums interpreted the trancelike utterings; angels were thought to have appeared. "Indian, Norwegian and Arabian spirits" swept through the communes. Hundreds of songs were written during this period. Scores of new dances were performed by children "with the grace and the precision of a machine." They were said to have been learned by "seraphs before the throne of God".

The Oneidas, though not spiritualists, also seem to have experienced a revival within a revival. But Noyes sternly controlled its course. The most singular, structural innovation within the Perfectionist communes represented a movement in a different direction. The system of complex marriage practiced from 1848 to 1869, stipulated absolute birth control. In 1869, however, Noyes announced that the experiment with male continence had been proven successful. The Perfectionists were now to embark upon a new experiment. The Onedian system of stirpiculture, a eugenics program, was initiated. A group of young men immediately announced in a written statement their willingness to participate. Noyes boldly justified his experiment by, among other sources, quoting Plato's defence of "breeding" in the *Republic*. Between 1869 and 1879 fifty-eight stirpiculture children were borne at Oneida by forty-four women. Parentage was approved (sometimes it was initiated) by committee.[29]

Is there a common significance in the Shaker revival-in-revival and the Oneidan stirpiculture? I think both inventive responses suggest that ultimately the commune, despite its creativity as a social form, is as transitional an institution as the revival camp and the protracted meeting. Of course communalists did not regard their experiments in this light. The Shakers believed that all America would be transformed into communes as the last and final advent drew near. Noyes argued that the proliferation of "all the socialisms that have sprung from the revivals" proved that "the theocratic principle . . . not Republicanism will at last triumph in some form here and throughout the world."[30]

But with the single exception of Mormonism (which itself had abandoned communal structure), this theocratic principle did not prove to be a permanent organizational invention. Part of the reason for this failure can be derived from the two examples we have discussed. I have argued that the American commune was an invention designed to give permanence and stability to the revival camp and the protracted meeting. However, the miniature "perfect societies" of the commune could not capture the singular ambiance of the revival camp because, simply put, the strength of the camp lay in its transitional character. As its inventive successor, the commune found itself straddling between two great organizational alternatives. On the one hand, lay the emotive solidarity of the revival, which broke through the carefully planned order of the Shaker commune. On the other, lay the bureaucratization of these little societies. The latter was the option which the Church of the Latter Day Saints eventually took. But while bureaucratization may be a logical alternative, it is inconsistent with the psychology of the commune. The commune, once bureaucratized, is a commune transformed into some other social form. The same can be said of the revival camp.

But the commune often did manage to avoid both alternatives through a psychically veiled "dirty little secret." Oneida, for instance, contained a potential revival-in-revival through the personal intervention of John Humphrey Noyes. It was Noyes himself, and there were others like him leading other communes, who held the commune between the two transforming alternatives. Like an awesome Freudian primal father, Noyes governed the Oneida as his patriarchal reserve. Freud's primal father forbid his sons sexual access to women of the horde, so did Noyes at Oneida. Enforced promiscuity has the same psychic effect as denial. Seen in this light, the stirpiculture experiment was a "new measure" analogous to the tactics of the protracted meeting. Noyes had controlled sexual union and demanded birth control. Now he was to control the number and parents of children as well. It is worth noting that in Noyes' absence the Oneidas could not maintain the stirpiculture system. The "perfect family" disintegrated into groups of "worldly marriages."

Chapter 7

Inventive Communities
Systemic Sources of Invention

We have discussed the history of five American inventions, suggested common types and organizational features. Each invention offered new communities for Americans. I would now like to suggest that these five inventions are themselves the creations of more complex and larger sets of institutions, if you will, "inventive communities." We can think of the telephone and the motel as examples of inventions produced by market communities, the penitentiary by reform communities, the pieced quilt by neighborhood communities, the revival camp by evangelical communities. These inventive communities are, I think, the basic agencies of change in America. Often they can be seen as communities in competition. Certainly, market institutions have assumed a hegemonic position in relation to the others. But there have been periods of bitter and sustained opposition to the tyranny of the market as well.

The Factory: "Pasteboard towns"

Many readers may wince at the description of capitalism as community. Does not capitalism despoil communities, shatter social bonds, reduce all relationships to a cash nexus? I shall return to this question in the next chapter, but here I would like to suggest that it is in the context of the market that Americans invent and re-invent social institutions, often in imitation of market mores and structures, sometimes in opposition to them. There is less argument, I think, on the question of the history of capitalism as an inventive system. Marx recognized capitalism as a radically transforming system, one which was historically unique in its incessant alteration of the instruments of production and "with them the whole relations of society."

With significant exceptions and periodic doubts, Americans have accepted capitalism as the necessary economic foundation of society. We no longer use terms such as the "natural order" of liberty, although public opinion still expresses this view inchoately. George Gilder has brilliantly restated the American belief in capitalism as an inventive community:

> Capitalists are motivated not chiefly by the desire to consume wealth or indulge their appetites, but by the freedom and the power to consummate their ideas. Whether piling up coconuts or designing new computers, they are the movers and shakers, doers and givers, obsessed with positive visions of change and opportunity. They are the men with an urge to understand and act, to master something and transform it, to work out a puzzle and profit from it, to figure out a part of nature and society and turn it to the common good. They are inventors and explorers, boosters and problem solvers: they take infinite pains and they strike fast.[1]

He continues by arguing that capitalists are not motivated by greed; money is only a means to express "their deep interest and engagement in the world beyond themselves, impelled by their imagination, optimism and faith."[2]

Gilder's romance and Marx' critique illustrate two aspects of capitalism as an inventive community: its explosive, liberating capacity in the invention of new products and its inventive reorganization of society into new forms of hierarchy and control.

We have only looked at two inventions of American capitalism. Both the telephone and the motel fit neatly with Gilder's presentation. Both were inventions of individuals with practical visions, both were "liberating" inventions which facilitated movement across time and space. Both inventions themselves produced or supported new and novel communities. Scores of other inventors and inventions fit this model: Henry Ford and the automobile, Isaac Singer and the sewing machine, the supermarket and the Pullman railroad car.

But inventiveness has hardly been limited to the creation of new commodities. Capitalism has proved to be at its most ingenious in its invention of new forms of production. It is true that Americans did not invent the factory. The origins of the factory as an economic

structure can be traced to medieval guilds. But American inventors
have created many major variants of the factory, from Francis
Lowell's creation of a community of women, to Bell's new electronic
public servant, to principles of "Fordism," to the Lordstown auto-
mation system. Let us take a brief look at these inventions, for they
offer us an insight, not only into capitalism as an inventive community, but also into the nature of American community in general.

Textiles were the wedge of American industrialization. They
were initially grossly outproduced by British industry, but the War
of 1812 temporarily curtailed British imports and permitted an
opening for American entrepreneurship. Francis Cabot Lowell
memorized British cotton weaving machinery and upon returning
to America was able to construct a workable machine. Lowell was
also able to form a group of Boston merchants as investors. The
result was the establishment of a textile factory at Waltham in 1814.
But Waltham represented more than a simple replication of British
weaving methods. It was the first "complete" textile factory in the
world. In England, weaving, dyeing, and finishing were coordinated
but separate enterprises. Waltham collected cotton from the South,
and out of the mills came cheap but serviceable cloth. Aided by a
tariff on low-cost imported cottons and by innovations in weaving
and calico printing, New England increased its spindlage from
eighty thousand in 1811 to 1.3 million in the early 1830s and
doubled the number of spindles between 1840 and 1860.[3]

It was the factory at Lowell, however, constructed in 1823 by
Lowell's associates, that attracted international attention. Here was
a town, wrote Michael Chevalier in 1836, that is "not like one of
our European towns that was built by some demigod, a son of
Jupiter, or by some hero of the Trojan War, or by the genius of an
Alexander or a Caesar, or by some saint attracting crowds by his
miracles, or by the whim of some great sovereign like Louis XIV or
Frederick, or by an edict of Peter the Great." Lowell had no such
"pious foundation," nor was it "an asylum for fugitives, nor a
military post." It was "one of the speculations of the merchants of
Boston," and it produced dividends from 10 to 12 percent.[4] Most
important, Lowell was an alternative to Manchester.

Chevalier, like all Europeans who visited Lowell, was extremely
impressed. Lowell was a "neat and decent, peaceable and sage"
town. When Chevalier held his "giddiness," however, he was often
perplexed. With its "steeple-crowned factories," it resembled a

Spanish town with its convents. But there were "no Madonnas or nuns, not even women in rags; instead there were pretty girls who, rather than working sacred hearts, spin and weave cotton."[5] But while he was excited by a system which could prevent the existence of a dangerous working class which threatened the security of "the rich and public order, as in Europe," Chevalier wondered about its permanence. The site itself reminded him of a "pasteboard town like those which Potemkin erected for Catherine along the road to St. Petersburg," and he wondered how long it could last. As long, he concluded, as wages were high. Chevalier was right.

At its height, Lowell employed thousands of young women in their teens to early twenties. They came from New England hamlets and farms. Many other companies copied the model of Lowell. The community which the directors of the Merrimack corporation invented was ingeniously complete. The "girls" would leave their families for a few years to return later to their hamlets with some education and a dowry. In many cases their services helped pay farm mortgages or put brothers through colleges. The company even sponsored a newspaper written and edited by the mill girls. At Lowell they would live in dormitories, strictly supervised by matrons and attend church services in the town. Here is a portion of the contract offered by the Lawrence Company in 1833:

> All persons employed by the Company must devote themselves assiduously to their duty during working-hours. They must be capable of doing the work which they undertake, or use all their efforts to this effect. They must on all occasions, both in their words and in their actions, show that they are penetrated by a laudable love of temperance and virtue, and animated by a sense of their moral and social obligations. The Agent of the Company shall endeavor to set to all a good example in this respect. Every individual who shall be notoriously dissolute, idle, dishonest, or intemperate, who shall be in the practice of absenting himself from divine service, or shall violate the Sabbath, or shall be addicted to gaming, shall be dismissed from the service of the Company.[6]

Lucy Larcom's *A New England Girlhood* (1889), written when she was sixty-five, contains an account of Lowell from the viewpoint of a young girl. Her feelings toward Lowell are openly ambiguous. She credits her contributions to the *Lowell Offering* as crucial to the development of her career as a writer and teacher. But she deeply resented the regimentation and separation from her family she endured. One theme that recurs in Larcom's recollections is her estrangement from nature: "I never cared much for machinery. . . . In sweet June weather I would lean out of the windows, and try not to hear the unceasing clash of sound inside."[7]

This yearning for rural life appears again and again in the writings of the young workers. One wrote: "When I went out at night, the sound of the mill was in my ears, as of crickets, frogs and Jews-harps, all mingled together in strange discord. After, it seemed as though cotton-wool was in my ears. . . ." Herbert Guttman believes that these pastoral metaphors were the result of "persons working machines in a society still predominantly a 'garden.' "[8] But the garden was more psychologically complex than a mere remembering of crickets and frogs. For Larcom, Lowell did represent an inverse pastoral. But nature, too, seemed bound up with tangles of affections and resentments. The idyll of a rural childhood had been shattered by the death of her father. After briefly leaving the mill to help her sisters, she now found nature "too passive." When she went back to Lowell, she found that she "enjoyed the familiar, unremitting clatter of the mill." The imagery remained pastoral, but now it was infused with new desires: "I liked to feel the people around me, even those whom I did not know, as a wave may like to feel the surrounding waves urging it forward, with or against its own will. I felt that I belonged to the world, that there was something for me to do in it. . . ."[9]

Such sense of achievement aside, the Lowell workers repeatedly protested—and lost. In 1834 and 1836, these "daughters of freemen" struck over wage cuts. Irish immigrants were to replace the original "Lowell girls."

As Lowell had provided jobs for the daughters of hard-pressed farmers, the invention of the telephone offered opportunities for young women of the post-Civil War middle class. Elementary schools no longer provided enough work for women, and war deaths had reduced the number of marriageable males. Boys had originally been used as telephone operators, following the model of the telegraph companies. But the telephone work required a more tethered and sedate employee. Boys swore at demanding customers, played practical jokes, and left the switchboard untended. In Grand Rapids women were hired to replace boys en masse when the latter were discovered shooting marbles on the job.[10] Thus began the "marriage" of the telephone to young women. It has been a curious relationship, inspiring, on the part of the employer, a combination of paternalism and ruthlessness not unlike the experience at Lowell.

Bell Telephone Company immediately set out to convince the public and parents that this new occupation was both respectable and important. Only single young women were hired. (Brenda Maddox contends that "virgins may not be too strong a word."[11]) The operators provided a major service, "the voice with a smile" was Bell's phrase, and recruits were encouraged to think and dress as schoolmistresses. Advertisements asked for "well-bred women" and "young women above the average in ability and ambition." Features of middle-class gentility were built around the new jobs: circulating libraries, reading clubs, flower and garden discussion groups.[12]

Beneath this campaign, however, was a less flattering view of women as new electronic public servants. Charles Garland saw women as ideally fit for telephone work. They came "cheap" and were "relatively docile." Moreover, "steady work at low pressure, and more or less mechanical in character, necessitating little or no judgment, seems to be admirably performed by women. . . ."[13] In 1902 the U.S. Bureau of the Census referred to the attraction of "many young women of Education to telephony" but noted the low rate of pay and "the simpler narrower range of work." Still, the reporters continued, duties were more varied than "watching machinery," hours were shorter, surroundings more pleasant, and "women did come in contact with the personalities of the subscribers."[14]

It was precisely this personal element in telephone service that Bell soon began to attack. The operator "must now be made as nearly as possible a paragon of perfection, a kind of human machine."[15] The automatic switch would eventually provide the "girlless phone." In the meantime, operators were required to respond to subscribers' requests through phrase books. Using one's own words was forbidden. Should a situation arise about which the phrase book was silent, the call was to be turned over to a supervisor. Women, of course, accepted the demands for efficiency and service. But there were more burdens: shocks from the headsets, neck cramps and, most of all, fatigue. The first electronic factory had been invented.

A 1915 government report had concluded that unionization of

"telephone girls is practically impossible." Turnover was too high, and Bell was convinced that a women's union would be especially irresponsible. But operators began joining the lineman and cable splicers union (IBEW) in such large numbers that men protested: "We can think of no rule of ethics or of human right which requires men handling the sting of electricity to submit forever to the rule of telephone operators. . . ."[16] A separate Telephone Operator's Department was formed. In 1947 the operaters joined the Communications Workers of America (CWA).

The automobile, along with the telephone, transformed time and space in America. But the production of cars initiated an alteration of time and space in the workplace that was just as profound. The Model T had been in existence only two years when the huge Highland Park plant was opened in 1910. The work of the auto mechanic had already changed a great deal. Several workers now made a car, each one responsible for a set of operations. But this division of labor would be obsolete within ten years. Using as models the principles of Frederick Taylor's scientific management, already being applied in the steel industry, and of the conveyor line of the Chicago meat-packing plants, Henry Ford set out to revolutionize auto production.

The initial problem revolved around the question of how to get the appropriate parts and tools to the mechanic. Tools were arranged in sequence and stockboys charged with the task of bringing parts to workers. Keith Swand provides this view of the assembly floor:

> The factory was growing by the hour; the larger the layout, the worse the confusion. Thousands were working on the production floor where hundreds had worked before. On final assembly, conditions approached pandemonium. Assemblers and stockboys were tripping over one another. Despite its advances, the new technique was still time-consuming. Strain as they might, up to the summer of 1913, Ford's men had never succeeded in putting a single Model T together in less time than twelve hours and twenty-eight minutes.[17]

Ford technicians temporarily compounded the problem by creating a makeshift conveyor for feeder lines (assemblies of motors and axles). The sub-assembly lifts produced a *Modern Times* effect, as parts and supplies piled up over and around harried workers.

In the summer of 1913 Ford applied the concept of a moving

assembly to the finish line. The new system of "constant motion" required new inventions to function. Carl Emde, a German-born craftsman employed by Ford, became the inventor of a whole series of new automatic single-purpose tools. New tools, including the automatic steel drill, were put in place in a period of less than six weeks. The overhead, endless chain conveyor was installed in Highland Park in January. The "Fordist" system could produce a car in ninety-three minutes, one tenth of the time it had taken in the previous spring.

One problem remained. Workers' skills had been demoted as well as their wages. The turnover of the workforce in 1913 was 380 percent, so high that Ford had to hire 963 men for every 100 he needed to employ. The IWW, which had struck at a Studebaker plant in that same summer of 1913, began to concentrate on Highland Park. On January 5, 1914, Ford announced his world famous "Five Dollar Day."

Ford was to refer to his plan as "one of the finest cost-cutting moves we ever made."[18] The "Five Dollar Day" wage as an industry-wide formula was never met. Workers on the six-month probation period did not qualify, and many were released on the day they were eligible. But the Ford plan did manage to produce almost immediately a more docile and permanent labor force.

The twin principles of Fordism, assembly-line auto production and "profit-sharing," revolutionized industrial production. Lincoln Steffens described Henry Ford as an American Lenin—"a prophet without words, a reformer without politics, a legislator, statesman, a radical." Lenin's own interest in Fordism is, of course, well known. What is as intriguing, however, were the inventive responses of the workers. Many of the reactions were individual and ad hoc acts of desperation. But even these efforts show imagination. For instance, Frank Marquart reports the practice of lying about skills, being fired a few days later, and repeating the process until a minimum skill level had been learned.[19]

Almost as soon as Fordism had been put in place, new formal structures were created. Some were borrowed from previous experiences like the Unemployment Councils of the Communists. Others, such as the unionization of "unorganizable" unskilled workers, were reinterpretations of responses to other conditions. The 1938 sit-down strikes which led to formal recognition of the UAW were an

inventive response to the problem of the employment of "scab labor" as strikebreakers.[20]

The innovations installed at the General Motors Lordstown
plant in Ohio in 1970 were in response to conditions as pressing as
those confronted by Ford in 1913. But this time the auto companies
acted, not from an effort to meet new demands, but rather as a
response to sagging sales resulting from foreign competition. Emma
Rothschild insists that Lordstown was "still a product of Fordist
practice."[21] In many respects she is correct. Lordstown still featured
the division of tasks into minute operations across a moving assembly. The measurement of time in "manseconds" continued, as did
the Fordist practice of "speedups." Yet Lordstown did represent the
germ of a new factory system, a "prototype" in the language of GM
managers that suggests future "post-industrial" organization.
Lordstown attempted to overlay new inventions upon Fordist structure and practice. Computer technology, including robots, was used
to facilitate production. The ALPACA computer system was designed
to create the "programmed responsive" plant, where "people
would be found doing many of the things they do now, but under
the direction of machines." The computer would replace the supervisor. The GM unimate robots replaced human welders whose
work had already been partially replaced by the welding gun.[22]

Lordstown attracted displaced miners, transient young workers,
and the sons and daughters of Ohio Valley industrial workers.
These groups derisively referred to one another as "hillbillies,"
"hippies," and "townies." Stanley Aronowitz notes the patterns of
hostility between these groups: hillbillies, regarded by townies as
ratebreakers, "hated hippies and Blacks with equal venom."[23] Despite these animosities, workers under the Lordstown system coop-
erated sufficiently to produce a series of wildcat strikes and acts of
sabotage which culminated in a major strike in 1972. Lordstown,
the prototype for the factory of the future, became a symbol of
worker alienation, a source of trouble for both union and management. Leonard Woodcock called Lordstown an "industrial Woodstock."

The modern factory is only one of the many generative inventions of capitalism. The corporation, now multinational in
form, challenges political structures in its power and complexity.
But the factory still remains at the center of capitalist invention.

Technological invention changes and transforms the factory; corporate infrastructure determines the allocation of investment. But both are still dependent on the factory for production. It is the factory that is the reproductive base of capitalism. Georges Sorel's 1921 remark still characterizes the factory today: "the modern factory is a field of experiment constantly enlisting the worker in scientific research."[24]

The inventors of Lowell, Highland Park, Lordstown, and the ubiquitous telephone exchanges purposefully created new communities. But their efforts at community building were narrowly conceived and, in most cases, hypocritical. Workers themselves saw the factory in the same manner. Factory life was regarded as temporary, a way station to other dreams. When permanence was recognized, community would be sought outside the factory, in the home and the neighborhood.[25]

This is not to say that workers were not able to forge some sense of community within the engineered society of the factory. Lucy Larcom wrote of these instant communities at Lowell: "One great advantage which came to these many stranger girls through being brought together, away from their homes, was that it taught them to go out of themselves, and enter into the lives of others."[26] The factory in America has been home to transient and marginal populations: farm girls, unmarried women, immigrants, some Southern blacks and whites, "hippies."

Of course, unions have provided a sense of community within the factory. Today we tend to see the union in bureaucratic terms. But the formation of unions themselves involved truly heroic efforts in creating common emotional bases among hostile and/or indifferent workers. But for all its successes, the union has never been able to transform the factory. The basic principles of Fordism remain intact today.

In *The Prison Notebooks* Antonio Gramsci offered a brilliant analysis of the significance of Fordism, the factory economic production, and community. Yet many of Gramsci's predictions rest upon a flawed analysis. Like many Marxists, Gramsci saw Fordism as part of a dialectical advance toward socialism. He contended that America was the logical location for the invention and application of Fordist practice because it lacked a feudal history. With the absence of "parasitic sedimentations" of earlier classes, America "nat-

urally" would produce a working class of "rational demographic
composition." Without the solidity of a peasantry and the aristo-
cratic demand for "quality" products, America could (and did)
invent a system of real mass production. This process was easily
achieved in America; all that was needed was a skilled combination
of force ("destruction of working class trade unionism on a territorial basis") and persuasion ("high wages, various social benefits,
extremely subtle ideological and political propaganda") to succeed
in "making the whole life of the nation revolve around production."
Gramsci concluded that "hegemony was born in the factory."[28] He
was especially impressed with how few professional political and
ideological intermediaries were required to institute Fordism in
America.

All the basic characteristics of American Fordism—quantity
production, minute measurement, radical division of labor, the
overall rationalization of society—were for Gramsci advances
which would create the conditions for worker revolution and socialist community. Fordism had "determined the need for a new
type of man" which capitalism could not provide. Two steps were
required to trigger this transformation. One was already nearly in
place. As mechanization advanced, work required little skill and
thought. Mechanization affects only "the physical gesture"; "the
brain of the worker, far from being mummified, reaches a state of
complete freedom." Gramsci believed that the Fordist creation of
the "trained gorilla" would eventually produce a revolutionary.
"Not only does the worker think," Gramsci surmised, "but the fact
that he gets no immediate satisfaction from his work and realizes
that they are trying to reduce him to a trained gorilla, can lead him
into a train of thought that is far from conformist."[29]

Gramsci was particularly impressed with what he called Ford's
"primitivism." He believed that monogamy performed a basic function in capitalism by maintaining a "psycho-physical equilibrium"
in the worker. But monogamy was suitable only for archaic econo-
mies, in which peasants' and artisans' labor required relative stability in sexual unions. The collectivization of labor would lead to
"the growth of a new form of sexual union shorn of the bright and
dazzling colour of the romantic tinsel typical of the petit bourgeois
and the Bohemian layabout."[30]

Two generations have passed since Gramsci's essay. No doubt

workers have thought. And there has been a "sexual revolution." But thinking and fucking have not produced a revolutionary labor force.

Marxists have not abandoned Gramsci's analysis. It is, in fact, the major theoretical tool of American Marxism. Gramsci's error lies not so much in an underestimation of hegemony as in an overestimation of the nature of the reorganization of society into a rational demography and the belief that Fordism would produce new and revolutionary collectivities. Americans had left settled communities by the thousands for the "liberation" of factory life. That process continues. Like Lucy Larcom (and as Gramsci prophesied), women have now further contributed to the creation of a rational demography by entering the labor force. They, too, have left a pastoral behind, for the image of family life is the only pastoral left which, in Gramsci's vocabulary, is not decorative. Those newly liberated discovered instant communities in the factory. These marginal populations then helped build formal institutional protection against the factory.

But the American worker has never submitted to the kind of psychological collectivization that Gramsci had outlined. The factory, for all its timed motion, has been regarded as a temporary institution despite its enormous transformations. Towns, and even cities, have been created by new factories and then discarded and razed. Those who can, move on. The aged and infirm are, of course, left behind. A labor force of "rational demographic composition" has not produced a revolutionary force. It has produced its own culture, as Gramsci had predicted, but it is not the culture he had conceived. When the last marginal group has been liberated by the factory, when we are no longer able to think of ethnicity, gender, or any conceivable collectivity, then Gramsci's rational geography will be complete. The factory will have fulfilled its historical purpose. The American factory appears to be part of a different Hegelian drama from that Gramsci had written. America's market communities have, through the dual aspects of invention—new products and new forms of production—smashed communities. Yet, however cynical and hypocritical were these new work structures, Americans have seen them as novel opportunities—opportunities for the creation of new individual lives and for the creation of new communities.

Of course, today Fordist mechanization has lost its glamor. The assembly line appears to be the organizational structure of decaying industries. In this respect, Lordstown appears, at least for one industry, to be a transitional invention. What produced the conflict was a freakish combination of mechanized and electronic organizational techniques. On the one hand, there was the robotization and the new expanded class of computer engineers, on the other, the Fordist techniques of speed-ups and routinized labor. The electronic factory of the future will have eliminated Ford's (and Gramsci's) trained gorilla. Basic production will be carried on by robots. Supervisory personnel would tend machines and computers. The "program responsive plant" would use systems analysis to replace the assembly line and Taylorism.

Nearly every segment of society anticipates the arrival of an electronic Ford. Venture capital seeks out new industries and the transformations of old ones. Politicians long for "re-industrialization" as a new tax base. Some liberals support the new electronic age because they see the possibilities of the destruction of the factory and the corporation and a return to new cottage industries.[31] Others see it as the completion of the creation of a new scientific class, the fulfillment of Simonian prophecy.[32] Young workers try to plan for new avenues of mobility.

It is too early to tell in what directions the electronic factory as an organizational invention will transform society.[33] There is some evidence to suggest that Fordist principles may be redesigned and incorporated into this new system. The secretary may now be in a position analogous to the early Ford auto worker. Her job is now being broken into specialized "de-skilled functions" (word processing, information retrieval, electronic filing).

A key to this transformation is the impact of the invention of the telephone. We noted how the phone both centralized and dispersed business and industrial organization. The electronic factory will produce the same effect. The advertising slogan "Reach out and touch someone" applied to industrial production extends a new kind of instant community to the reproductive base of the capitalist system.

We tend to think of the revival camp as a relic of America's past. But the camp, although as traditional and fragile as a revival itself, remains the central institutional invention of evangelical Protestantism. The revival camp is generationally replicated by the American evangelistic community. Of course, its history is a jerky one; the camp form veritably explodes during American awakenings and recedes during periods in which conventional expressions of religiosity are predominant. The revival can unexpectedly cut a swath through any local community, igniting renewed fervor and new sects. The modern Pentecostal movement, led by Charles Parham, began at a revival in Galena, Kansas, and spread to Missouri and Texas (25,000 people and 60 preachers attended one rally), then to Alabama, and western Florida from 1905 to 1906. In 1901, the black congregation at the Azusa Street Methodist Ministry in Los Angeles underwent a revival that spread across the country through camps.

The same features that characterized the camps of the Great Revival have been present in the twentieth century. Modern Finneys and Cartwrights—Dwight Moody, Billy Sunday and Aimee MacPherson—have employed a colloquial speech many found disturbing. A condition of Billy Sunday's revival campaign involved the closing of local churches in order that congregations could assemble en masse to the "tabernacles" to be revived. Conversion was "guaranteed" the "instant" a sinner rose from his seat.

Some conditions have changed since the Second Great Awakening. Business interests rather than a competitive clergy assumed the role of the elite exercising control of modern revivals. A population of salesgirls, clerks, and emigrees to cities could better "adjust" to industrial life under a commitment to evangelical Christianity. Timothy Smith, however, has argued that despite this financial and ideological support, the new revival camps, now held in auditoriums or newly built tabernacles, still prepared a base for the Social Gospel Movement.[34] Moreover, even the political ideology of the revivalists themselves offered only mixed support for the new industrial order. Moody, for instance, would maintain "that men and women saved by the blood of Jesus rarely remain the subjects of charity," but rise at once to comfort and respectability. Billy Sunday would complain that "the trouble with the church, the YMCA, and the Young Peoples' Societies is that they have taken up sociology and settlement work but are not winning souls to Christ."[35] But the "social question" lay barely submerged at these revivals. Questions of social justice were rarely formulated in terms of class; the focus of the revivals of Moody, Sunday, and MacPherson was on restoration: restoration of concepts of personal responsibility and cultural uniformity in an ordered and stable society. Though they might be used by corporate elites, these values were really not the stuff from which an industrial society was to be built. Ironically, it may have been those who met the dislocations of industrialization head on who unwittingly smoothed the transition to the new order. Thus acceptance of the new industrial values of professional responsibility, environmental causation, and systemic integration, however humanized, helped integrate the needs of the new society and the goals of evangelism. Thus, writes William McLoughlin, those middle-class urban educated citizens who combined "progressive orthodoxy in religion and progressive politics in society" became "the bureaucratic managers of technocracy," combining "their new guidelines into a new vision of manifest destiny under new prophets."[36] But in either case the choice was not an easy one, there was confusion everywhere in the evangelistic community, so much so that McLoughlin argues that the division "weakened both sides, leaving a vacuum into which agnostic humanitarianism, professional altruism and behaviorist social engineering slipped in as a surrogate religion."[37]

Yet, however bourgeois-rustic the new revivalists appeared to some contemporaries, the new versions of the camps borrowed heavily from both the incipient electronic society and the techniques of the new industrial order. It was from these two sources that the twentieth century revival camp invented its own "new measures." Aimee MacPherson invented a dial-a-prayer service and founded a radio station. She was the first revivalist to assume the role of a media celebrity. What amounted to an evangelical form of Fordism and Taylorism was enthusiastically developed. Moody had initiated a quantification of salvation by reporting conversions. Those who "came forward" were shunted to a "prayer room" to fill a "decision card" to be used as a part of a "follow-up" record. Billy Sunday employed "revival machinery" which included the use of "conversion tables" as a public relations device. Thus, the conversion as a personal experience, which is, after all, the center of the revival camp and evangelical Christianity in general, was at least partially subsumed under new bureaucratic imperatives.

Despite the success of revivalists between 1890 and 1930, the camp, at least in its traditional form, appeared to be an invention in need of adaption. Evangelist radio, synonymous with the invention of the medium, flourished in the 1920s and 1930s. Charles Fuller's "Old Fashioned Revival Hour," broadcast from a California parish, was a prime example. Oral Roberts, a pentecostal preacher from Oklahoma, had used the camp form until 1967. While he still attracted large audiences, Roberts came to the conclusion that "the tent was ceasing to be an asset." People would no longer "pack up the babies and grab the old ladies." They had become used to "cushioned chairs and air conditioning and to watching television."[38] Roberts cancelled his camp circuit and turned to television with a concept of electronic revivalism. Other ministries underwent similar transformations. Robert Schuller has experimented with new forms. In 1955 he rented a drive-in theater in California and preached atop its refreshment stand. He had invented the ("come as you are in your family car") "drive-in church." Later, Schuller went electronic; the "Hour of Power" is still one of the most popular Christian television programs.

But some of the basic principles of the camp meeting still survive in this new structure. We witnessed in the 1970s a kind of electronic revival that illustrates the capacity of this invention to reinvigorate itself through new linkages. Frances Fitzgerald has made this historical connection: ". . . for those who believe that salvation can be achieved by a sudden spontaneous leap to faith, television serves as the equivalent of a vast revival tent. . . ."[39]

The recent growth of fundamentalist denominations preceded the use of the new "electronic church." A major turning point, however, occurred when evangelists began buying time on Sunday morning television. This time slot is known to executives for its notoriously small audiences. It had been "given away," as required by the FCC to public service religious programming. The willingness of evangelists to pay for this time, even at the low rates, drew objections from "mainstream" denominations who refused to solicit contributions on the air. But the FCC ruled that paid religious programs satisfied the public service requirement. The more aggressive evangelists thus captured the air waves. By 1980 over 90 percent of all religious television programming was commercial.[40]

Cable television, with its selective audience base, accelerated this development. Currently there are thirty religious television stations and four religious networks owned and run by this new electronic evangelistic community. All are supported by audience contribution. Rev. Falwell's daily radio and television broadcasts cost only 9 million dollars a year. Computer technology with its telephone banks and "personalized" solicitations permits small donations to be cost-effective.

The differences between the new evangelists' electronic church and the revival camp and protracted meeting are significant. Television provides only an indirect sort of social interaction. Audience and preacher do not "see" one another in a personal sense. The audience itself is privatized. Each viewer sits alone in his/her living room. The contagion fostered by the revival camp is significantly altered. Yet there are functional substitutes. New electronically based "little bands of sisters" appear on the screen relating in the most personal terms their conversion experiences. Telephone volunteers promise an instant therapeutic community to listeners. Direct and personal support groups for the electronic revival have blossomed. Rev. Falwell's Thomas Road Baptist Church was founded in 1956 in an old factory building. Now it consists of a Christian Academy (K-12), a house for alcoholics, a children's summer camp, a Bible institute, seminary and college, and a home for unwed teenage mothers.

No contemporary electronic minister has been more inventive in this regard than Robert Schuller. Schuller holds institutes in "successful church leadership" at his "Crystal Cathedral," as well as "video workshops" led by his staff at local churches. His *Your Church Has Real Possibilities* is an amazingly frank manual for the development of successful new churches. Schuller lists six principles for growth, all blatantly framed in terms of marketing analyses. Schuller finds the shopping center, "one of the most phenomenal successes of American business in the twentieth century," to be the perfect model of Christianity.[41] It is readily accessible and has surplus parking—so must the local church. It has service departments—so must the local church. It has visible advertising—so must the local church. And it has a good cash flow—so must the local church.

Still, the features of the Great Revival have reappeared: the promise of instant and complete conversion, the flood of printed material, the constant "unseemly" requests for donations, the plain speech and use of everyday metaphors by preachers, the proliferation of new entrepreneurial ministers. Television is regarded, and rightly so, as an invention that has transformed our social and political lives. However, in an important sense, revivalism has transformed television. It has linked itself to this electronic invention and used it for its own purposes.

It is difficult to say in which political and social direction the electronic revival camp will lead. Has American Protestantism again become a battleground for shifting class conflicts as it was during the Great Revival and the Moody era? So argues Peter Berger.[42] The latest revival involves a competition between two elites, one the old business class and the other the new class of professionals, bureaucrats, and intellectuals. The old industrial class still holds to conventional bourgeois virtues of economic initiative and moral authority, while the knowledge class, secular or liberal Protestant, seeks to expand the welfare state and promote cultural pluralism. The problem with Berger's analysis is that it does not take account of the fundamental contradictions in both coalitions. As Joseph Schumpeter, as well as other writers, has shown, industrial capitalism has eroded the culture upon which it rests. It relentlessly destroys all avenues toward autonomous and stable social institutions. The home, the neighborhood, the family, are all subservient to corporate imperatives. The politico-ethical perspective of the New Class is as inconsistent. The new managers demand a service community to replace capitalist individualism, but at the same time support a hyper-pluralism in cultural life. Community is to be extended to benefits and economic regulation. In individual life, abortion is promoted, as are sexual preference and freedom of speech. The correspondence between the political beliefs of the electronic ministry, if it is to be seen as in the control of the old business elite, and that of the electronic congregations may not be congruous. The evangelical (even the fundamentalist) rank and file is not firmly committed to the economic agenda of the revival clergy. A 1979 Gallup poll asked electronic congregations what were their needs in order of importance. Salvation was the most common priority, followed by physical well-being, love, and meaning in life.[43] Economic needs were not high on the list—so little so that Kevin Phillips sees a potentially explosive populist (even fascist) potential in this latest awakening.[44]

In addition, there is a strange similarity between the supporters
of both the old and New Class. Members of the New Class seek
salvation as well as the traditional elites have, although in different
ways. Their conversions are uniformly modernist, but the repeated,
even obsessive, searches for sexual identity and fellowship are examples of attempts at individual transformation as well. This connection between two American strata has been observed by a
number of writers.

Jeremy Rifkin, student radical and director of the People's Bicen-
tennial commission, sees the latest wave of religiosity, including the
electronic revival, as a continuation of the critique offered by the
New Left. Both emerged as an attempt to create a "postliberal
ethics" which rejects the principles of a society based upon mate-
rialism and economic growth. Rifkin reviews the history of the
goals of evangelistic Christianity in America and argues that the
Christian doctrines can replace the ruthless tenets of capitalist expansion. The concepts of biblical creation and stewardship can
form the basis for a real sense of personal virtue and public good.
Rifkin sees the public interest movement in America (contrary to
Berger's analysis) in fundamental agreement with the evangelical
vision: "For the evangelists, the gap between the larger whole and
the sum of its parts is God's love. . . . For the ecologist, the difference or gap between the whole and its parts is a nonquantifiable
bonding or interrelationship that exists with all life. Both evangelicals and ecologists assume then that there are aspects to life that
can never be measured."[45]

Jane Fonda, Tom Hayden, Ralph Nader, Jerry Falwell and Oral
Roberts on the same stage and in the same movement? It does seem
unlikely. But this is what William G. McLoughlin, a historian of
religion, suggests as well, although more cautiously. He admits that
"too much narrow-minded authoritarianism and obscurantism is
heard" from the current generation of evangelicals. Their world
view is "essentially an escape from the seemingly insoluble, tension-
ridden social and political problems."[46] Yet he still believes there is
a connection between the modernist search for the authenticity of
the sixties, which he calls a Third Great Awakening, and the electronically based evangelism of the seventies. The convergence may
occur in the next generation:

At some point in the future, early in the 1990's at best, a consensus will emerge that will thrust into political leadership a president with a platform committed to the kinds of fundamental restructuring that have followed our previous awakenings—in 1776, in 1830, and in 1932. . . . Such a reorientation will most likely include a new sense of the mystical unity of all mankind and of the vital power of harmony between man and nature. . . . Sacrifice of self will replace self-aggrandizement as a definition of virtue; helping others will replace competitiveness as a value; institutions will be organized for the fulfillment of individual needs by means of cooperative communal efforts rather than through the isolated nuclear family.[47]

What so captivates both Rifkin and McLoughlin is the inventive capacity of evangelical communities. Rifkin regards the evangelical infrastructure (schools, churches, communication networks) as the only "permanent set of institutions in this society that are viable enough to offer an alternative base from which to challenge the existing order." The evangelicals have succeeded at the point at which the New Left failed:

. . . Woodstock Nation was simply lacking in the essential ingredients necessary to create a truly alternate society. The counterculture did not control its own communications and never developed a meaningful infrastructure. As a result, there was always a great deal of talk about creating a sense of community, but the community never went much beyond pitched tents, makeshift campsites, good dope, electric rock and mellow memories. . . . The evangelical movement is very different. . . . It is backed up by a historical tradition firmly embedded in the popular mind and an infrastructure that is strong enough to offer an alternative.[48]

While Berger's elite analysis overemphasizes economic motivation, this interpretation may misinterpret the capacity for political transcendence in the evangelical communities. As we indicated in our discussion of the electronic revival camp, ministerial strategy is deeply embedded in an expansionist technological and economic mentality. The reliance on the persuasive machinery of the electronic arena is not simply a question of tactics. The new revivalists have adopted the language of technological society as well as its organizational imperatives. Rifkin is not aware of this point: James Bakker's and Pat Robertson's fascination with satellite technology has become "a near obsession—one might even say idolatry."

But how different are the evangelicals from the counterculturalists in terms of infrastructure? Richard Quebedeaux, in his sobering book, *By What Authority*, raises doubts. He argues that the concept of the "celebrity leader" has always existed in American Protestantism. Certainly Cartwright, Finney, Moody, and MacPherson all fit this description. But Quebedeaux contends that the electronic revival has carried this phenomenon to disturbing extremes:

> Theirs is a leadership of influence, based on appeal; and influence is power, albeit indirect and unstructured in character. Television evangelists stage their shows, select their guests, gear their message, and market their product in ways conceived to meet the needs and wants of present and prospective viewers. In testimony and in song, preaching and teaching, the leaders of the electronic church . . . offer a simple, rational—though experiential—pragmatic technique of acquiring salvation in one's personal life, in the family, and in the church. The religion of mass culture asserts that everything is remediable. It had better be! Here the medium shapes the message, but so does the message.[49]

While the electronic age has been able to produce a revival, the evangelical communities have not produced true leaders. For, according to Quebedeaux, celebrities exist only to be "celebrated"; they produce "fans," not disciples. Thus the electronic church is not a real church and Quebedeaux wonders if, should fans' attention lapse, the evangelical infrastructure may collapse like a stack of cards (or more accurately, disappear like the image on an unused television). For a real revival, real leaders are necessary, "pragmatic" leaders who minister to individual and community needs, and even heroic leaders who help redefine our conception of our selves.

Quebedeaux' analysis is fundamentally correct, for if the electronic church is really an electronic revival camp, its impact, while extraordinary, will still be a limited one. The most important question is: isn't this the kind of community that Americans really want anyway?

The Town: "A kind of invisible roof"

The quilt was an invention, albeit a minor and supporting one, of neighborhoods. I have discussed how the culture's nostalgic affection for the quilt obscures the reality of historical American community. The quilt, as craft and as social invention, was a response to incessant efforts to change the environment. In part, it was the result of forsaken communities. Much the same can be said for the larger basic unit invented by Americans, the town.

The American affection for the town is as intense as the affection for the quilt, one of its remnant inventions. In fact, no other single institution is the recipient of so much love. It is, it turns out, a love renounced, and renounced repeatedly. But the men and women who left, even who built careers chronicling the repressive conformity of the American town, have still paid it tributes of unabashed sentimentality. Thomas Wolfe remembered "quiet streets, the time-enchanted spell and magic of full June, the solid liquid lonely shuffle of men in shirt-sleeves coming home, the leafy fragrance of the cooling turning greens and screens that slammed. . . ."[50] Sherwood Anderson, who would write of the savage consequences of sexual repression in American communities, would still reflect to the idyllic portion of Freudian romance: "the people who lived in the towns were to each other like members of a family. . . . A kind of invisible roof beneath which every one lived spread itself over each town."[51] Even those who, like Edgar Lee Masters, were ruthlessly critical of the American town often responded so because they felt this form of community represented promises unfilled.

What is the source of the intensity of feeling for the American town? It lies, I think, in the realization that the American town represented a home, a place of nurture and tranquility, composure and permanence. As Lewis Atherton writes, "people were born into the small town as they were once born into a church." They "belonged by their very presence. . . ."[52] No other American institution has offered these values. The town itself has never fully been able to live up to its image. As we suggested, Americans have historically rejected towns in favor of the increased economic opportunity or liberation of cosmopolitan life. Yet for almost two centuries both choices, home and success, were thought to be available (at least to many Americans). One could accept the institution of the town *or* create new homes, more prosperous and as nurturing. Of course, the trading-in of homes would eventually defeat the very idea of a home. An instant community bears only some of the features of a home. As a result, the community that one left as a young adult or child, became the real home, its nurturing and harmonious capacities magnified by a fragmented and perhaps guilt-ridden memory.

But this image of community as home, unchanging and tranquil, covers an aspect of the town as an institution that is contrary to cultural memory. The American town represented a highly inventive form of community.

The American version of the town itself was the invention of emigrees.[53] It was, in a sense, a restorative invention, an attempt to recreate in the New World the village that had been threatened by enclosure and engrossment in the old. Special efforts were made to create a kind of "classless" community. Land was parceled out on a freehold basis. Common land for fishing, hunting, and grazing was set aside. But there was a tremendous difference between the early American town and the English village. In America, common and freeholder rights did not rest upon ancestral usage; these were covenanted towns, planned with a legalistic precision. The New England town was a community by contract. However much this reality was imbued with a utopian religious purpose, the implications of an instant community would continually reappear. Disengagement from the town would first come from population pressures, then from greed, and finally from the siren of economic mobility. Towns were suspicious of "outlivers" (those who purchased and farmed larger tracts far from the meetinghouse). Secessionist disputes raged on at town meetings, often requiring intervention by the legislature.

But the model of the "city on a hill" has its own tenacity. Generation after generation of communities devised inventions to keep the idea of covenanted towns intact. Perhaps the most important invention in this regard was the town meeting. An expansion of the English village parish organization, the town meeting still holds the American political imagination. It is now regarded as a purer, more reliable form of individual expression, less corruptible than a system of representation.[54] But the orientation of the town meeting was collectivist:

> In the towns of provincial Massachusetts, government by consent meant something more—and less—than majoritarianism. Majoritarianism implies a minority, and towns could no more condone a competing minority by their values than they could have constrained it by their police power.[55]

Zuckerman's study of eighteenth century New England towns finds an obsessive concern with peace and tranquility through consensus, with the use of the town meeting as an agency of accommodation to, in the words of a Braintree resident in 1703, "prevent any further Trouble in the Town."[56]

The meeting, then, was an invention designed to maintain a harmony of interests. Even our supreme cultural model of the neighborhood community, the New England Town, was often mired in conflict and discord. Lockridge, in his history of Dedham, finds an astounding turnover of selectmen.[57] John Demos has uncovered a very large number of suits and countersuits among New England townspeople.[58] Zuckerman, by implication, proves this case. If the town was so harmonious and conflict-free, what explains its obsession with institutions of consensus? The point, I think, that the town as neighborhood community can illustrate, is that conflict, even corrosive personal conflict, can be diluted through inventive institutions that are public and community based. Such conflict does not necessarily require distillation through representation or the anonymity of the marketplace. But our very affection for the town obscures this point. For instance, consider this passage from Mansbridge's book:

> While an abrasive personality may turn the townspeople away from some proposal, a friendly explanation of why the books are not balanced can meet with sympathy. Moreover, the citizen who manages to attend town meeting year after year will collect a set of memories— sitting down to the home-cooked dinner, laughing or wondering at Wally Tyson's jokes, watching the mother of the family down the road try to keep her son quiet and follow the report at the same time. . . .[59]

See how the measured defense of the town meeting as a political institution quickly slips into the language of a utopian idealization of town life. Common interests, technically correct decisions, and the subduing of abrasive people are transferred into home-cooked dinners, smiles, and love. No institution can survive this sort of adoration. For the achieving of such harmony is in reality the result of both empathy and restraint and is often very hard work.

The greatest inventions of the American town were, however, social rather than political. Even the selectman-town meeting system, with its emphasis upon consensus, was an invention which used social ties to actually restrict "political" activity: "The reality of local politics rested in a hundred humble conversations, across fences and tavern tables, quietly allusive, subtly suggestive, endlessly tactful. If all went well, an almost silently shared understanding

would be reached among the inhabitants, and there would be no
contest at all. . . ."[60]

Small town inventions appear today to be either quaint or
smugly moralistic. But the town school was an American invention.
It was locally financed and controlled and open to all. State cen-
tralization of the teaching profession and curriculum came spo-
radically and relatively late in American history. No doubt the
quality of education varied enormously among town schools. James
West, for instance, found schooling in Plainville, a pseudonymous
Midwestern town, to be a dismal affair, with only music and vocational agriculture well taught.[61] Still, Americans were determined
that no class of peasants would emerge from this constant transpor-
tation to new towns.

Between 1850 and 1900 Americans bought 100 million copies of
McGuffey's reader.[62] No other single fact reveals more about the
character of the local school. The messages of the lessons were
service and piety and the mutual interdependence of community. In
the 1857 revised edition there emerged a tone of embattlement in
the presentation of eternal values. Longfellow's admonition was
offered ("Let me envy not the great/Since true pleasures may be
seen/On a cheerful village green"). The vices of the city were paraded before schoolchildren: drinking, gambling, theft. Ironically,
the diluted Puritan values of the McGuffey reader created its own
executioners. The turn-of-the-century small town did not produce a
generation of robber barons. On the contrary, the high school and
small college graduate entered the scientific, legal, and managerial
professions. Page Smith has argued that it was "the psychology of
the small town" that produced an ideal of "professional calling,
fluidity of the social organization, and an ethic of service to the
larger good that, in an increasingly materialistic and secular society,
made science a most attractive field for younger men from thousands of small town communities."[63] This progressive elite may
have subconsciously attempted to apply the ideals of the small town
to reform, but in the process they nationalized American society
and thus contributed to the demise of the small town.

The service ideology that was inculcated in the school fanned out
across the entire structure of the town. The Sunday School, which
took on the character of a movement in the nineteenth century, the
women's organizations which functioned as adjuncts to the churches, the lodges and civic organizations—all of them layered out

interlocking networks delicately balanced between social control and pure sociality.

Central to the small town, and a basis for its inhabitants' collective affection, was its treatment of the holiday. There were scores of official celebrations, one for nearly every month of the year: Christmas and New Year, Easter, Arbor Day, May Day, Memorial Day, High School Graduation, Independence Day, Old Settlers' Day. Fairs and elections also assumed the character of mass celebration. In addition were the revivals, lawn socials, suppers, Sunday School picnics and innumerable fund raising affairs. There was, of course, an inevitability to these events, the same speeches, the same food, the same people, and it is this aspect that so enchants memory. But what remembrance conveys, it also alters. For there was a deliberate character to these holidays and they were in part efforts to achieve communal solidarity and sociality. These events were long affairs. A high school graduation might consist of a week of activities. Some, like May Day, reflected remnants of English village customs. But many were purely American attempts to provide some link with the past. Memorial Day was one such holiday. Let me report two recollections of this celebration. One is William Allen White's account of a parade in Kansas:

> Here may be a place where I can set down the photograph upon my child's mind of the first memorial parade I ever saw. It was headed by the Eldorado silver cornet band in splendid regalia—splendid to my child's eye at least. Following that was the volunteer fire department pulling the old pumping engine that took its water from the great cistern at the corner of Central and Main streets. Then in the town's one open carriage sat Peter Telyea, a veteran of the War of 1812—a man well into his nineties who owned the town carriage works, and who toiled amid his lathes and shavings every day until he died. Behind him, on horseback, were the veterans of the Mexican War. Colonel Gibson, our town banker, rode at the head of that small squadron of fifty men or so, all bearded. Then, in order of rank, were the veterans of the Civil War. General Ellet, the hero of Island Number Ten in Grant's campaign on the Mississippi, led the long line. After the general came the half-dozen colonels we had, and captains, all sashed and horsed and panoplied in military pomp; and following them walked the blue-clad soldiers of the lower ranks. Behind them marched citizens' on foot, and women's organizations. It was a long parade—a picture I shall never forget. And my father, who had no part in the military glory, held my hand as we stood on the sidewalk. He explained to me the meaning of it all, and left to me no

great sense of the pomp and circumstance of glorious war. My Uncle
Frank Hatten, my mother's brother, captain in the First Michigan Caval-
ry, who enlisted and reenlisted three times, and after the war went West
to fight the Indians, rode in the parade. My father clapped for him, and
so did I; but he dismissed certain sections of the parade with the phrase,
"A lot of damn bounty jumpers!" and carefully explained to me that a
"bounty jumper" was a man who was paid to substitute for a drafted
man, and who then deserted from the army with his bounty in his
pocket, turned up in another part of the country, got another bounty,
and enlisted again. It was a fairly profitable career in a country which
had a wide, unsettled frontier to which the "bounty jumper" could go,
and from which he could return to ply his trade in a new and strange
community.[64]

Another is Bruce Catton's memoir of a Memorial Day in a Michigan small town:

> One of the pleasantest holidays of the year was Memorial Day, uni-
> versally known then as Decoration Day because it was the day when you
> went out to the cemetery and decorated graves. This day of course
> belonged to the Civil War veterans, although as years passed it more and
> more became a day to put flowers on the grave of any loved one who had
> died, and when it came just about everyone in town went to the cemetery
> with a basket of lilacs. Lilacs grow like weeds in our part of the country,
> and most farmers planted a long row of lilacs as windbreaks around
> their houses; in town almost every house had lilacs in the yard, and in
> late May the scent of them lay on the breeze. To this day I never see lilac
> blossoms without remembering those Decoration Day observances of
> long ago.
>
> The Civil War veterans were men set apart. On formal occasions they
> wore blue uniforms with brass buttons and black campaign hats, by the
> time I knew them most of them had long gray beards, and whatever they
> may have been as young men they had an unassuming natural dignity in
> old age. They were pillars, not so much of the church (although most of
> them were devout communicants) as of the community; the keepers of
> its patriotic traditions, the living embodiment, so to speak, of what it
> most deeply believed about the nation's greatness and high destiny.

White's memories, while no less vivid and emotional than Catton's rip the gauze of affection to reveal a sense of the tension even in
this communal event. Could it be that some of these grand figures
had been opportunistic transients? The Memorial Day Catton describes occurs later. His soldiers were not Allen's figures ten years
away from the war—"men in their thirties and forties, husky, full-

throated, happy. . . ." For Catton, the yearly parading of these old men represented a "faith in the continuity of human experience." But both accounts illustrate the inventive character of the local celebration as an attempt to preserve the memory of the past for the next generation by gathering a community together for a day. William Maxwell has written that "with the Middle Western American family, no sooner do you begin to perceive the extent of the proliferation of the ancestors backward into time than they are lost from sight. Every trace of them disappears, through the simple erosion of human forgetfulness. They were in movement in a new century. . . ."[66] A holiday like Memorial Day was an attempt to stave off that forgetfulness.

But as inventive as it was, the small town could not maintain itself as a viable unit. At the turn of the century it frantically attempted to import culture and entertainment, to entice new industries, to halt the massive exodus of its young. But the attrition continued, despite all these efforts. Central to this decline was the destruction of the autonomy (social, political, and economic) of the small town. This loss of autonomy came from all directions. The telephone, and then the automobile, cinema, and radio not only facilitated transience, but promised new forms of community. Worse, at least from the perspective of the town, was the systematic penetration of urban and market values and institutions into the town itself. The franchise, the shopping mall, and the factory smashed small industry and business. A psychic diminution infected every small town. The litany of attacks on the small town reflected and then magnified these changes.

Other conceptions of neighborhood did emerge. Small-town residents from farmers to intellectuals reconstructed some of the features of the small town in cities. In these cultural oases, they invented their own festivals and political institutions, and these, too, have produced nostalgic literary evocations. But the urban neighborhood has also been eroded both by internal and external forces. The suburb, regarded by some as capturing only the worst elements of small town life, was nevertheless an attempt to invent new covenanted neighborhood communities.

There is some evidence of an actual return to the small town. And the search for some functional equivalent to the small town still continues as well. But it is blocked, not only by a failure to invent a new institution with a cohesive social, political, and economic base, but also by the temptation to find instant community, some set of relationships from which a sense of "home" can be immediately grasped.

The Reform Group:
"A restless, prying, conscientious criticism"

Reform groups in America show a resilience and a creativity that should never be underestimated. We saw how the penitentiary was invented and re-invented by groups of urban reformers. The Philadelphia Society drew up the appropriate legislation and administered the new prison themselves. In chapter 3 we discussed promotion groups and their role in the dissemination of successful inventions. Reform groups are themselves promotion groups devoted to social and political change through invention. Sometimes these groups have taken concepts or institutions from other inventive communities and reapplied them, as, for example, the Philadelphia reformers applied the notion of penitence to the criminal justice system. Often reform groups create their own inventions.

What gives reform groups such power and creativity in America is a unique set of elements. In general, liberal societies provide opportunities for a continual reorganization of opinion. In America the potential for change is increased because of the relative absence of stable classes which can insulate opinion. Emerson spoke of this phenomenon in 1844. In America, and especially New England, there had been a "keener scrutiny of institutions and domestic life than we had known . . . a restless, prying, conscientious criticism broke out in all quarters." "The spirit of protest" had produced "a congress of kings, each of whom had a realm to rule, and a way of his own that made concert unprofitable. . . . What a fertility of projects for the salvation of the world!"[67]

There has always been, of course, an underside to this tendency. The "spirit of protest" walks across America with a middle-class gait. The reform group is a precipitate of class, although its middle-class outlines are rarely perceived by either its members or the society at large. Thus the reform group can take forms that are viciously anti-bourgeois, but this is itself part of the spirit of self-criticism sometimes characteristic of the middle class.

The original simplicity of the American reform group is a testimony both to its huge potential and to its own failures. As a systemic source of invention, the reform group contains three basic features: networks of small groups, programmatic agendas and implementation, and supervisory agencies. Let me briefly review the nature of the reform group as a base of invention by referring to aspects of four reform movements in American history: the antislavery crusade, the settlement house movement, the New Left, and the contemporary feminist movement. Of course each of these examples contains unique features and each has left its own legacy. But there are common features.

Each movement began as a collection of small groups and confederations. In each case organizational growth was phenomenal. The first group committed to the immediate abolition of slavery was the New England Anti-Slavery Society formed in 1832. Shortly later, the American Anti-Slavery Society was formed in Philadelphia. By 1838 it had more than thirteen hundred chapters and a membership of a quarter million people. In 1891 there were six settlement houses in the United States; by 1900 there were more than one hundred; by 1910, more than four hundred.[68] More recently, the Students for a Democratic Society experienced a membership growth that was so sudden its board could only guess at the number of chapters.[69] Feminist reform arose from the sexual tensions of the New Left. Beginning first as caucuses within radical groups, five feminist organizations were created in 1967 in different cities. The National Organization of Women was formed independently of these efforts a year earlier from a few small chapters. Between 1967 and 1974 NOW expanded from fourteen chapters to more than seven hundred. In seven years its membership rose from one thousand to forty thousand members.[70]

In all these cases membership growth was startlingly rapid. Massive organizations were built in less than ten years. Activists even complained that membership growth was achieved too easily. While all of these groups had national organizations, their governing boards were usually representatives in a loose confederative structure. It is the small group that is the reproductive base of the reform group. Luther Gerlack and Virginia Hine have described the infrastructure of such movements as "decentralized, segmentary and reticulate."[71] Chapters in these organizations contained fewer than three hundred people and invariably included an activist core of fewer than fifty. Jo Freeman, in her analysis of the feminist movement, has listed four common characteristics of small groups. They are, I think, features of the American reform group in general:

(1) It is task oriented. . . . It is the task that basically structures the group. By determining what needs to be done and when it needs to be done, it provides a guide by which people can judge their actions and make plans for future activity.

(2) It is relatively small and homogenous. Homogeneity is necessary to ensure that participants have a "common language" of interaction. People from widely different backgrounds may provide richness to a consciousness-raising group where each can learn from others' experience, but too great a diversity among members of a task-oriented group means only that they continually misunderstand one another.

(3) There is a high degree of communication. Information must be passed to everyone, opinions checked, work divided up, and participation assured in the relevant decisions. This is possible only if the group is small and people practically live together for the crucial phases of the task.

(4) There is a low degree of skill specialization. Not everyone has to be able to do everything; but everything must be able to be done by more than one person in order for no one to be indispensable. To a certain extent, people must become interchangeable parts.[72]

What these features illustrate is the nature of the reform group as a community that is literally invented. All of the features are the result of complex longings for friendship, solidarity, and commitment.

An appreciation of the psychic basis of the reform group should not be regarded as undercutting the integrity of its commitment to justice or its outrage at unacceptable institutions or policies. The American reform group is what James Q. Wilson has called a "redemptive organization," one which "not only seeks to change society and its institutions, but also to change its members by requiring them to exemplify in their own lives the new order."[73] The therapeutic value of meetings was openly discussed by the abolitionists.[74] But no American writer has been more perceptive in analyzing the relationship between these motivations for reform group activity than Jane Addams. In "The Subjective Necessity for Social Settlements," Addams argued that a sense of loneliness so infected the middle class that "many are buried beneath mere mental accumulation with lowered vitality and discontent." She tells a story of an educated young woman. Upon her return from college, "the family claim is strenuously asserted." The desire for service and community is unfulfilled, and "The girl loses something vital out of her life. . . . She is restricted and unhappy; her elders, meanwhile, are conscious of the situation, and we have all the elements of a tragedy."[75] Addams had recognized this subjective necessity for herself, and in 1889 she established the first American settlement house in Chicago. The settlement was designed to meet the need for community on the part of the sons and daughters of the bourgeoisie as much as it was to aid the poor. In fact, many of the early activities of the settlements were middle-class functions (teas, reading groups, lectures, concerts) now carried to the education of the poor.

The same desire for the creation of a service community is poignantly expressed in the "Port Huron Statement" of 1962. The generation "bred in at least modest comfort" saw a world of "loneliness, estrangement, isolation" that must somehow be transformed into one of "reason, love, and freedom." The political principles of the SDS program were generalizations based upon the newly invented community of its own small groups, wherein it was mandated that

> decision-making of basic consequence be carried on by public groupings;
> politics be seen positively, as the art of collectively creating an acceptable pattern of social relations;
> politics has the function of bringing people out of isolation and into community, thus being a necessary, though not sufficient, means of finding meaning in personal life;
> the political order should serve to clarify problems in a way instrumental to their solution; it should provide outlets for expression of personal grievance and aspiration. . . .[76]

The very nature of the issue of gender makes feminist reform groups a perfect illustration of Wilson's concept of redemptive organizations. I will quote here a few excerpts from an autobiographical fragment detailing the experience of a consciousness-raising group.

> When I joined a consciousness-raising group last fall, I believed that I was in women's liberation for my daughters' sakes—to make a better world for them. At our first meeting one woman said, "The exciting thing about this movement to me is that finally women are doing some-

thing for themselves. That's how change really comes about. I mean, for the first time in my life I am my own cause."

My consciousness jumped up a foot. Later I realized that this is where the energy of the movement is coming from: we are working to liberate ourselves.

Our group, culled spontaneously from a larger meeting and a few telephone calls around the neighborhood, consisted of ten women, all over thirty-five, and all mothers. Some of us were artists, tucking our work in around the edges of the children's schedules; others supported ourselves in the business world at jobs which would have paid a man of the same age and background at least double what we made. Most of us were politically cynical.

We had all been in psychoanalytic and/or encounter therapy; we tacitly agreed that our consciousness-raising sessions were to be something else: as a group, we would refuse to consider the charge that we were personally inadequate, neurotic, or not pretty or smart enough. For me the charge was exposed as ridiculous when I saw the other nine women—however inept, sick, ugly or dumb *I* might feel, *they* were obviously here for no such reason; they probably thought the same of me, where then did the charge originate? Where did the definitions of what women are come from?

We asked the question everywhere during the week and discovered that once you have changed the question you have changed the world. There was no way to un-see what we had begun seeing. How? Why? Where did the idea get started? Every scrap of our lives was infected with the fact that we were women and someone else had decided for us what being a woman was.

A month later the group was disbanded. But members had left the "mother-group to join other, action groups."

If each reform group is an invented community, like all communities it harbors secrets and self-deception. The polycephalous character of the reform group still requires some leadership both for organizational goals as well as organizational maintenance. But the small group's homogeneity and its developed sense of friendship create conditions, psychological as well as structural, in which leadership is treated with suspicion. After all, the group had been successfully invented by strangers in order to meet needs for community. But however alert groups may be, a leadership emerges. Marge Piercy looked back on her experience in the SDS and discovered that each chapter was actually organized around subtle but pervasive reform leaders: "The typical Movement institution consists of one or more men who act as charismatic spokesmen, who speak in the name of the institution, and negotiate and represent that body in and outside the Movement, and who manipulate the relationships inside to maintain his or their position. . . . Most prestige in the Movement rests not on having done anything in particular, but in having visibly dominated some gathering, in manipulating a certain set of rhetorical counters well in public or in having played some theatrical role. . . ."[78]

While considerations such as funding, cooptation and even the response to repression are all crucial to the formation of leadership in the reform group, it is the availability of an individual's time—defined as energy and commitment to a group—that forges the edge between the sometime attender and the activist. In general, time is the basic resource of the reform group itself.[79] It propels individuals into the group and allows them to continue in it. Each reform leader "gives," "makes," "saves," "offers" time to the group. As an invented commodity, time is an individual demonstration of the existence of this new community. This new use of a public- and group-oriented time involves a re-ordering of individual person-alities, as the feminist autobiography cited above illustrates. Those who offer the most of themselves in the service of the reform group's tasks possess the necessary qualifications for leadership. Rush's Elam's the Grimkes', Hayden's seemingly endless travels estab-lished their claim to leadership within the group.

But the emergence of time as a political resource is only part of the dynamic of the reform group. Part of the standard critique of the New Left revolves around its antagonism to leaders, but this at-titude characterizes all reform groups. Still, when leadership emerges—and it always does—it is based upon the only available resource other than the creative use of time: an ideological articula-tion of the reform communities' tasks. An individual claims lead-ership by drawing out the most radical implications of the reform group's tenets. This behavior precipitates an organizational crisis, such as Garrison instigated over the women's and Sabbath question, Mark Rudd over the issue of violent action, Charlotte Bunch over the "lesbian question." It is on these sets of issues that the reform group is especially vulnerable. For the raison d'être of the communi-ty that has just been established is common commitment to a set of organizational goals. When it is argued that these goals require new or extended responses, doubters are placed in the position of ap-

pearing to surrender newly established bounds. The history of each
reform group is short. It is difficult to make rebuttals of questions of
policy based on tradition. In paraphrase of the papal injunction,
there is no salvation outside the group.

Groups of prison reformers have a much longer history. But we
saw how these groups have undergone periodic reformations in the
direction both of advocating for more "total" institutions or of
demanding that existing ones be abolished. I think, however, that
the difference between the prison reformers and the settlement
house workers on the one hand and the abolitionists, New Leftists,
and feminists on the other, is that the former were able to invent
new institutions. Whatever objections one may have to the penitentiary, it has been an extremely productive institution as a focus for
new techniques and organizations and as a creator of new professions and supporting institutions. There is a tendency today to
belittle the settlement house as an ineffective institution. But the
settlement house was a very successful invention. It was used as an
educational institution (for both neighborhood residents and reformers), and it provided child and health care, vocational training,
and even university courses. Hull House became a center for political reform as well as a lobby for parks, clubs, and housing.

Other reform groups have had greater difficulty with institutional invention. Of course, the abolitionists were devoted to "de-
inventing" slavery. But they had tremendous difficulties in linking
up with any institutional structures. Energies were focused upon
the invention of new strategies and tactics, a direction which only
increased organizational instability. The New Left underwent a
similar course. The SDS had its Economic Research and Action
Project (ERAP), a kind of contemporary version of the settlement
house. But it never could invent a stable institutional base to extend
and solidify sympathies that were just as vague as those of the
settlement workers. The draft counseling center was an innovative
service for the Movement's own class constituency, but it foundered
on questions of what constituted morally acceptable alternatives.
The feminist movement, still in the process of development, shows
signs of inventive activity: battered women shelters, abortion
clinics, credit unions.

The failures of American reform groups can, in part, be seen as
an incestual problem. The small group structure centers around a
public problem (slavery, poverty, war, sexism). It is itself an in-

vention, the result of great personal anxiety and effort. For an activist to forsake the small group in favor of allegiance to any other institution is to risk strenuous resistance by other members.[80] This resistance frequently takes the form of opposition to institutions in general. The small group is seen as a "natural" group, anti-institutional and morally untainted. The basic institutional structures of society are already responsible for slavery, poverty, etc., and hence are not seen as viable alternatives.

Anti-institutionalism is reflected in the agendas of reform groups. Garrisonians moved from a critique of slavery, to a condemnation of the Constitution, to an opposition to government in general. Stanley Elkin has complained about the abolitionists on this point. "Slavery might have been approached not as a problem in pure morality but as a question of institutional arrangements—a question of those institutions which make a difference in men's relationships with one another. . . ."[81] The programs of the New Left followed a similar process of escalation from reform to radicalism and then, in some cases, to terrorism.

What is intriguing about the New Left, however, is the frantic nature of its attempts to create new institutions. Every major event in the decade of its prominence was interpreted as a new institutional invention: People's Park, Woodstock, teach-ins, street theatre. In actuality, these were all more strategic exhibitions of groups than new institutions. Yet after the decline of the Movement, theoretical advances in regard to this problem were finally made.

The concept of participatory democracy was the New Left's contribution to a radical organization theory. Seen from our perspective, it was an attempt to articulate and to maintain the new-found community of group members. As the Movement gravitated first toward a strategy of resistance and then revolution, another formulation emerged. The idea of "liberated zones" seems to have evolved from two sources: a critique of America as an imperialist power and the awareness of the mutual cultural animosity between the New Left and "bourgeois America." Like much of the New Left thought, the concept of "liberated zones" was less a theory than an analogy. The United States was a colonial power and its destruction could be hastened by conceiving of portions of the American population as internal colonies of the mother country. The idea of liberated zones was consistent with the demands of black nationalists as well as the demands of students for free universities. More impor-

tantly, it represented an effort to extend the concept of group solidarity to the invention of new institutions. At one point, Tom Hayden was a proponent of this idea and it will be useful if we briefly
note his own conception before we discuss his latest book, *The*
American Future.

In 1970, Hayden argued that "free territories" have "four common points of identity": (1) "They will be utopian centers of new
cultural experiment . . . the nuclear family would be replaced by a
mixture of communes, extended families, children's centers, and
new schools. . . . Drugs would be commonly used as a means of
deepening self-awareness. Urban structures would be destroyed to
be replaced with parks, closed streets, expanded backyards inside
blocks, and a village atmosphere in general would be encouraged."
(2) "The territories would be internationalist. . . . Solidarity committees to aid all Third World struggles would be in constant motion. Each territory would see itself as an 'international city'; the
flags, music, and culture of other countries and other liberation
movements would permeate the territory. Travel and foreign
cultures would be commonplace." (3) "The territories will be centers of constant confrontation, battlefronts inside the Mother country." (4) "They will be centers of survival and self-defense. . . .
Training in physical self-defense and the use of weapons would
become commonplace as fascism and vigilantism increase."[82] Hayden insisted that the establishment of liberated zones would prove
"once and for all" that Americans would "no longer be able to
think comfortably of themselves as a homogeneous society with a
few extremists at the fringes."

Ten years later, Hayden is still writing about the imminent collapse of a "center" that has held together American life. But obser-
vations are offered in the earlier style of the "Port Huron Statement": "The emerging morality will begin by recognizing an
ancient truth—that the great moral and religious philosophers
throughout history have tended to promote inner rather than outer,
rewards, modesty rather than status hunger, love rather than domination." As in the early days of the SDS, the traditional Left is
dismissed as old-fashioned, outmoded, and lacking moral vision.
Socialism is only "a useful introduction to the continuing search for
answers. "Without major re-examination," the socialist tradition is
of "declining relevance." Work in a Leningrad steel factory is "just
as alienating as work at the River Rouge plant in Detroit."[83]

Hayden identifies two cultural views that have existed through-out American history. One sees America as an endless frontier; first, in terms of geographic expansion, then in terms of infinite material progress. Domestic consumption has become a kind of "supplementary frontier." Supporting and propelling this Faustian economics is "capitalist expansion, investment and profit." Hayden finds the epitome of the frontier mentality in the figure of General Custer. The Custer legend produced a "mythical romantic heroism" that covered the "true racist venality and avarice" that led to his humiliating destruction. All this is standard New Left pamphleteering. Incendiary rhetoric is employed to expose the immoral underbelly of liberal aspirations and to solidify personal leadership.

It is this destructive, jeremiadic posturing that overwhelmed the Movement. But now Hayden has recovered the progressive element of an Enlightenment that flashed so brightly in the "Port Huron Statement." Reason, love, and a belief in the future return. Americans have always had a belief in an "inner frontier" as a space for moral rebirth, and Hayden re-outlines the redemptive vision of reform. Thoreau is the key articulator, according to Hayden, if not the father, of this other view. He was the opposite of Custer and denounced "both the corporate industrial age from Walden Pond and the Mexican War from a prison."[84] Of course, Thoreau could not subvert the dominant institutions derived from the Custerite mentality. But now the capitalist vision of the American frontier has run its course, and it remains for Hayden to outline political movements and institutional structures that will bring the Thoreauean and New Left critique to life.

Hayden has reconstructed the concept of liberated zones within American political culture. His political program is based upon the American's emotional preference for local administration and antagonism to authority. Hayden argues that the New Left discovered that government bureaucracy was an "obscene burden" long before the neo-conservative critiques began to do so. Major responsibility for certain programs and services must be returned to voluntary organizations. Energy policy must be built by a movement toward decentralization. Hayden's proposals include solar power, corporate divestiture, community energy self-sufficiency. Cancer research should be supported in small foundations and not the huge R&D corporate laboratories. Corporations must be democratized and subject to legal restrictions, both internal and external. The former

New Left proposal to smash international capitalism is replaced by
a global strategy for a "common international front of workers and
consumers against the policies of the multi-nationals."[85] As to inflation, there is "no responsible human response to inflation except
to realize that less *is* more and the best things in life are free."[86] The
cultural tenets of Woodstock Nation are left unmentioned by Hayden. Instead we are reminded that the Protestant Ethic can now be
used as a basis for a "politics of frugality" in an era of limits.

According to Hayden, two political forces can bring about these
transformations. One is a "new majority governing coalition" ("enlightened" bankers and industrialists, labor, minorities, and wom-
en). The other is the collection of populist groups (Hayden's own
CED, anti-nuclear power organizations, local citizen action organizations like ACORN). The "governing coalition" would be "pushed
by, and in return exercise a restraining influence over, the saner
progressive movements for further change."[87]

Ironically, the first group is the New Deal coalition of "corporate
liberalism" that had previously so enraged the New Left. The latter
is, of course, a reincarnation of the movement itself, circa 1965.
Hayden, in the true spirit of the reformer, believes that the coalition
could move toward national power in the 1990s, making America
an economic democracy and a solar society by the year 2000.

Hayden's first effort in *The Trial*, for all its bravado, had not
progressed beyond a vision of the small groups of SDS. *The American Future* makes the transition to the creation of new institutions,
with the CED functioning as a laboratory for invention.

Harry Boyte's *The Backward Revolution: Understanding the
New Citizen Movement* is another example of the continuing
search for transcendence through participatory democracy and liberated zones.[88] His vision is based upon what he believes is a growing neighborhood movement of protest against corporations, public utilities, and unresponsive governmental bodies. Most of Boyte's
efforts go toward establishing that enough local groups exist with
common goals to deserve the characterization of a movement. As
we noted, the SDS had attempted, without much sustained success,
to create local action groups. Boyte's implicit argument is that thousands of ERAPs have flowered from the remains of the New Left. The
COSH (Committee on Occupational Safety and Health) groups,
working women's organizations (9 to 5, Pittsburgh Working Wom-
en, Cleveland Women Working, etc.), ACORN (Association of Com-

munity Organizations for Reform Now), support networks for community organizations (National Association of Neighborhoods, Rural America, Center for Community Change, etc.) and many others form a new "democratic culture" spread along "social networks."[89]

On the basis of his analysis of these groups, Boyte develops a theory of social change. For the first time in the history of the New Left, the search for institutional transcendence seems to be pointed in an outward direction. The concepts of participatory democracy and liberated zones are merged in Boyte. These citizens' groups are arenas of direct democracy. Boyte quotes one community organizer: " 'We've got ordinary people who came from public housing projects, retirement centers and churches, who've never spoken before a crowd, who are now sitting down and talking to the governor, to legislators, to the heads of utility companies and who are learning the skills of active citizenship.' "[90]

As these groups manage to create a degree of organizational autonomy in relation to the corporate state, they support and nurture a complex process of cultural autonomy. At this point, Boyte presents a rebuttal to the Marxist (and New Leftist) analysis of social change. The traditional leftist view sees the origin of revolt in those places in which the process of modernization and industrialization have most rationalized individual lives. The factory is, for Marx, the model economic invention of the new capitalist order and the basis from which a new society will be built. Protest against the dissolution of the family, small business, and church are seen as conservative, even reactionary, movements which, in the words of Marx and Engels, "try to hold back the wheel of history." Boyte contends that this left-wing view of social movement is "simply wrong." Protest derives from the desire to protect "free spaces, . . . those organic relations that modern life has not completely collectivized, rationalized and refashioned in the image of the market place."

The chances are slim that citizen groups will become a democratic movement, that "free space" will not collapse internally into oligarchy or externally into services provided by the welfare state, or that the leftist vision will not be rejected by the groups themselves.[91] But Boyte's *Backyard Rebellion* is nevertheless a theoretical achievement, and one that proves that even the New Left,

perhaps the most self-destructive of all American reform groups,
still has the capacity to bestow a legacy on the next generation.

But if American reform groups naturally incline toward incestuous self-destruction, efforts to create inventions and/or to create the linkages we described in chapter 3 can produce problems from an opposite direction. This process is usually referred to as "cooptation." Yet in modern political systems, cooptation has become a major structural problem which faces every reform group. Michael Walzer has outlined this process in terms which I hope are too deterministic, but which effectively indicate the nature of the problem. In "The Pastoral Retreat of the New Left," he criticizes the application of New Left strategies to the political issues of the 1980s that we have just discussed. Groups like the CFD mistakenly believe that they are imparting dignity and independence to the powerless. Walzer argues that, in fact, they are collaborating with the agents of the welfare state. These reformers are "bureaucrats without offices," "agents of entitlement . . . acting in behalf of members of powerless and dispersed social groups."[92]

Walzer's thesis has historical parallels. The penitentiary, conceived as an institution of humane liberation from criminal compulsion, was quickly transformed into a massive establishment of political control. Every effort to invent the public school and its curriculum has served to strengthen its functional connections to the welfare state. The settlement house movement was turned into the social work profession. Black power became institutionalized as affirmative action. Feminism frequently appears to be dissolving into an agency for individual career advancement using the Service State as its structural support.

In the language we have been employing, the inventions of reform groups have become supporting inventions of the American welfare state. The reform group takes on the role of supervising and extending programs for its clientele. Just as the union has been unable to transform the factory, the reform group has been unable to transcend the service ideology of the welfare state. But is the choice only between dissipation as a redemptive community of small groups or transformation into an accrediting bureaucracy of the welfare state? We shall have more to say on this question in our concluding chapter. But for now, this much can be said: In an Aristotelean sense, the purpose of the American reform group is not the completion of the welfare state. Its function is service-oriented, but with the goal of redeeming both its "clients" and its members through new forms of community. The welfare state can never fulfill this objective. In Walzer's own words, the ultimate goal of the welfare state is a system in which "everyone will be known not to each other but to the specialists in such knowledge, not personally but statistically."[93] "Subjective necessity" has always required a different goal. The invention of service institutions independent of the Service State has been within the vision, if not the grasp, of the reform group. Ironically, the reform group, even in its historical role as a supporting invention of the service state, still has the potential for dismantling that state's very foundations by replacing its structure with new inventions.

Chapter 8

Conclusion

What generalizations can we offer about these inventions? And what, if any, lessons do they ofer for the future of invention in America?

Instant Community

First, we must repeat that all these inventions were created in the context of an unstable and fluid society. Frequently they provided relief from the consequences of such extreme movement; but in some cases, they perpetuated and even accelerated it. The telephone, as technological invention, permitted new forms of communications between scattered settlements and among those who emigrated from towns and cities. But the telephone also brought into existence electronic neighborhoods, larger but shallower kinds of community. The modern prison is American liberalism's adventure with political invention. It was, and still is, offered as an institution which will transform wayward individuals through a radical alteration of environment. The revival camp in all its forms, from protracted meeting to recent electronic variations, was an invention that also attempted to capture and organize people who were seen to have been shaken from conventional moorings. The camps did, and still do, offer solace and commitment, even personal transformation. The motel was a supporting invention for auto travel. But it was also an invention designed to deal with complex longings for geographic mobility and comradely adventure. As an unintended consequence the motel contributed to a basic alteration in sexual morality. The quilt, as craft form and household invention, maintained a psychic link to forsaken communities and helped build new ones.

Second, each of these inventions, despite major differences in function and type, represented attempts to create a novel kind of community. For the examples we have discussed illustrate the establishment of "instant communities." Despite the uniqueness of the American experience and of modernity in general, our language of community has remained remarkably continuous with that of the past. Community contains the following elements: (1) a territorial base, whether home, town, ethnic group, or parish; (2) primary relationships (face-to-face encounters); (3) stability; (4) some conception of a principled commitment to a collectivity.[1] A large number of writers have attempted to re-evaluate these features of community. For instance, Emile Durkheim contended that the concept of territorial base was outmoded: "The provincial spirit has disappeared never to return; the patriotism of the parish has become an archaism that cannot be restored at will."[2] Perhaps, Durkheim argued, professional associations and other organizations, now incipient, could provide substitutes for this lost territorial base. There has also been disagreement as to how inclusive a commitment is required for a community to be said to exist. Liberals in particular have emphasized the desirability of a limited "general will." Other writers have explored the extent to which secondary relationships can coexist with primary structures in a community.

Still the basic definition remains intact. Communities are characterized by a local economy (Weber's *oikos*), a mutuality in social relationships (Tonnies' *Gemeinschaft*), and a self-contained area (Simmel's *autarkic* society). Other organizations employ an expansive, functional use of space, a market economy, and contractual relationships based upon rational calculation.

The patterns of relationships created by the inventions we have studied have challenged even the most loosely tethered interpretations of community. These instant communities contain substitute concepts. To say that they are not territorially based understates the novelty of these inventions. The telephone, the penitentiary, the revival camp, the quilting bee, the motel not only disregard geographic organization but in some cases defy any conception of natural space. The telephone offers a potential community at the sound of a ring. The revival camp offers an instant church as its

inventive spin-off, the commune, offers instant society. The penitentiary offers reform through architecture, and more recently through
drugs. The auto camp and then the motel and the recreational
vehicle offer comradeship through travel. The quilting bee offered
instant neighborliness.

If one thinks for a moment about telephonic, penal, tourist,
evangelistic, and quilting communities, one can see how strange
and unusual are the settings of their participants. Relatives and old
friends maintain ties through an electronic form of communication
that is blind but instantly available. People travel to forest clearings
to save their souls. Emigrees quilt together. Prisoners sit in scientifically designed cells and await therapy. Motorists, strangers a
moment before, enjoy a sunset or a historical marker together.

This radical reorganization of social space produces a different
kind of commitment derived from primary relationships, one different from either Tonnies' service contract or *Gemeinschaft*. It is what
I would call an "intimate anonymity," and it pervades all the inventions we have discussed.

Many participants in the Western revival camps barely knew one
another. Yet under the exhortations of a new clergy they formed an
immediate and common bond. Similar emotions arise today when
the electronic preacher and his/her bands of sisters offer community. After we stripped away the American romance of the quilt and
the bee, we discovered that this supporting institution was designed
to meet the needs of strangers. Sewing is not as emotionally intense
an activity as conversion, but the bee does involve work in close
proximity. It was alleged that convention permitted more intimate
conversation as the quilt was folded into smaller and smaller sections. We saw how the autocamp participants reveled in the informality of a new form of travel and how they preferred to avoid last
names and discussion of occupations—all this while men and wom-
en shared toilet and eating facilities in close quarters. We argued
that the motel involved a conscious movement away from sociality.
But this movement paradoxically opened up new possibilities for
intimate anonymity in the sexual encounter. It is difficult to imagine
how a society could attach more psychic importance to this new
form of sexual behavior. "The stranger calls" phenomenon of the
telephone requires an immediate kind of intimacy as well. The
prison carries the process of intimate anonymity to extreme and

grotesque proportions: on the one hand there is the impersonal but totalitarian supervision; on the other the brutal, submissive demands of the inmate subculture.

Both of these features, the unusual use of social space and the special kind of intimacy, have produced in the inventions under consideration a unique mixture of public and private modes of activity. The traditional approach emphasizes the absence of privacy in communities. Townspeople, families, religious authorities assure in intricate ways a narrow sphere of freedom, and it is rather the citydweller, anonymous and unsupervised, who is the private man or woman. However, the communities that these inventions have created alter this framework.

One way to appreciate this phenomenon is to review Erving Goffman's concept of "front" and "back" regions of institutions.[3] Goffman argues that all institutions contain these two spheres. The front portion is a public region. Examples would include the eating area of a restaurant, a stage in a theatre, reception alcoves in a business, even the living room of a home. The "back" encompasses areas like kitchens, boiler rooms, garages, dressing rooms, any place where individuals need not perform according to their public roles as actors, waiters, secretaries, etc. Of course, the back region is not without its own social or ritualized element, and Goffman is quite adept at exploring these subtleties. My point here, however, is that the front and back regions of the inventions we have been considering are strangely interwoven, more intensely supervised than the traditional watchful community yet oriented toward private needs as well.

What, for example, is the back area of a revival camp? Critics insisted darkly that in the answer to this question lay the real attraction of the camps. Still, instances of sexual activity under the podiums hardly explained the camps' popularity. Ministers may have occasionally walked outside the grounds to prime themselves for sermons, and Finley reported meeting groups of drunken men in the woods outside Cane Ridge. But for the most part, the camp and the protracted meeting were designed without a back region. Escape required egress from the whole affair, much more so than did the traditional church service. The goals of the revival were much more demanding and absolutist than those of conventional religion, and both the camp and the commune which attempted to extend its life were intensely public institutions. At the same time they required complete expression of private feeling, one through the conversion, the other, at least in the case of Oneida, through mutual criticism and sexual management.

Of course, as transitional institutions, camp and commune were by nature limited in duration. But the same unusual conflation of front and back occurs during the telephone conversation. It is very difficult to talk to a person in one's physical presence while speaking to another on the telephone. One can, of course, page through a magazine or wash dishes or watch television while telephoning—but with only limited success. Other forms of behavior like making love, exercising, or reading a novel become ludicrous or comical. The telephone commands attention, but only for short intervals. There are occasions when we ache to "get off the phone" and be freed from a demanding relative or whining friend. When we are finally successful, the interaction ends as abruptly as it began. Yet all this is, of course, a "private conversation." A skeptic might note that the telephone is simply an instrument. But we saw how the use of this instrument reflected and also transformed our conception of community.

Similarly, we reviewed in our analysis of Capra's film how the motel dissolves and then reorganizes our conception of privacy. In another sense the motel, and the tourist industry in general, inverts front and back. The design of the motel attempts to create the feeling of a back region. Motifs which recreate English taverns, log cabins, and fishing shacks are efforts to convey an aura of living in some previously inaccessible setting, doubly so because the themes are frequently borrowed from the past. Yet this carefully reconstructed back region is really the front. Not only are the rough-hewn beams across the ceiling made of plastic, but the "real" back region is the stainless steel kitchen where frozen food is prepared. Nabokov appreciated this phenomenon, and he paralleled his growing knowledge of the front nature of this allegedly back region with his acquisition of carnal experience.

The penitentiary reveals the same structure in its most brutal form. Certainly the inmate subculture is a back region. Or is it? It is to the outsider who tries to discover its mores. But the set of behaviors that constitutes this subculture is so routinized and all-encompassing that it functions more as another competing front region to the official one.

One final feature of these instant communities: To say that they are voluntary communities is commonplace. It is natural that a culture based upon Lockean premises would invent communities that one joins rather than inherits. That evangelism feverishly attempts to support "old" values while at the same time it seeks new and voluntary individual commitments shows that it has more in common with the "secular humanism" of the reform group than participants in either would be willing to admit. It is no accident then that these inventions produced communities that individuals more or less consciously choose.

What is so disturbing about these communities is their fragility. In an attempt to redefine community in modern society, Israel Rubin suggests that territorial space need not constitute part of the concept of community, but he readily admits the need for some kind of stability: "we barely need to belabor the point that organization must endure for a considerable stretch of time, that an ad hoc structure cannot function as a community . . . the individual must belong to the organization for a significant portion of his adult life."[4] Significance these communities do have; permanence they do not. In fact, this is the trade-off (although it is not seen as such by participants) that an instant community can offer. While specific communities are notoriously unstable, the model itself is emminently replicable. Towns (later to be described so endearingly) were cast off for better communities. An auto worker from Detroit can join an evangelist group (as did his rural ancestor) in Houston and immediately partake of some kind of community.

Social Invention
and the Liberal Future

Given the obvious limitations of these inventions, do we need not more invention, but less? Even the great systemic sources of American invention, the factory, the town, the evangelistic churches, the reform group—all of them exhibit the same features that characterize the inventions they have produced. I have hesitated to refer to the communities produced by these inventions as corruptions of community, as pathological formulations, but a critic could indeed draw such conclusions. There are, however, two sets of arguments that lead away from an assessment of this sort. First, each of the inventions, with the exception of the penitentiary, still illustrates that men and women are able to reconstruct their lives through inventive responses. Many of the inventions we have mentioned have managed to imbue people's lives with some kind of social element. Often these inventions were created under extreme conditions of loneliness (the quilt, the revival). Sometimes they were constructed with great vision (the town meeting, the commune), sometimes under conditions of great hardship and sacrifice (the union, the settlement house). Even those arising from less heroic motives like bourgeois ennui (the autocamp) or with less than successful results (the prison) show an admirable effort at invention.

It is the covenanted aspect of these inventions (whether the "city on the hill" or telephonic crisis counseling) that is at once so corruptible and so exhilarating. For American men and women have historically produced "new foundings" through social invention. That these inventions are not fully susceptible to elite manipulation is also a cause for some optimism. The revival camp never quite served as an agency of elite control, and, while we saw how no social invention has been able to fundamentally reorganize the factory, it is still true that Americans have been able to resist the psychological collectivization both corporate elites and Marxists have hoped for.

But let me also state the argument negatively. In the context of such extreme geographical and economic movement, political and economic inventions take on a frighteningly aggressive character. The fact that we can even imagine what a world composed only of penitentiaries and factories would be like indicates a possible future.

Let me conclude this essay by focusing upon ways in which the conditions for social invention can be established. First, it must be recognized that, contrary to previous periods in the history of American liberalism, social space must be won. It must be wrested and torn away from economic and political institutions. New supporting inventions must be invented from the remaining social institutions that now exist. In other instances, transitional and even generative inventions are necessary to replace or significantly alter existing institutions. Those inventions we have discussed that contain a social element—quilting, the revival camp, even motel travel—as well as the systemic sources of these inventions themselves have not been able to create communities that could fully resist the growth of economic and political institutions. For a time the American town and the urban neighborhood was sufficiently inventive to do so. The reform group illustrates how men and women can form social bonds and, when they are able to reach beyond their new-found comradeship, establish new social institutions. But incestual temptations and a preoccupation with political goals has limited its inventive capacities in this regard. We noted in chapter 6 the ambivalent position of American evangelism on this question. Yet the potential for social renewal still exists. American communities will never assume the solidity of a peasant village. But perhaps if the social sphere could be expanded through invention, instant communities might develop into more promising forms.

For while the modern liberal agenda has promoted the expansion of political and economic invention, Americans have desperately attempted to create community. The four sources of American invention we have just discussed still have the capacity to create social inventions. Sets of new social institutions centered around work, home, religion, and mutual commitment are at least conceivable. It is not possible to re-invent the American town, but some equivalent conception of home can still be a goal. The electronic factory will certainly not automatically produce the kind of social invention that will transform the heart of a market society. The creation of viable social inventions to contain elite control and redirect technological changes is an essential task. Despite the tremendous efforts of trade unions, the American labor movement has suffered severe setbacks in the so-called second wave of industrial expansion. Perhaps an unacknowledged partnership of reform group and evangelists could play a major role in such a project.

Let me illustrate by discussing the possibilities for social invention in three areas: the renovation of existing social institutions, the approach to new social inventions, the de-invention of existing economic institutions.

The current status of the American family is typical of the status of social institutions in general. In many ways the modern family is itself a liberal invention. The conception of the modern family, as it emerged from the seventeenth century, is of a nuclear, child-centered institution, grounded in an emotional and erotic relationship between relatively equal spouses. This notion was itself based upon the pedagogy of liberals or was the result of political and economic changes advocated by liberals. Today that version of the family is undergoing a major transformation. The new average American family is quite small (household size was 2.73 in 1981) and in-

creasingly it is headed by a single parent. The shrinkage in family
size itself limits the character of social relationships. In some ways,
this feature is counteracted by the creation of new forms of extended
familiies (divorced parents, then new partners and children). John-
ny is now said to have benefited from divorce. He now has a "new"
mom or dad and "new" brothers and sisters. But there is no question that the character of familial social relationships has been
altered. Moreover, the entry by women into the work force, the rise
of marriage contracts, and the increase in rates of illegitimacy suggest that the family is ceasing to function as a social institution. The
problem is not, as some critics argue, the result of the flight of
working women from the home. The problem, at least in part, lies
in the nature of work itself in modern society. Work is assigned
individually, physically away from the home, and according to a
precise schedule. Yet the demands of liberal reform do not seek to
recover the social element in family life but seek rather to replace it
with new supporting political and economic institutions such as the
public or employee day-care center or expanded school programs.
In a recent study of family policy reform, the authors remind us that
future policy must be premised upon full labor participation regardless of sex and that "society does not owe an equal standard of
living to those that prefer to trade the home contributions of one
partner against income from work."[5]

One would hope that liberals would examine the consequences
of this new absorption of both adults and children by new institutions. An example of one such approach is an article by Elizabeth
Jones and Elizabeth Prescott.[6] They have focused their concern on
the impact of adult role model behavior in day-care centers. Day-
care staff frequently change jobs within the system, which naturally
is designed to accommodate change: "A bureaucracy—and most
day care is becoming bureaucratic in design—is organized to promote efficient task accomplishment through clear definition of
roles, so that individuals can be replaced without interrupting the
task." Competent care is, of course, assured but "when a day-care
giver moves, she says goodbye. And the child mourns—or learns
not to care." If one couples this behavior with the high divorce rates
of the new American family, there is cause for a complete evaluation
of the bureaucratic alternative to child-rearing. Jones and Prescott
note that one recurrent finding of day-care studies is that children in
day care appear to be more oriented to peers than to adults. They

noted that "peers are able to give children a sense of the present—but not of the future.[7] Any alternative to day care must include the creation of "a coherent sense of community, in which adults can act with purpose and commitment, and children can absorb and internalize this mode of being in the world."

The creation of new communities with "purpose and commitment" should indeed form the future agenda of liberalism. In the case of family policy the most immediate task must include the creation of social space itself through attempts to restrict the economic demands placed upon employees. One such proposal has been offered by Z. I. Giraldo, who has recommended borrowed paid time for parents with young children.[8] We may find that the expansion of social space itself will reveal immanent social structures. For example, Alice Collins and Diane Pancoast have argued that in every human setting there exist "natural helping networks," linkages among relatives, friends, and acquaintances. These networks revolve around a "central figure," "natural neighbor," or gatekeeper who "acts as an exchange agent or a match-maker for needs and resources, and also offers direct advice, support, and practical help to members of a network."[9] They contend that such social networks are being rediscovered and studied and that they hold real promise for positive intervention in human problems on a large scale at a feasible cost. The resuscitation of these networks (which these writers admit are often unknown to health and service professionals) could provide a condition for social invention.

The family is an existing institution in need of social expansion. As we have noted, American society continuously invents new social institutions. We described the way revival camps tore apart and rebuilt established churches and how the revival spawned even more utopian efforts at creating new communities. While there are significant differences between the new institutions of the Great Revival and the current electronic revival and the emergence of new "cults," enough of a parallel exists for us to be able to assess the kinds of positions a liberal theorist can assume in regard to the invention of new communities in general.

It is certainly not difficult to conclude that the Children of God, the Unification Church, the Krishnas, and the Church of Scientology do not fit the model of a liberal theory of voluntary association. Membership is exclusive, not overlapping; converts "leave" society and drastically alter their previous beliefs and life-styles.

Recruitment methods generally involve at least some initial decep-
tion; initiation rites are severe (so much so that the term "brainwashing" is used to describe the conversion process). Eccentric and,
in some cases, venal leaders abound who combine the features of
Freud's primal father and those of corporate entrepreneurs. Fund-
raising activities are suspect. It is no wonder then that the liberal
mind recoils at these new groups and that there are efforts to curb
the proliferation of these new communities. Twice legislation has
been introduced and passed in New York state that would allow the
court to be appointed as temporary guardian to any person who
has undergone "substantial behavioral change and lacks substantial capacity to make independent and informed decisions or to
understand or control his conduct." Any new institution, so argues
one approach to liberal theory, which destroys individual autonomy is a pathological form of community that must be restricted.

Another approach, also quite consistent with liberal theory, is to
assert that citizens ought to be indifferent to the invention of any
new community. For instance, Thomas Robbins contends that since
free will is a "philosophical premise which underlies our legal system" we must "routinely assume behavior which is not overtly
coerced or drugged or which does not manifest signs of extreme
disorganization . . . to be autonomous." We must not assume that
a person who is not "hysterical, violent, drugged, or under physical
restraint and who talks coherently albeit dogmatically" is a "zom-
bie" who requires legal "deprogramming."[10]

Both approaches possess a great deal of internal consistency and
are equally derived from liberal theory precisely because neither
attempts to include any concept of the social in their accounts. Both
positions are in essence economic theories of group behavior, one
insisting that members of new religions must demonstrate capacity
for autonomous choice, the other insisting that, barring physical
force or drugged-induced behavior, all decisions must be considered autonomous. One approach then argues for a kind of consumer rights model of group membership in which "truth in pack-
age" warnings are posted and a "cooling off" period is required, and
the other assumes a position of caveat emptor.

But the on-going debate concerning economic choice need not,
and should not, be applied to new forms of social organization. As
we tried to show in our discussion of the Shakers and Oneidas, the
invention of new little societies is part of a general process of social

experimentation in which people participate for a variety of complex reasons. The impulse to reject current social forms and to feverishly attempt to invent a whole new social order in miniature can be evidence of the vitality of a society as much as evidence of its disintegration. Certainly, as we discussed, the chances for the long-term survival of these "little societies" is quite small. Drastically different organizational alternatives must eventually be considered. But in the process of this kind of invention, individuals are able to literally create new ways of living with a larger social sphere than liberal society can offer and to provide examples for those who are justifiably hesitant to participate directly in this form of experimentation. But more importantly, the point that liberal theory fails to appreciate is that people in part seek these new communities *because* they have already rejected individual autonomy as the central value to be maximized in their lives. Other goals are sought: solidarity, other-wordly contemplation, cooperation. As one commentator has written:

> We who are part of mainstream religious traditions should consider why so many young adults are attracted to the new cults. What do the cults offer that we do not? One insidious technique of which certain cults have been accused is called "love-bombing." Potential converts are showered with attention and affection by group members . . . how many religious organizations have grown too comfortable to bother to love-bomb anybody?[11]

All of this is not to say that a laissez-faire attitude toward the invention of new communities is justifiable. The experience of Jonestown clearly illustrates the necessity for liberal theory to be able to call some experiments pathological. For if a central goal of liberalism in our time is the expansion of the social, the liberal theorist must be able to judge whether certain new forms are instances of attempts to form new communities or instead new institutions of oppression. If some liberals are unable to recognize that any association that does not require the limited allegiance that one gives to say, a credit union, may be valuable, others are unable to distinguish between the practices of monasterial retreat and the brutality and insanity of the Peoples' Temple. It will not do, for instance to argue that the differences between "deviant" and "variant" behavior is simply a question of whose "prevailing mores" are in question, that "communes in which children are allowed access

to the sexual and drug-taking practices of their parents . . . might
be viewed as 'abuse' in other contexts."[12] Toleration there must be,
even sympathy for new kinds of community. But while there will
always be cases in which there are disagreements over the kinds and
methods of restriction to be applied to new miniature societies
when they appear to be so insufferable as to require intervention,
certainly the liberal must be able to distinguish a convent from a
private concentration camp.

Most new invented communities in America do not attempt to
create whole new societies. They are, like the model of the craft of
quilting, makeshift inventions designed to provide temporary support for people. Left to themselves, these attempts at creating a
social space are peculiar forms of community in which the principle
of intimate anonymity suffices for communal bonds. Transitional
inventions disappear; supporting inventions change form or also
decline in use. One example we did not discuss, but which illustrates the potential of these types, is the crisis counseling center.
Suicide is the most direct and poignant response to the absence of
community. In the 1950s a suicide prevention center was opened in
Los Angeles, and soon the counseling function proliferated. General crisis centers appeared with twenty-four hour services. Specialization has flourished. There are now hotlines for drug abuse,
poison information, rumor control, and community services;
hotlines focus upon needs for special groups such as teen counseling, aid to the elderly (Boston's Rescue, Inc.), counseling for homo-
sexuals, victims of rape, child abuse. More commercially driven are
radio and cable television shows offering call in psychological
counseling. There is, of course, a dark side to this as to all invention.
Dial-a-Porn and hate group hotlines offer outlets and encourage-
ment to needs that might be best left alone.

Crisis counseling is clearly an inventive response to not only the
atomization process of a liberal society but also the inability of
professional institutions, both public and private, to meet communal needs. One study of the Los Angeles suicide prevention center
discovered that one-half of the people who used the service were
currently receiving traditional psychological treatment.[13] The telephone itself offers what some researchers have called an "equaliza-
tion of power" between client and counselor.[14] The caller is anonymous, can terminate the session whenever he or she chooses, can
avoid the gauntlet of passing the receptionist, and the inevitable

vulnerability of the face-to-face encounter with an authority figure. Of course some of these features may ultimately be necessary for resolving the problems of the caller, but the hotline provides an alternative to the impasse of enduring either continual private anguish or impersonal professional service.

But the unavoidable question here is how can this network of "strangers calling strangers" for help in dealing with the most personal problems avoid the paths traveled by so many American social inventions: absorption by the market (a pay-for-service hotline system), or absorption by the service state (requirements for licensing counselors and limiting the role of volunteers), or continued existence as an instant community that deals with only the most extreme consequences of atomization. Can this form of community become a generative invention in its own right or at least serve as a transitional or supporting institution for new forms of community? Only a few guidelines can be offered, and these are themselves fraught with obstacles.

Somehow the crisis center must create structures which transcend the initial pattern of intimate anonymity while still avoiding the Scylla and Charybdis of the market and the service state. A physical place for refuge is essential. As Jane Addams knew from her own efforts, the counseling center cannot be designed to be a home, but it can aspire to be a temporary refuge as well as an adjunct to one. Many centers have attempted to fulfill this objective. Most impressive in this regard are the efforts of groups that provide places of refuge for battered wives. In an attempt to avoid the route of professionalization of the counselor, this sort of helping activity must be aggressively democratized. Existing social groups, especially churches, can make consulting services a central role of the parishioner. Indirect funding is the only way social inventions can employ the resources of the service state without openly losing autonomy. Even this alternative creates problems. It is conceivable that helping activity can be subsidized in a democratic context by providing for tax deductions for service. Or it is possible to envision a large program for youth as an alternative to conscription. This alternative, however, raises problems which liberals should rightly fear: The nationalization of caring, even in the name of democracy, may serve to erode social space. Voluntary participation in helping activities could be employed as credits toward financing college or vocational education. No doubt all these possibilities create condi-

tions for the absorption of social invention. There will be questions
raised by professionals, mistakes by volunteers, as well as instances
of carelessness and sporadic service. But we must remember that
these problems already pervade existing institutions.

Most importantly the democratization of caring, while it shifts
the focus of the liberal agenda, nevertheless can draw upon the
repository of liberal theory. From J. S. Mill to John Dewey, liberals
have constructed theories of the role that democratic political participation plays in personal development. The possibilities for the
expansion of concrete qualities of empathy and concern offer the
liberal an equivalent theory in the social sphere.

Finally, there is the necessity for de-inventing political and economic institutions in order to open up space for the invention of
social institutions. We have discussed the attempts to de-invent the
penitentiary and the problems raised by this effort. Yet concerted
reform group activity can employ America's unique social and economic structure to successfully challenge the hegemony of political
and economic institutions. The key to any effort of this kind, however, is to simultaneously offer new social institutions to take the
place of that targeted for de-invention. The opponents of the penitentiary have faced especially difficult problems in this regard. But
without social invention, opposition becomes part of the perpetual
dialectic that so afflicts American reform. Efforts to dismantle the
welfare state are made in the name of the superiority of market
incentives. Privatization benefits some groups and disadvantages
others. New initiatives are pressed, calling for public responsibility
for claims for universally recognized needs. Entitlement programs
are implemented only to be again challenged by those who wish to
experiment with market incentives. Throughout this process the
social sphere shrinks.

One successful example of de-invention, however, is the home-
birthing movement. The counterculturists of the 1960s had begun
to explore more "natural" methods of childbirth when newly
emerging feminist groups challenged the phenomenology of the
maternity ward of the hospital in works like *Our Bodies/Ourselves:*

> There we are separated at a crucial time from family and friends. We and
> our present children suffer from this sudden absence. In the hospital we
> are depersonalized; usually our clothes and personal effects, right down
> to glasses and hairpins, are taken away. We lose our identity. We are
> expected to be passive and acquiescent and to make no trouble. (Pas-

sivity is considered a sign of maturity). We are expected to depend not on ourselves but on doctors. Most often for the doctor's convenience, we are given drugs to "ease" our labor. . . .[15]

Nancy Stroller Shaw in her aptly named book *Forced Labor* concluded that the reason women are "isolated, stripped, emptied, drugged, immoblized, and 'delivered'" is because the organizational goals of the hospital directly conflict with the needs of the pregnant woman and her family.[16] Some historians argue that the dramatic shift to hospital births in this century represented more the dominance of a male medical profession than a triumph of reason.[17]

Women began to have babies at home; midwifery rose as a new underground profession. Home-birth manuals attempted to transfer what had come to be specialized knowledge to women at large. An early effort in this regard was Patricia Carter's *Come Gently, Sweet Lucinda,* partly an autobiographical account of home birth, which borrowed from delivery tests intended for students and policeman and offered a do-it-yourself approach.[18] The vocabulary of childbirth was consciously altered. Babies were not delivered but "caught."

In 1969 Lester Hazell in *Commonsense Childbirth* recommended the invention of what he called "maternity motels" as an alternative to hospital deliveries.[19] The analogy is especially intriguing in light of our discussion in chapter 5. In offering the idea of the maternity motel, Hazell echoed some of the same reasons for abandoning the formality of the hospital as had been used to criticize the hotel in the 1920s. He envisioned a team of midwives, doctors and volunteers who would become acquainted not only with the mother but the husband and present children. The maternity motel would contain a restaurant, cocktail lounge, game room. After a birth a family would stay the night or weekend.

Maternity motels do not now dot our landscape, but the home-birthing critiques, along with associated movements such as those led by Fernand Lamaze, Elizabeth Bing, and Frederick Leboyer, did reach the hearts and minds of the vast American middle class. Many hospitals now do have "birthing rooms" constructed very much along the lines of the maternity motel; Lamaze classes are regularly offered by hospital staff; midwives are recognized by the American College of Obstetrics and Gynecologists. Is the hospital now "hu-

manized"? Certainly not, but in one small area the old maternity
ward is being de-invented and enriched by those with a social vision. Other political and economic institutions have even stronger
imperatives and are even more deeply entrenched than that in this
example. But as invention always implies de-invention, social
spheres now contracted can be expanded.

One should not expect nor should one hope that liberalism alter
its basic beliefs. These beliefs admit of a great number of variations,
some of which are historically untried. Nor should one expect that
liberalism will not always have a preference for social institutions
that are loosely joined and limited in scope. But liberals must develop a philosophy that is truly social as well as one which recognizes
the inventive capacities of men and women. They must learn that a
world that has an expanded social element is not one which restricts
individual vision and fosters what John Stuart Mill called "ape-like
imitation." A world rich in sociability need not be a static and
insulated place, as so many conservatives implicitly assume. On the
contrary, it can be a world of proliferating social inventions, a world
which sees what Jean Bethke Elshtain has called a "redemption of
everyday life," a world which truly encourages a utopian spirit of
association.[20]

Notes

Chapter 1

1. See George Kateb, *Utopia and Its Enemies* (New York, 1963), and Barbara Goodwin and Keith Taylor, *The Politics of Utopia: A Study of Theory and Practice* (New York, 1982) for defenses of this tradition.

2. Robert Nozick, *Anarchy, State and Utopia* (New York, 1974), 19.

3. See, for instance, John Kenneth Galbraith, *Economics and the Public Purpose* (New York, 1973). Galbraith has now moved to an overtly socialist perspective, but his position on this question remains the same.

4. Ivan Illich, *Deschooling Society* (New York, 1971), *Toward a History of Needs* (New York, 1977).

5. Wendell Berry, *The Unsettling of America: Culture and Agriculture* (New York, 1978); Lawrence Goodwin, "Organizing Democracy," *Democracy* (Jan., 1981), 41–60.

6. Harry Boyte, *The Backyard Revolution* (Philadelphia, 1980); Jeremy Rifkin, *The Emerging Order* (New York, 1979). For discussions of Boyte and Rifkin, see chs. 6 and 7.

7. Hannah Arendt, *On Revolution* (New York, 1965).

8. Robert Nisbet, *The Twilight of Authority* (New York, 1975), 279.

9. Edmund Burke, "Reflections on the French Revolution," in *The Collected Works of Edmund Burke*, II (London, 1854), 366.

10. Arthur Bestor, Jr., "Patent-Office Models of the Good Society," *American Historical Review* 58 (April 1953), 505–26.

11. Nisbet, *Twilight of Authority*, 280.

12. See Vivian Gornick's *The Romance of American Communism* (New York, 1977).

13. Cited in Ernst Nolte, *Three Faces of Fascism* (New York, 1963), 382.

14. See Michael Walzer, *Radical Principles* (New York, 1980). Walzer insists the welfare state is a liberal invention.

15. Irving Kristol, "On Corporate Capitalism in America," in *The*

American Commonwealth, ed. Nathan Glazer and Irving Kristol (New York, 1976), 125.

16. Ibid., 140.

17. Robert Dahl, *After the Revolution: Authority in the Good Society* (New Haven, 1970), 116.

18. Michael Novack, *The Spirit of Democratic Capitalism* (New York, 1982); George Gilder, *Wealth and Poverty* (New York, 1981).

19. Robert Dahl, *Modern Political Analysis,* 4th ed. (Englewood Cliffs, N.J., 1984), 130.

20. John Rawls, *A Theory of Justice* (Cambridge, Mass., 1971), 521.

21. Ibid., 522.

22. Ibid., 528.

23. Ibid.

24. Ibid.

25. Nozick, *Anarchy,* 314.

26. Ibid., 302.

27. Alexis de Tocqueville, *Democracy in America,* ed. J. P. Mayer (Garden City, N.Y., 1969), 507.

28. Ibid., 691–92.

29. David Truman, *The Governmental Process* (New York, 1970), 51–52.

30. Robert Dahl, *After the Revolution,* 12.

31. John H. Schaar, "The Case for Patriotism," *New American Review* 17 (1973)—also see citations below; Wilson Carey McWilliams, *The Idea of Fraternity in America* (Berkeley, Calif., 1973); Christopher Lasch, *The Culture of Narcissism* (New York, 1978).

32. Schaar, "The Circles of Watergate Hell," *New American Review* 21 (1974), 38.

33. Lasch, *The Culture of Narcissism,* 50.

34. John H. Schaar, "Power and Purity," *New American Review* 19 (1974), 121.

Chapter 2

1. Henry M. Boettinger, *The Telephone Book* (New York, 1976).

2. David A. Hounshell, "Elisha Grey and the Telephone: On the Disadvantages of Being an Expert," *Technology and Culture* 16 (1975), 159.

3. Ithiel de Sola Pool, ed., *The Social Impact of the Telephone* (Cambridge, Mass., 1977), Appendix, 156.

4. Ibid.

5. Sidney H. Aronson, "Bell's Electrical Toy: What's the Use? The Sociology of Early Telephone Usage," in *Social Impact of the Telephone*, 22.

6. John E. Kingsbury, *The Telephone and Telephone Exchanges* (New York, 1972), 74.

7. American Telephone and Telegraph Co., *Events in Telephone History* (New York, 1971), 9, 14, 20.

8. For an account which emphasizes the European origins of the penitentiary, see Dario Melossi and Massimo Pavarini, *The Prison and the Factory* (Totowa, N.J., 1981).

9. Michael Foucault, *Discipline and Punish: The Birth of the Modern Prison* (New York, 1979), 37.

10. Negley K. Teeters, *The Cradle of the Penitentiary: The Walnut Street Jail at Philadelphia, 1773–1835* (Philadelphia, 1955), 27.

11. Benjamin Rush, *An Inquiry into the Effects of Public Punishments . . .* reprinted in *A Plan for the Punishment of Crime* (Philadelphia, 1954).

12. Ibid., 40.

13. Ibid., 42–43. Also see Harry Barnes, *Evolution of Penology in Pennsylvania* (Indianapolis, 1927) for reactions of contemporaries.

14. Nathan Goodman, *Benjamin Rush* (Philadelphia, 1934), 282.

15. Negley K. Teeters and John D. Shearer, *The Prison at Philadelphia, Cherry Hill* (New York, 1957).

16. Cited in W. David Lewis, *From Newgate to Dannemora: The Rise of the Penitentiary in New York, 1796–1840* (Ithaca, N.Y., 1965), 57.

17. Ibid., 69.

18. Ibid., 79.

19. Gustave de Beaumont and Alexis de Tocqueville, *On the Penitentiary System in the United States and Its Application to France* (1833), trans. Francis Lieber (Carbondale, Ill., 1964), 91.

20. Ibid., 79.

21. Melville Ferguson, *Motor Camping on Western Trails*, (New York, 1925), 271.

22. Warren Belasco, *Americans on the Road: From Autocamp to Motel, 1910–1945* (Cambridge, Mass., 1979), 46.

23. Ibid., 8–17.

24. Ibid., 117.

25. Earl May, "The Argonauts of the Automobile," *Saturday Evening Post*, August 9, 1924, p. 24.

26. Belasco, *Americans on the Road*, 115.

27. Clara Keyton, *Tourist Camp Pioneering* (Chicago, 1960).

28. Paul Lancaster, "The Great American Hotel," *American Heritage* (June–July, 1982), 100.

29. See M. Cerallo and Phyllis Ewen, "Having a Good Time: The American Family Goes Camping" *Radical America* 16, nos. 1 and 2 (1986), 13–44 is a shrill critique, but it does capture the phenomenology of the contemporary family vacation.

30. Benjamin Franklin, *Autobiography* (1790), ed. Russell Nye (Boston, 1958), 97.

31. William Ellery Channing, *Unitarian Christianity* (Baltimore, 1819).

32. *Autobiography of Rev. James B. Finnley* (Cincinnati, 1858), 287.

33. *Autobiography of Peter Cartwright, The Backwoods Preacher* (New York, 1856).

34. Charles A. Johnson, *The Frontier Camp Meeting* (Dallas, 1955), 51.

35. Ibid.

36. Finnley, *Autobiography*, 166.

37. Ibid., 167.

38. Ibid.

39. Cartwright, *Autobiography*.

40. Whitney Cross, *The Burned-Over District* (New York, 1950), 163.

41. Margaret Bayard Smith, *The First Forty Years of Washington Society* (New York, 1906), 158.

42. Thomas Hamilton, *Men and Manners in America* (New York, 1833). Also see the discussion in Winthrop Hudson, *Religion in America* (New York, 1981), 138–141.

43. *Memoirs of Charles G. Finney* (New York, 1876), 81. Compare this position to Finney's own conversion as an experience in expressive liberation (27–29).

44. Cross, *The Burned-Over District*, 158.

45. Ibid.

46. Finney, *Memoirs*, 90.

47. For the significance of the Great Revival for women see: Mary P. Ryan, "A Woman's Awakening: Evangelical Religion and the Families of Utica, New York, 1800–1840," in *Women in American Religion*, ed. Janet Wilson James (Philadelphia, 1980), 89–110; and Nancy F. Cott, "Young Women in the Second Great Awakening in New England," *Feminist Studies* (Fall 1975), 14–29.

48. E. M. Forster, "Mount Lebanon," in *Two Cheers for Democracy* (New York, 1938), 337–40.

49. Lenice Ingram Bacon, *American Patchwork Quilts* (New York, 1973), 25.

50. Jonathon Holstein, *The Pieced Quilt: An American Design Tradition* (Greenwich, Conn., 1973).

51. Patricia Cooper and Norma Bradley Buferd, *The Quilters: Women and Domestic Art* (Garden City, N.Y., 1977), 51.

52. Ibid.

53. Frances Lichten, *Folk Art of Rural Pennsylvania* (New York, 1946), 168.

54. Katherine Hall Travis, "Quilts of the Ozarks" *Southwest Review* (Jan. 1930), 239.

55. Cooper and Buferd, *The Quilters*, 154.

56. Ibid., 49.

57. Holstein, *The Pieced Quilt*, 84.

58. Herwin Schaefer, *Nineteenth Century Modern* (New York, 1970), 66.

59. Ibid.

60. Dorothy Seiberling, "A New Kind of Quilt," *New York Times Magazine*, Oct. 3, 1982, pp. 42–50.

61. Note the following explanation for this resurgence: "Tourism and travel have become a great industry. People are on the move. People want hobbies that go on trips with them. . . ." Alfred Allan Lewis, *The Mountain Artisans Quilting Book* (New York, 1973), ix. "Pioneering" continues, in new forms of course, but the problems of travel remain.

Chapter 3

1. Thomas Kuhn, *The Structure of Scientific Revolution* (Chicago, 1962).

2. Lewis, *From Newgate to Dannemora*, 70–76.

3. Louis B. Wright, *Everyday Life on the American Frontier* (New York, 1968).

4. Marilyn Lithgow, *Quiltmaking and Quiltmakers* (New York, 1974), 22.

5. Arthur Schlesinger, *The Rise of Modern America, 1905–1951* (New York, 1951), 66.

6. Eric Foner, *Tom Paine and Revolutionary America* (New York, 1976), 40.

7. Benjamin Franklin, *Autobiography and Other Writings* (Boston, 1958).

8. Ronald G. Walters, *American Reformers, 1815–1860* (New York, 1978), 33.

9. J. C. Stevens, "Tourist Court Organization," *Tourist Court Journal* (Aug. 1938), 25. Hotels had begun to formulate plans to imitate features of the motel. See: "How We Make Folks Like Small Hotels," *Hotel Manage-*

ment (Aug. 1932), 80–82; "How to Capitalize on the Current Craze for Miniature Golf," *Hotel Management* (Nov. 1930), 409–12.

10. Belasco, *Americans on the Road,* 170.

11. Lewis, *From Newgate to Dannemora,* 109.

12. Tocqueville and Beaumont, *On the Penitentiary System,* 130.

13. Lewis, *From Newgate to Dannemora,* 133.

14. Ibid.

15. Charles A. Johnson, *The Frontier Camp Meeting,* 57.

16. Cooper and Buferd, *The Quilters,* 140.

17. AT&T, *Events in Telephone History,* 8, 10.

18. For one account, see Robert O'Brien, *Marriot* (Salt Lake City, 1977), 224–30.

19. "Invisible Jail," *Detroit News* (Sept. 1982) 20. Over thirty states have new prisons planned or under construction supported in part by federal grants. Other linkages continue. A federal pilot project now permits private corporations to contract for prison labor, a practice that was once the bane of prison reformers. "The Nation's Prisoners Join the Labor Force," *New York Times,* Aug. 28, 1983, p. 6 F.

20. Richard H. Niebuhr, *The Social Sources of Denominationalism* (New York, 1929), 17.

Chapter 4

1. Edward A. Ackermann, *Geography as a Fundamental Research Discipline* (Chicago, 1958), 26; Jean Gottman, *Megalopolis* (New York, 1961).

2. Ithiel de Sola Pool et al., "Foresight and Hindsight: The Case of the Telephone," in *Social Impact of the Telephone,* 141.

3. P. W. Daniels, *Office Location* (London, 1975).

4. Cited in J. K. Mumford, "This Land of Opportunity: The Nerve Center of Business," *Harper's Weekly* 52, Aug. 1, 1908, p. 23.

5. Ronald Abler, "The Telephone and the Evolution of the American Metropolitan System," in *Social Impact of the Telephone,* 326.

6. Peter Cowan et al., *The Office* (London, 1975); Nicholas Johnson, *How to Talk Back to Your Television Set* (New York, 1970).

7. Suzanne Keller, "The Telephone in New (and Old) Communities," in *Social Uses of the Telephone,* 296.

8. John Brooks, *The Telephone: The First Hundred Years* (New York, 1975) 117.

9. *Understanding Media* (New York, 1962).

10. Should the telephone assume video capabilities, the instantaneous

demand may well intensify. The "ring" would require instant presentability.

11. "Sequencing in Conversational Openings," *American Anthropologist* 70 (1968), 1075–95.

12. "Latent Functions of the Telephone: What Missing Extension Means," in *Social Uses of the Telephone,* 246–61.

13. Ibid., 256. Also see Sidney Aronson's "The Sociology of the Telephone," *International Journal of Comparative Sociology* 12 (Sept. 1971), 153–67.

14. Norval Norris, *The Future of Imprisonment* (Chicago, 1974).

15. William G. Nagel, *The New Red Barn: A Critical Look at the Modern Prison* (New York, 1973).

16. U.S. Department of Justice, *Sourcebook of Criminal Justice Statistics* (Albany, N.Y., 1978).

17. Lewis, *From Newgate to Dannemora.*

18. Foucault, *Discipline and Punish,* 239.

19. Donald Clemmer, *The Prison Community* (Boston, 1940) was based upon a case study of the Illinois State Penitentiary at Menard. Gresham Sykes' *The Society of Captives* (Princeton, 1958) was an analysis of a New Jersey facility.

20. Jack Henry Abbott, *In the Belly of the Beast: Letters from Prison* (New York, 1981).

21. Even this position contains a cultural "loop." If prisons are unsuccessful, perhaps it is because supporting structures in society do not instill respect for authority and a sense of self-restraint. See James Q. Wilson for a current statement of this position. "Crime and American Culture," *Public Interest* (Winter, 1982).

22. James V. Bennet, *I Chose Prison,* (New York, 1970), 226.

23. Jessica Mitford, *Kind and Unusual Punishment. The Prison Business* (New York, 1973), 141.

24. Ibid.

25. Ibid., 147.

26. Edgar Schein, "Man Against Man: Brainwashing," *Corrective Psychiatry and the Journal of Social Change* 8, no. 4 (1962), 102.

27. Mitford, *Kind and Unusual Punishment,* 136.

28. James V. McConnell, "Criminals Can Be Brainwashed—Now," *Psychology Today* (April 1970), 10.

29. Robert Summer, *The End of Imprisonment* (New York, 1976).

30. David Fogel, *We Are the Living Proof: The Justice Model of Corrections* (Cincinnati, 1975).

31. Ibid.

32. Robert Martinson, "Restraint in the Community: A Modest Proposal," *Criminal Justice Newsletter* 24, Dec. 8, 1975, pp. 4–5. For an

extension of the surveillance model, see Lawrence W. Sherman, "Watching: New Directions for Police," *Journal of Contemporary Studies* 5 (Fall 1982), 87–101.

33. Walter Berns, *For Capital Punishment* (New York, 1979).

34. Ibid., 134.

35. Ibid.

36. Ibid.

37. Ernest van den Haag, *Punishing Criminals: A Very Old and Painful Question,* (New York, 1975).

38. William Matrias, Richard Rescorla, and Eugene Stephens, *Foundations of Criminal Justice,* (Englewood Cliffs, N.J., 1980), 539.

Chapter 5

1. Daniel Bell, *The Cultural Contradictions of Capitalism* (New York, 1976) 67.

2. Robert S. Lynd and Helen M. Lynd, *Middletown* (New York, 1929). The Lynds also speculated that the impact of an auto purchase on the family budget had important implications for group sanctions (254).

3. Norman Hayner, *Hotel Life* (Chapel Hill, N.C., 1936) 6.

4. Cited in David L. Lewis, "Sex and the Automobile" in David Lewis, ed., *The Automobile and American Culture* (Ann Arbor, Mich., 1980), 58.

5. *Tourist Court Journal* (Aug. 1939) 18.

6. Belasco, *Americans on the Road,* 97.

7. Melville Ferguson, *Motor Camping on Western Trails* (New York, 1925) 25.

8. Vladimir Nabokov, *Lolita* (New York, 1955), 147.

9. Ibid.

10. Harriet Beecher Stowe, *The Minister's Wooing* (Boston, n.d.).

11. Cooper and Buferd, *The Quilters,* 143.

12. Christiana Holmes Tillson, *A Woman's Story of Pioneer Illinois* (Chicago, 1919), 93.

13. Lithgow, *Quiltmaking and Quiltmakers,* 23.

14. Tillson, *A Woman's Story,* xv.

15. Hamlin Garland, *A Son of the Middle Border* (New York, 1914), 236–37.

16. Ibid., 238.

17. William Bradford, *Of Plymouth Plantation,* ed. Harvey Wish (New York, 1982) 214.

18. Cited in Richard Power, *Planting Corn Belt Culture* (Indianapolis, 1953), 49.

19. Eliza Farnham, *Life in Prairie Land* (New York, 1846), 100.

20. Merle Curti et al., *The Making of an American Community: A Case Study of Democracy in a Frontier County* (Stanford, Calif., 1959).

21. Richard Lingeman, *Small Town America* (Boston, 1980), 479.

22. Kathryne Hall Travis, "Quilts of the Ozarks," *Southwest Review* (Jan. 1930), 240–42.

Chapter 6

1. *The Autobiography of Peter Cartwright, The Backwoods Preacher* (New York, 1856), 51.

2. *Memoirs of Rev. Charles G. Finney,* 182.

3. Ibid., 78.

4. Ibid., 79.

5. On this point see John L. Hammond's careful analysis of voting patterns in his *The Politics of Benevolence* (Norwood, N.J., 1979). John B. Boles chronicles the failure of the revival to confront the slavery question in his *The Great Revival, 1787–1805* (Lexington, Ky, 1972). Also see the discussion in ch. 7.

6. Charles G. Finney, *Lectures on Revivals on Religion* (New York, 1935) 369.

7. Alice Felt Tyler, *Freedom's Ferment* (New York, 1944), 77.

8. Finnley, *Autobiography,* 372.; Edward Denning Andrews and Faith Andrews, *Work and Worship* (New York, 1974), 45. Also see a Shaker's own account in Charles Nordoff, *The Communistic Societies of the United States* (New York, 1975) 158–59.

9. Constance Noyes Robertson, *Oneida Community: An Autobiography, 1851–1876* (Syracuse, 1970), 3.

10. Nordhoff, *Communistic Societies of the United States,* 269.

11. Letter, Noyes to Dixon, March 1867, in Dixon, *Spiritual Wives,* II (London, 1868), 176–77.

12. Cited in Andrews and Andrews, *Work and Worship,* 28.

13. William Dean Howells, *Three Villages* (Boston, 1884), 110.

14. William Hepworth Dixon, *New America* (Philadelphia, 1867), pp. 304–5.

15. Noyes, "Confessions" in Dixon, *Spiritual Wives,* 36.

16. Ibid., 37.

17. John Humphrey Noyes, *Male Continence* (Oneida, 1872), 7.

18. Ibid.

19. Ibid., 8.

20. Ibid., 16.

21. Maren Lockwood Carden, *Oneida: Utopian Community to Modern Corporation* (Baltimore, 1969), 25–26.

22. Nordhoff, *Communistic Societies in the United States*, 286.

23. Ibid., 290–92.

24. Ibid., 292–93.

25. Ibid., 293.

26. Ibid., 232–33.

27. Ibid., 245.

28. John Humphrey Noyes, *Essay on Scientific Propagation* (Oneida, 1875), 2.

29. Carden, *Oneida*, p. 63. For members' accounts see: Allan Estalke, *The Oneida Community* (London, 1900); Robertson, *Oneida Community*, 335–55.

30. Dixon, *Spiritual Wives*, 184.

Chapter 7

1. George Gilder, *Wealth and Poverty* (New York, 1981), 30.

2. Ibid., 31.

3. Catherine Fennely, *Textiles in New England* (Sturbridge, Mass., 1961).

4. Michael Chevalier, *Society Manners, and Politics in the United States* (1836), ed. John William Ward (Garden City, N.Y., 1961), 131–32.

5. Ibid., 137.

6. Ibid., 140.

7. Lucy Larcom, *A New England Girlhood* (Boston, 1889), 154.

8. Herbert Guttman, *Work, Culture and Society* (New York, 1976), 29.

9. Larcom, *New England Girlhood*, 193.

10. Michigan Bell, *History of the Telephone in Michigan* (Detroit, 1970), 10.

11. Brenda Maddox, "Good Jobs for Girls," *Telecommunication Journal* (Dec. 1975), 710.

12. Elizabeth Faulkner Baker, *Technology and Women's Work* (New York, 1964), 70.

13. Charles H. Garland, "Women as Telegraphists," *Economic Journal* 11 (June 1901), 258–59.

14. Cited in Baker, *Technology and Women's Work*, 69.

15. Katherine Schmitt, "I Was your Old 'Hello Girl,'" *Saturday Evening Post*, July 12, 1930, p. 3.

16. Jack Burbash, *Unions and Telephones* (New York, 1952), 18.

17. Keith Swand, *The Legend of Henry Ford* (New York, 1948), 35.

18. Henry Ford, *My Life and Work* (Garden City, N.Y., 1922), 147.

19. Frank Marquart, *Auto Workers' Journal* (University Park, Pa., 1975), 13–14.

20. The following illustrate the inventive character of worker responses: Peter Friedlander, *The Emergence of a UAW Local, 1936–1939* (Pittsburgh, 1975); Claude Hoffman, *Sit-down in Anderson* (Detroit, 1968); Victor Reuther, *The Brothers Reuther* (Boston, 1976); Sidney Fine, *Sit-Down,* (Ann Arbor, Mich., 1969).

21. Emma Rothschild, *Paradise Lost: The Decline of the Auto-Industrial Age* (New York, 1973), 104.

22. Ibid., 112.

23. Stanley Aronowitz, *False Promises* (New York, 1973).

24. Georges Sorel, *The Illusion of Progress* (Berkeley, Calif., 1969).

25. This point is argued forcefully in Ira Katznelson's *City Trenches* (Chicago, 1981).

26. Larcom, *New England Girlhood,* 178.

27. Antonio Gramsci, "Americanism and Fordism," in *The Prison Notebooks* (New York, 1971).

28. Ibid., 285.

29. Ibid., 309–10.

30. Ibid., 304.

31. Robert Reich, *The Next American Frontier* (New York, 1983).

32. Daniel Bell, *The Coming of Post-Industrial Society* (New York, 1973), 165–265.

33. See: John Holusha, "The New Allure of Manufacturing," *New York Times,* Dec. 18, 1983, pp. 2, 30.

34. Timothy Smith, *Revivalism and Social Reform* (New York, 1957). Also see James Findlay, *Dwight L. Moody* (Chicago, 1969).

35. William McLoughlin, *Billy Sunday Was His Real Name* (Chicago, 1955).

36. William G. McLoughlin, *Revivals, Awakenings, and Reform* (Chicago, 1978), 153.

37. Ibid.

38. Richard Quebedeaux, *The New Charismatics* (Garden City, N.Y. 1976), 87.

39. Francis Fitzgerald, "A Disciplined Changing Army," *New Yorker,* May 18, 1981, p. 59.

40. Ibid., p. 52.

41. Robert Schuller, *Your Church Has Real Possibilities,* (Glendale, Calif., 1974); also see Lyle Schaller, *Assimilating New Members* (Nashville, 1978) for a frank discussion of evangelical strategy.

42. Peter L. Berger, "The Class Struggle in American Religion," *Christian Century,* Feb. 25, 1981, pp. 194–99.

43. George Gallup and David Poling, *The Search for America's Faith,* (Nashville, 1980), 134.

44. Kevin Phillips, *Post-Conservative America* (New York, 1981), 196–97.

45. Jeremy Rifkin, *The Emerging Order: God in an Age of Scarcity* (New York, 1979), 270.

46. McLoughlin, *Revivals, Awakenings,* 214.

47. Ibid.

48. Rifkin, *Emerging Order,* 103.

49. Richard Quebedeaux, *By What Authority: The Rise of Personality Cults in American Christianity* (New York, 1982), 75.

50. Thomas Wolfe, *Of Time and the River* (New York, 1935), 898.

51. Sherwood Anderson, *Poor White* (New York, 1974), 36.

52. Lewis Atherton, *Main Street on the Middle Border* (Chicago, 1966), 355.

53. In his study of Sudbury, Massachusetts, Sumner Chilton Powell is so impressed with the "inventive" character of the New England town that he asks: "How many men today, founding a 'godly plantation' on the moon or on any inhabitable planet, would make as many significant alterations in religion, in social organization, in local government, and in attitude and values generally?" *Puritan Village* (Middletown, Conn., 1963).

54. For example, see: Daniel Kramer, *Participatory Democracy* (Cambridge, Mass., 1972); Robert Paul Wolff, *In Defense of Anarchism* (New York, 1970).

55. Michael Zuckerman, *Peaceable Kingdoms: New England Towns in the Eighteenth Century* (New York, 1970), 94.

56. Ibid., 131. Janet Mansbridge has found that the town meeting is still devoted to this purpose. *Beyond Adversary Democracy* (Chicago, 1983).

57. Kenneth A. Lockridge, *A New England Town: The First Hundred Years* (New York, 1970), 125.

58. John Demos, "Developmental Perspectives on the History of Childhood," in *The Family in History,* ed. Theodore K. Rabb and Robert I. Rotberg. (New York, 1971), 127–39.

59. Mansbridge, *Adversary,* 74.

60. Zuckerman, *Peaceable Kingdoms,* 182.

61. James West, *Plainville, U.S.A.* (New York, 1945), 75–81.

62. Atherton, *Main Street,* 65.

63. Page Smith, *As a City Upon a Hill* (New York, 1966), 251.

64. *The Autobiography of William Allen White* (New York, 1946), 72–73.

65. Bruce Catton, *Waiting for the Morning Train* (Garden City, N.Y., 1972), 189.

66. William Maxwell, *Ancestors* (New York, 1971), 41.

67. "New England Reformers," in *Ralph Waldo Emerson* (New York, 1962), 144–47.

68. Ronald G. Walters, *American Reformers, 1815–1860* (New York, 1978), 80. Allen F. Davis, *Spearheads for Reform: The Social Settlements and the Progressive Movement, 1890–1914* (New York, 1967), 23–24.

69. Kirkpatrick Sale, *SDS* (New York, 1973), 175–76.

70. Jo Freeman, *The Politics of Women's Liberation* (New York, 1975), 123–24.

71. Luther B. Gerlach and Virginia Hine, *People, Power, Change: Movements of Social Transformation* (Indianapolis, 1970), 33.

72. Freeman, *Women's Liberation,* 123–24.

73. James Q. Wilson, *Political Organizations* (New York, 1973), 47.

74. Aileen S. Kraditor, *Means and Ends in American Abolitionism* (New York, 1967), 261.

75. Christopher Lasch, ed., *The Social Thought of Jane Addams* (Indianapolis, 1965), 38.

76. "Port Huron Statement," in *Reflections in American Political Thought,* ed. Philip Abbott and Michael P. Riccards (New York, 1973), 266–67.

77. June Arnold, "Consciousness Raising," in *Women's Liberation,* ed. Sookie Stambler (New York, 1970), 155–56.

78. Marge Piercy, "The Grand Coolie Dam," in *Sisterhood is Powerful* (New York, 1970).

79. Time as a political resource is discussed in Mansbridge, *Beyond Adversary Democracy,* 186–89; Robert Dahl, *After the Revolution,* (New Haven, Conn., 1970); Michael Walzer, "A Day in the Life of a Socialist Citizen," *Dissent* (May–June 1968).

80. In this sense, the commune which we discussed in ch. 5 represents an abdication to incestual desire. Of course the problem for the communards still remains, although in different form.

81. Stanley Elkins, *Slavery* (Chicago, 1959), 28.

82. Tom Hayden, *The Trial* (New York, 1970), 161–63.

83. Tom Hayden, *The American Future* (Boston, 1980), 184.

84. Ibid., 24.

85. Ibid., 237.

86. Ibid., 82.

87. Ibid., 300.

88. Harry Boyte, *The Backyard Revolution* (Philadelphia, 1980).

89. Ibid., 186.

90. Ibid., 38.

91. There is also the problem that leftist organizers do not sincerely

accept the agenda of the groups themselves. There are, in fact, traces of a "united front" morality in Boyte's own work (see 204–7).

92. Michael Walzer, *Radical Principles,* 182.

93. Ibid.

Chapter 8

1. George A. Hillery, Jr., "Definition of Community: Some Areas of Agreement," *Rural Sociology* (1955), 111–23. Also see Carl J. Friedrich, "The Concept of Community in the History of Political and Legal Philosophy" in *Community: NomosII,* ed. Carl J. Friedrich (New York, 1959), 3–24, for a masterful discussion of the strains in definitions in community.

2. Emile Durkheim, *Division of Labor in Society* (Glencoe, Il., 1964), 27.

3. Erving Goffman, *The Presentation of the Self in Everyday Life* (Garden City, N.Y., 1959), 112 ff.

4. Israel Rubin, "Function and Structure of Community: Conceptual and Theoretical Analysis," *International Review of Community Development* (1969), 118.

5. Sheila B. Kamerman and Alfred J. Kahn, *Family Benefits and Working Parents: A Study in Comparative Policy* (New York, 1981), 251.

6. Elizabeth Jones and Elizabeth Prescott, "Day Care: Short or Long-Term, Solution?" *The Annals of the American Academy of Political and Social Science* 461 (May 1982), 91–101.

7. Ibid., 95.

8. Z. I. Giraldo, *Public Policy and the Family* (New York, 1980), 210.

9. Ernice C. Watson and Alice H. Collins, *Natural Helping Networks* (Washington, D.C., 1976), 18.

10. Thomas Robbins, "Cults and the Therapeutic State," *Social Policy* (May–June 1979), 45. Also see Harvey Cox's introduction to David Bromley and Anson Shupe, *Strange Gods* (Boston, 1981), xi–xv.

11. Donald L. Drakeman, "Cult Members: Converts or Criminals?" *The Christian Century,* Feb. 15, 1984, p. 165.

12. Teresa D. Marciano, "Variant Family Forms in a World Perspective" *Family Coordinator* 24, Oct. 24, 1975, 409–10. For a discussion of the inability to distinguish the pathological from the desirable in social forms see my *The Family on Trial* (University Park, Penn., 1981), 149–53.

13. See: S. A. Husain and Trish Vandiver, eds., *Suicide in Children and Adolescents* (New York, 1984), 166.

14. P. Nathan, S. Smith and A. Rossi, "Experimental Analysis of a Brief Psycho Therapeutic Encounter," *American Journal of Orthopychiatry* 38 (1908), 482–492.

15. Boston Women's Collective, *Our Bodies, Ourselves* (New York, 1973), 243.

16. Nancy Stroller Shaw, *Forced Labor* (Elmsford, N.J., 1974), 134.

17. Mary P. Ryan, *Womanhood in America* (New York, 1975), 186.

18. Autobiographical accounts function as a source of legitimatation for de-invention. *Come Gently, Sweet Lucinda* was self-published. Also see: Donald Sutherland, "Childbirth is Not for Mothers Only," *Ms.* (May 1974); Barbara Grizutti Harrison, "Men Don't Know Nothin' 'Bout Birth-in' Babies" *Esquire* (July 1973); Marjorie Karmel, *Thank You, Dr. Lamaze* (Philadelphia, 1959).

19. Lester D. Hazell, *Commonsense Childbirth* (New York, 1959).

20. Jean Bethke Elshtain, *Public Man, Private Woman* (Princeton, N.J., 1981), 333; also see Michael Walzer's treatment of the social in *Spheres of Justice* (New York, 1983).

Bibliography

Abbott, Jack Henry. *In the Belly of the Beast: Letters from Prison.* New York: Random House, 1981.

Abbott, Philip. *The Family on Trial.* University Park: Pennsylvania State Univ. Press, 1981.

———. *Furious Fancies: American Political Thought in the Post Liberal Era.* Westport, Conn.: Greenwood Press, 1980.

Abbott, Philip, and Riccards, Michael P., eds. *Reflections in American Political Thought.* New York: Chandler Publishing Co., 1973.

Ackermann, Edward A. *Geography as a Fundamental Research Discipline.* Chicago: Univ. of Chicago Press, 1958.

American Telephone and Telegraph Co. *Events in Telephone History.* New York: AT&T, 1971.

Anderson, Sherwood. *Poor White.* New York: Viking Press, 1974.

Andrews, Edward Denning, and Andrews, Faith. *Work and Worship.* New York, New York Graphic Society, 1974.

Arendt, Hannah. *On Revolution.* New York: Viking Press, 1965.

Aronowitz, Stanley. *False Promises.* New York: McGraw-Hill, 1973.

Aronson, Sidney. "The Sociology of the Telephone." *International Journal of Comparative Sociology* 12 (Sept. 1971).

Atherton, Lewis. *Main Street on the Middle Border.* Chicago: Quadrangle Books, 1966.

Bacon, Lenice Ingram. *American Patchwork Quilts.* New York: William Morrow, 1973.

Baker, Elizabeth Faulkner. *Technology and Women's Work.* New York: Columbia Univ. Press, 1964.

Barbash, Jack. *Unions and Telephones.* New York: Harper & Row, 1952.

Barnes, Harry Elmer. *The Evolution of Penology in Pennsylvania.* Montclair, N.J.: Patterson Smith, 1927.

de Beaumont, Gustave, and de Tocqueville, Alexis. *On the Penitentiary System in the United States and Its Application to France (1833)* Carbondale: Univ. of Illinois Press, 1964.

Belasco, Warren. *Americans on the Road: From Autocamp to Motel, 1910–1945*. Cambridge, Mass.: MIT, 1979.

Bell, Daniel. *The Coming of Post-Indusrial Society*. New York: Basic Books, 1973.

―――. *The Cultural Contradictions of Capitalism*. New York: Basic Books, 1976.

Bennet, James V. *I Chose Prison*. New York: Knopf, 1970.

Berger, Peter L. "The Class Struggle in American Religion." *Christian Century*, Feb. 25, 1981.

Berns, Walter. *For Capital Punishment*. New York: Basic Books, 1979.

Berry, Wendell. *The Unsettling of America: Culture and Agriculture*. San Francisco: Sierra Books, 1977.

Bestor, Arthur Jr. "Patent-Office Models of the Good Society." *American Historical Review* 58 (April 1953).

Boettinger, Henry. *The Telephone Book*. New York: Harper & Row, 1976.

Boles, John B. *The Great Revival, 1787–1805*. Lexington: Univ. Press of Kentucky, 1972.

Boston Women's Collective. *Our Bodies, Ourselves*. New York: Simon & Schuster, 1973.

Boyte, Harry. *The Backyard Revolution*. Philadelphia: Temple Univ. Press, 1980.

Bradford, William. *Of Plymouth Plantation*. Ed. Harvey Wish. New York: Charles Scribner's Sons, 1982.

Bromley, David, and Shupe, Anson. *Strange Gods*. Boston: Beacon Press, 1981.

Burke, Edmund. "Reflections on the French Revolution." in *The Collected Works of Edmund Burke*. London: J. M. Dent & Sons Ltd., 1854.

Carden, Maren Lockwood. *Oneida: Utopian Community to Modern Corporation*. Baltimore: Johns Hopkins Univ. Press, 1969.

Cartwright, Peter. *Autobiography of Peter Cartwright, the Backwoods Preacher*. New York: Carlton & Porter, 1856.

Catton, Bruce. *Waiting for the Morning Train*. Garden City, N.Y.: Doubleday, 1972.

Cerallo, M., and Ewen, Phyllis. "Having a Good Time: The American Family Goes Camping." *Radical America* 16 (1968).

Channing, William Ellery. *Unitarian Christianity and Other Essays*. New York: Liberal Arts Press, 1957.

Chevalier, Michael. *Society, Manners and Politics in the United States*. Ed. John William Ward. Garden City, N.Y.: Doubleday, 1961.

Clemmer, Donald. *The Prison Community*. Boston: The Christopher Publishing House, 1940.

Cooper, Patricia and Buferd, Norma Bradley. *The Quilters: Women and Domestic Art*. Garden City: Doubleday, 1977.

Coser, Lewis. *Greedy Institutions*. New York: Free Press, 1974.

Cott, Nancy F. "Young Women in the Second Great Awakening in New England." *Feminist Studies* (Fall 1975).

Cowan, Peter. *The Office*. London: Heinemann Educational Books, 1975.

Cross, Whitney. *The Burned-Over District*. New York: Harper & Row, 1950.

Curti, Merle, et al. *The Making of an American Community: A Case Study of Democracy in a Frontier County*. Stanford, Calif.: Stanford Univ. Press, 1959.

Dahl, Robert. *After the Revolution*. New Haven: Yale Univ. Press, 1970.

———. *Modern Political Analysis*. Englewood Cliffs, N.J.: Prentice-Hall, 1984.

Daniels, P. W. *Office Location*. London: Bell & Sims, 1975.

Davis, Allen F. *Spearheads for Reform: the Social Settlements and the Progressive Movement, 1890–1914*. New York: Oxford Univ. Press, 1967.

Dixon, William Hepworth. *New America*. Philadelphia: Lippincott, 1867.

———. *Spiritual Wives*. Vol. II. London: Hurst & Blackett, 1868.

Drakeman, Donald R. "Cult Members: Converts or Criminals." *The Christian Century*, Feb. 15, 1984.

Durkheim, Emile. *Division of Labor in Society*. Glencoe, Ill.: Free Press, 1964.

Elkins, Stanley. *Slavery*. Chicago: Univ. of Chicago Press, 1959.

Elshtain, Jean Bethke. *Public Man, Private Woman: Women in Social and Political Thought*. Princeton: Princeton Univ. Press, 1981.

Emerson, Ralph Waldo. *Ralph Waldo Emerson: Selected Prose and Poetry*. Ed. Reginald Cook. New York: Holt, Rinehart & Winston, 1962.

Estlake, Allan. *The Oneida Community*. London: Redway, 1900.

Farnham, Eliza. *Life in Prairie Land*. New York: Harper & Brothers, 1846.

Fennely, Catherine. *Textiles in New England*. Sturbridge, Mass.: Old Sturbridge Village, 1961.

Ferguson, Melville. *Motor Camping on Western Trails*. New York: Century, 1925.

Findlay, James. *Dwight L. Moody*. Chicago: Univ. of Chicago Press, 1969.

Fine, Sidney. *Sit-down*. Ann Arbor: Univ. of Michigan Press, 1969.

Finney, Charles G. *Lectures on Revivals of Religion*. New York: Cambridge-Belknap Press of Harvard Univ. Press, 1960.

———. *Memoirs of Charles G. Finney*. New York: F. H. Revell, 1876.

Finnley, James B. *Autobiography of Reverend James B. Finnley*. Cincinnati: Cranston and Curts, 1858.

Fitzgerald, Francis. "A Disciplined Changing Army." *New Yorker*, May 18, 1981.

Fogel, David. *We Are the Living Proof: The Justice Model of Corrections.* Cincinnati: Anderson Publishing Co., 1975.

Foner, Eric. *Tom Paine and Revolutionary America.* New York: Oxford Univ. Press, 1976.

Ford, Henry. *My Life and Work.* Garden City, N.Y.: Doubleday, 1922.

Forster, E. M. "Mount Lebanon." In *Two Cheers for Democracy.* New York: Harcourt Brace, 1951.

Foucault, Michael. *Discipline and Punish: The Birth of the Modern Prison.* New York: Vintage Press, 1979.

Franklin, Benjamin. *Autobiography.* Ed. Russell Nye. Boston: Houghton Mifflin Co., 1958.

Freeman, Jo. *The Politics of Women's Liberation.* New York: David McKay, 1975.

Friedlander, Peter. *The Emergence of a UAW Local, 1936–1939.* Pittsburgh: Univ. Of Pittsburgh Press, 1975.

Friedrich, Carl J., ed. *Community.* New York: Liberal Arts Press, 1959.

Galbraith, John Kenneth. *Economics and the Public Purpose.* New York: New American Library, 1973.

Gallup, George, and Poling, David. *The Search for America's Faith.* Nashville: Abingdon, 1980.

Garland, Charles. "Women as Telegraphists." *Economic Journal* 11 (June 1901).

Garland, Hamlin. *A Son of the Middle Border.* New York: Grosset & Dunlop, 1914.

Gerlach, Luther B., and Hine, Virginia. *People, Power, Change: Movements of Social Transformation.* Indianapolis: Bobbs-Merrill Co., 1970.

Gilder, George. *Wealth and Poverty.* New York: Basic Books, 1981.

Giraldo, Z. I. *Public Policy and the Family.* Lexington, Mass.: Lexington Books, 1980.

Goffman, Erving. *The Presentation of the Self in Everyday Life.* Garden City, N.Y.: Doubleday, 1959.

Goodman, Nathan. *Benjamin Rush.* Philadelphia: Univ. of Pennsylvania Press, 1934.

Goodwin, Barbara, and Taylor, Keith. *The Politics of Utopia, A Study of Theory and Practice.* New York: St. Martins Press, 1982.

Goodwin, Lawrence. "Organizing Democracy." *Democracy* (Jan. 1981).

Gornick, Vivian. *The Romance of American Communism.* New York: Basic Books, 1977.

Gottman, Jean. *Megalopolis.* New York: Twentieth Century Fund, 1961.

Gramsci, Antonio. *The Prison Notebooks.* New York: Harper & Row, 1971.

Guttman, Herbert. *Work, Culture and Society.* New York: Knopf, 1976.

Hamilton, Thomas. *Men and Manners in America*. New York: Russell & Russell, 1968.

Hammond, John L. *The Politics of Benevolence*. Norwood, N.J.: Ablex Publications, 1979.

Harrison, Barbara Grizutti. "Men Don't Know Nothing 'Bout Birthin' Babies." *Esquire* (July 1973).

Hayner, Norman. *Hotel Life*. Chapel Hill: Univ. of North Carolina Press, 1936.

Hazell, Lester. *Commonsense Childbirth*. New York: G. P. Putnam's Sons, 1959.

Hillery, George A., Jr. "Definition of Community: Some Areas of Agreement." *Rural Sociology* (1955).

Hoffman, Claude. *Sit-down in Anderson*. Detroit: Wayne State Univ. Press, 1968.

Holstein, Jonathon. *The Pieced Quilt: An American Design Tradition*. Greenwich, Conn.: New York Graphic Society, 1973.

Holusha, John. "The New Allure of Manufacturing." *New York Times*, Dec. 18, 1983.

Hounshell, David A. "Elisha Grey and the Telephone: On the Disadvantage of Being an Expert." *Technology and Culture* 16 (1975).

Howells, William Dean. *Three Villages*. Boston: J. R. Osgood & Co., 1884.

Hudson, Winthrop. *Religion in America*. New York: Charles Scribner's Sons, 1981.

Husain, S. A., and Vandiver, Trish. eds. *Suicide in Children and Adolescents*. New York: S. P. Medical and Scientific Books, 1984.

Illich, Ivan. *Deschooling Society*. New York: Harper & Row, 1971.

James, Janet Wilson. *Women in American Religion*. Philadelphia: Univ. of Pennsylvania Press, 1980.

Johnson, Charles A. *The Frontier Camp Meeting*. Dallas: Southern Methodist Univ. Press, 1955.

Johnson, Nicholas. *How To Talk Back to Your Television Set*. New York: Little, Brown, 1970.

Jones, Elizabeth, and Prescott, Elizabeth. "Day Care: Short or Long Term Solution?" *The Annals of the American Academy of Political and Social Science* 461 (May 1982).

Kamerman, Sheila, and Kahn, Alfred J. *Family Benefits and Working Parents: A Study in Comparative Policy*. New York: Columbia Univ. Press, 1981.

Karmel, Marjorie. *Thank You, Dr. Lamaze*. Philadelphia: J. B. Lippincott Co., 1959.

Kateb, George. *Utopia and Its Enemies*. New York: Free Press of Glencoe, 1963.

Katznelson, Ira. *City Trenches*. Chicago: Univ. of Chicago Press, 1981.

Keyton, Clara. *Tourist Camp Pioneering*. Chicago: Adams Press, 1960.

Kingsbury, John E. *The Telephone and Telephone Exchanges*. New York: Arno Press, 1972.

Kraditor, Aileen S. *Means and Ends in American Abolitionism*. New York: Vintage Books, 1967.

Kramer, Daniel. *Participatory Democracy*. Cambridge, Mass.: Schenkman Publishing Co., 1972.

Kristol, Irving. "On Corporate Capitalism in America." In *The American Commonwealth*. Ed. Nathan Glazer and Irving Kristol. New York: Basic Books, 1976.

Kuhn, Thomas. *The Structure of Scientific Revolutions*. Chicago: Univ. of Chicago Press, 1962.

Lancaster, Paul. "The Great American Hotel." *American Heritage* (June–July 1982).

Larcom, Lucy. *A New England Girlhood*. Boston: Houghton-Mifflin Co., 1889.

Lasch, Christopher. *The Culture of Narcissism*. New York: W. W. Norton Co., 1978.

Lasch, Christopher, ed. *The Social Thought of Jane Addams*. Indianapolis: Bobbs-Merrill Co., 1965.

Lewis, Alfred Allan. *The Mountain Artisans Quilting Book*. New York: Macmillan, 1973.

Lewis, W. David. *From Newgate to Dannemora: The Rise of the Penitentiary in New York, 1796–1840*. Ithaca: Cornell Univ. Press, 1965.

Lichten, Francis. *Folk Art of Rural Pennsylvania*. Charles Scribner's Sons, 1946.

Lingeman, Richard. *Small Town America*. Boston: Houghton-Mifflin Co., 1980.

Lithgow, Marilyn. *Quiltmaking and Quiltmakers*. New York: Funk & Wagnalls, 1974.

Lockridge, Kenneth A. *A New England Town: The First Hundred Years*. New York: W. W. Norton Co., 1970.

Lynd, Robert S. and Lynd, Helen M. *Middletown*. New York: Harcourt Brace, 1929.

McConnell, James V. "Criminals Can Be Brainwashed Now." *Psychology Today* (April 1970).

McLoughlin, William. *Billy Sunday Was His Real Name*. Chicago: Univ. of Chicago Press, 1955.

———. *Revivals, Awakenings and Reform*. Chicago: Univ. of Chicago, 1978.

McWilliams, Wilson Carey. *The Idea of Fraternity in America*. Berkeley: Univ. of California Press, 1973.

Maddox, Brenda. "Good Jobs for Girls." *Telecommunicator Journal* (Dec. 1975).

Mansbridge, Janet. *Beyond Adversary Democracy.* Chicago: Univ. of Chicago Press 1983.

Marciano, Teresa. "Variant Family Forms in a World Perspective." *Family Coordinator* 24, Oct. 24, 1975.

Marquart, Frank. *Auto Worker's Journal.* University Park: Penn State Univ. Press, 1975.

Martinson, Robert. "Restraint in the Community: A Modest Proposal." *Criminal Justice Newsletter* 24, Dec. 8, 1975.

Matrias, William; Rescorla, Richard; and Stephens, Eugene. *Foundations of Criminal Justice.* Englewood Cliffs: Prentice-Hall, 1980.

Maxwell, William. *Ancestors.* New York: Alfred A. Knopf, 1971.

May, Earl. "The Argonauts of the Automobile." *Saturday Evening Post,* Aug. 9, 1924.

Melossi, Dario, and Pavarini, Massimo. *The Prison and the Factory.* Totawa, N.J.: Roman and Littlefield, 1981.

Michigan Bell. *History of the Telephone in Michigan.* Detroit: Michigan Bell, 1970.

Mitford, Jessica. *Kind and Unusual Punishment: The Prison Business.* New York: Vintage Books, 1973.

Mumford, J. K. "This Land of Opportunity: The Nerve Center of Business." *Harper's Weekly* 52, Aug. 1, 1908.

Nabokov, Vladimir. *Lolita.* New York: Putnam, 1955.

Nagel, William G. *The New Red Barn: A Critical Look at the Modern Prison.* New York: Walker and Co., 1973.

Nathan, P., Smith, S., and Rossi, A. "Experimental Analysis of a Brief Psycho Therapeutic Encounter." *American Journal of Orthopsychiatry* 38 (1968).

Niebuhr, Richard H. *The Social Sources of Denominationalism.* New York: Meridian Books, 1929.

Nisbet, Robert. *The Twilight of Authority.* New York: Oxford Univ. Press, 1975.

Nolte, Ernst. *Three Faces of Communism.* New York: Holt, Rinehart & Winston, 1963.

Nordhoff, Charles. *The Communistic Societies of the United States.* New York: Hillary House, 1975.

Norris, Norval. *The Future of Imprisonment.* Chicago: Univ. of Chicago Press, 1974.

Novak, Michael. *The Spirit of Democratic Capitalism.* New York: Simon & Schuster, 1982.

Noyes, John Humphrey. *Male Continence.* Oneida: AMS Press, 1974.

Nozick, Robert. *Anarchy, State and Utopia.* New York: Basic Books, 1974.

O'Brien, Robert. *Marriot.* Salt Lake City: Deseret Book Company, 1977.

Phillips, Kevin. *Post-Conservative America.* New York: Random House, 1981.

Pool, Ithiel de Sola., ed. *The Social Impact of the Telephone.* Cambridge: MIT Press, 1977. ·

Powell, Summer Chilton. *Puritan Village.* Middletown Conn.: Wesleyan Univ. Press, 1963.

Power, Richard. *Planting Corn Belt Culture.* Indianapolis: Bobbs-Merrill Co., 1953.

Quebedeaux, Richard. *By What Authority: The Rise of Personality Cults in American Christianity.* San Francisco: Harper & Row, 1982.

———. *The New Charismatics.* Garden City: Doubleday, 1976.

Rabb, Theodore, and Rotberg, Robert I., eds. *The Family in History.* New York: Harper & Row, 1971.

Rawls, John. *A Theory of Justice.* Cambridge, Mass: Harvard Univ. Press, 1971.

Reich, Robert. *The Next American Frontier.* New York: New York Times Books, 1983.

Reuther, Victor. *The Brothers Reuther.* Boston: Houghton-Mifflin Co., 1976.

Rifkin, Jeremy. *The Emerging Order: God in an Age of Scarcity.* G. P. Putnam's Sons, 1979.

Robbins, Thomas. "Cults and the Therapeutic State." *Social Policy* (May– June 1979).

Robertson, Constance Noyes. *Oneida Community: An Autobiography, 1851–1876.* Syracuse: Syracuse Univ. Press, 1970.

Rothschild, Emma. *Paradise Lost: The Decline of the Auto-Industrial Age.* New York: Random House, 1973.

Rubin, Israel. "Function and Structure of Community: Conceptual and Theoretical Analysis." *International Review of Community Development* (1969).

Ryan, Mary P. *Womanhood in America.* New York: New Viewpoints, 1975.

Sale, Kirkpatrick, *SDS.* New York: Vintage Books, 1973.

Schaar, John H. "The Case for Patriotism." *New American Review* 17 (1973).

———. "Power and Purity." *New American Review* 19 (1974).

Schein, Edgar, "Man Against Man: Brainwashing." *Corrective Psychiatry and the Journal of Social Change* 8 (Nov. 1962).

Schesloff, Emmanuel. "Sequencing in Conversational Opening." *American Anthropologist* 70 (1968).

Schlesinger, Arthur, *The Rise of Modern America 1905–1951*. New York: Macmillan Publishing Co., 1951.

Schmitt, Katherine. "I Was Your Old 'Hello Girl.'" *Saturday Evening Post*, July 12, 1930.

Schuller, Robert. *Your Church Has Real Possibilities*. Glendale Calif.: G/L Publications, 1974.

Seiberling, Dorothy. "A New Kind of Quilt." *New York Times Magazine*, Oct. 3, 1982.

Shaw, Nancy Stroller. *Forced Labor*. Elmsford, N.J.: Pergamon, 1974.

Smith, Margaret Bayard. *The First Forty Years of Washington Society*. New York: Fungar Publishing Co., 1906.

Smith, Page. *As A City Upon a Hill*. New York: Knopf, 1966.

Smith, Timothy. *Revivalism and Social Reform*. New York: Abingdon, 1957.

Sorel, Georges. *The Illusion of Progress*. Berkeley: Univ. of California, 1969.

Stambler, Sookie, ed. *Women's Liberation*. New York: Ace Books, 1970.

Stevens, J. C. "Tourist Court Organization." *Tourist Court Journal* (Aug. 1938).

Stowe, Harriet Beecher. *The Minister's Wooing*. Ridgewood, N.J.: Gregg Press, 1968.

Summer, Robert. *The End of Imprisonment*. New York: Oxford Univ. Press, 1976.

Sward, Keith. *The Legend of Henry Ford*. New York: Rhinehart & Co., 1948.

Sykes, Gresham. *The Society of Captives*. Princeton: Princeton Univ. Press, 1958.

Teeters, Negley K. *The Cradle of the Penitentiary—The Walnut Street Jail at Philadelphia, 1773–1835*. Philadelphia: Penn Prison Society, 1955.

Teeters, Negley K., and Shearer, John D. *The Prison at Philadelphia*. Cherry Hill, N.J.: Temple Univ. Publications, 1957.

Tillson, Christiana Holmes. *A Woman's Story of Pioneer Illinois*. Chicago: R. R. Donnelley & Son, 1919.

de Tocqueville, Alexis. *Democracy in America*. Ed. J. P. Mayer. Garden City, N.Y.: Doubleday, 1969.

Travis, Katherine Hall. "Quilts of the Ozarks." *Southwest Review* (Jan. 1930).

Truman, David. *The Governmental Process*. New York: Knopf, 1970.

Tyler, Alice Felt. *Freedom's Ferment*. Minnesota: Univ. of Minnesota Press, 1944.

Van den Haag, Ernest. *Punishing Criminals: A Very Old and Painful Question*. New York: Basic Books, 1975.

Walters, Ronald G. *American Reformers, 1815–1860*. New York: Hill & Wang, 1978.

Walzer, Michael. "A Day in the Life of a Socialist Citizen." *Dissent* (May–June 1968).

———. *Radical Principles*. New York: Basic Books, 1980.

Watson, Ernice C., and Collines, Alice H. *Natural Helping Networks*. Washington D.C.: NASW Press, 1976.

West, James. *Plainville USA*. New York: Columbia Univ. Press, 1945.

White, William Allen. *The Autobiography of William Allen White*. New York: Macmillan Publishing Co., 1946.

Wilson, James Q. "Crime and American Culture." *Public Interest* (Winter 1982).

———. *Political Organizations*. New York: Basic Books, 1973.

Wolfe, Thomas. *Of Time and the River*. New York: Charles Scribner & Sons, 1935.

Wolff, Robert Paul, *In Defense of Anarchism*. New York: Harper & Row, 1970.

Wright, Louis B. *Everyday Life on the American Frontier*. New York: G. P. Putnam's Sons, 1968.

Zuckerman, Michael. *Peaceable Kingdoms: New England Towns in the Eighteenth Century*. New York: Vintage Books, 1970.

Index